MARY
Mother of the Lord, Figure of the Church

By the same author:

EUCHARIST AT TAIZE (Faith Press)

CONFESSION (S.C.M. Press)

MARRIAGE AND CELIBACY (S.C.M. Press)

EUCHARISTIC MEMORIAL (Lutterworth Press and John Knox Press)

MODERN MAN AND SPIRITUAL LIFE (Lutterworth Press. World Christian Books)

VISIBLE UNITY AND TRADITION (Helicon Press)

MAX THURIAN
Frère de Taizé

MARY
Mother of the Lord
Figure of the Church

TRANSLATED BY NEVILLE B. CRYER

THE FAITH PRESS
7 TUFTON STREET LONDON S.W. 1

FIRST PUBLISHED IN 1963

This translation © Neville B. Cryer, 1963

Translated from the French

MARIE. MERE DU SEIGNEUR, FIGURE DE L'EGLISE

© 1962 Les Presses de Taizé, Taizé (S.-et-L.) France

PRINTED IN GREAT BRITAIN
in 10pt. Times by
THE FAITH PRESS LTD
LEIGHTON BUZZARD

Contents

Introduction

There would be no point in a study of the vocation of the Virgin Mary, the Mother of the Lord, if the significance of it were merely historical; and still less if its motive were merely polemical, stemming from a desire to prove that those of our Christian brethren whose doctrines we do not wholly share were in error. We have better things to do than to fight among ourselves at this time when we are maturing ecumenically and when more than ever the world is waiting for us to reveal our unity in the essential verities and in supernatural love so that it may believe.

Instead of being a cause of division amongst us, Christian reflection on the rôle of the Virgin Mary should be a cause for rejoicing and a source of prayer. Too often, through fear and contrariness, Protestants have not dared to meditate freely on what the Gospel tells us about the Mother of our Lord. Because she played a distinguished part in the incarnation of the Son of God, it is both theologically essential and spiritually profitable to consider the vocation of Mary with some freedom.

It is both the spiritual necessity of giving the Mary of the Gospels her rightful place in our devotions, and also a concern for the work of ecumenical edification, which means trying to help the personal piety of every kind of Christian, that now compel us to write these pages about her whom Elizabeth, the mother of John the Baptist, called 'Blessed . . . among women' and whom all generations proclaim as 'blessed' (Luke 1: 42, 48).

It is true that on the subject of Mary problems have arisen between Christians, but what they already share by way of common belief is sufficient to unite them, especially when it is attended by the hope of growing up together into the fullness of the truth which is in Jesus Christ, the Word of God made flesh. It is not therefore our intention to treat here, for example, the doctrines of the

7

Immaculate Conception and of the Assumption. We trust our Catholic brethren will not be shocked at this, but granted the difficulties raised by these issues for those in the Reformed Churches, we would not be able to deal with these two points of doctrine without taking note of all the Protestant objections. We likewise trust that our Protestant brethren will not be shocked by these omissions. Our intention is not to repeat criticisms which have already been made several times, and are sufficiently well known to all who are interested. We simply wish to hear what the Gospel has to say, trying meanwhile to avoid every echo of polemic.

There is everything to be gained by soaking ourselves together in the living 'waters' of our common faith. Some have thought it proper, in all good faith, to admit that there have been doctrinal developments in this field, the legitimacy of which others have challenged, but this is not the place to weigh their arguments. An exhaustive historic and dogmatic study would be necessary for that. We do not wish to offend any, but to urge all the greater faithfulness to the *Scriptural* sources of their Faith, in full solidarity with the Church which has fed them with the Word of God and with the Sacraments of His Presence, like a Mother who cares for their eternal welfare and salvation.

This study is divided into chapters of varying length, depending on the relative difficulty of the problems raised by different aspects of Mary's vocation. This inequality, however, should not be regarded as an attempt to lay greater emphasis on some of these aspects at the expense of the others. We are greatly indebted to the numerous Mariological studies of recent decades, and lay no claim to originality in our solution of various exegetical or dogmatic problems. Nor do we imagine that we can teach anything new to those who have recently applied their hearts and minds to the very often delicate problems which Mariology raises. The proper nature of this study is a balance, which we have sought to maintain, between the diverse aspects of Mary's vocation and an ecumenical longing to set the Marian problem in relation both to Catholic tradition on the one hand, whilst maintaining solidarity with Reformed thought on the other. Our desire has been to produce a biblical and ecumenical study which would provide for the spiritual edification of the contemporary Christian! [1]

Let no one misunderstand our purpose however. We are not advocating a theology of easy accommodation or of cheap compromise. These pages are intended to witness to a faith based on the results of biblical exegesis and dogmatic thinking. They spring from a desire to partake in daily devotion of the fruits of a theological enquiry which may well appear to some to deal with a matter on the periphery of what is essential to the Faith: and we no longer have the right to produce theology which is irrelevant to contemporary needs. It seems to us, however, that a consideration of Mary's vocation is intimately linked with our Church life, and the life of men who are suffering, striving and seeking for a sign of true brotherly love among us. Do not, however, let us delude ourselves. May it not be that we prefer theology to a real concern both for the welfare of our brother-men, and their salvation both now and eternally?

Neither the Gospel nor past Christian tradition have been able to separate Mary and the Church. To speak of Mary is to speak of the Church. The two are united in one fundamental vocation—maternity.

At the third Ecumenical Council at Ephesus in 431, Mary received the greatest title ever given to her—'theotokos, Mother of God'—a title which was then made explicit in the liturgy, 'Mother of our God and Saviour, Jesus Christ.' This status of Motherhood in relation to the Son of God, which she received as a unique privilege by the pure grace of her Creator, is the starting-point for understanding her whole vocation and history.

The Church, likewise, has no truer or greater title than that of 'Mother.' St. Paul wrote of her: 'The Jerusalem above is free, and she is our mother' (Gal. 4: 26). John Calvin here comments beautifully, 'the heavenly Jerusalem, which has its beginning in heaven, and by faith inhabits the realms above, is she who is the mother of the faithful. For she has preserved the seed of unending life, by which she forms us, conceives us in her womb, and then gives birth to us. She, moreover, has the milk and solid food with which she supplies us continually, once she has given us birth. That is why the Church is called the Mother of the faithful. And, indeed, whoever refuses to be a child of the Church will in vain expect to have God as his Father. For it is only by the ministry of the Church that God gives birth to his children, and nurtures them, until they have grown up and reach manhood.' [2]

9

And elsewhere he writes, 'But as it is now our purpose to discourse of the visible Church, let us learn from her single title of "Mother" how useful, nay how necessary, the knowledge of her is, since there is no other means of entering into life unless she conceives us in the womb. . . .'[3] Then he describes how the Church bears, nourishes and keeps the faithful 'under her charge and government, until, divested of mortal flesh, we become like the angels (Matt. 22: 30). For our weakness does not permit us to leave school until we have spent our whole lives as scholars.'

Thus Mary and the Church are united in this vocation of 'maternity'; the one enables us to understand the other, for the one is the 'type' of the other. Mary, the Mother of our God and Saviour, Jesus Christ, is a 'type' of the Church, the mother of the faithful. Everything that Mary was and experienced, the Church is and should experience, except for what is bound up with Mary's unique vocation in the incarnation of the Son of God.

Yet the maternity, both of Mary and of the Church, is a product of faith. As St. Augustine says, 'Mary was more blessed in receiving the faith by Christ than in conceiving the flesh of Christ. . . . The maternal bond would have been of no avail to Mary, had she not been more pleased to bear Christ in her heart, than to bear him in her body.'[4] This remark, which sets the whole maternal vocation of the Virgin Mary in the context of faith, underlies her close connection with the Church, which is also a mother by faith, which bears Christ in her heart and which can therefore also give birth to the children of God.

The vocation of the Virgin Mary is at once made explicit from St. Luke's account of the Annunciation (Luke 1: 26–38). 'In the sixth month the angel Gabriel was sent from God to a city of Galilee named Nazareth, to a virgin betrothed to a man whose name was Joseph, of the house of David; and the virgin's name was Mary. And he came to her and said, "Hail, O favoured one, the Lord is with you." But she was greatly troubled at the saying, and considered in her mind what sort of greeting this might be. And the angel said to her, "Do not be afraid Mary, for you have found favour with God. And behold, you will conceive in your womb and bear a son, and you shall call his name Jesus.

"He will be great, and will be called the Son of the Most High;
  And the Lord God will give to him the throne of his father
  David,
  And he will reign over the house of Jacob for ever
  And of his kingdom there will be no end."
And Mary said to the angel, "How can this be, since I have no
husband?" And the angel said to her,
  "The Holy Spirit will come upon you
  And the power of the Most High will overshadow you;
  Therefore the Child to be born will be called holy, the Son
  of God.
"And behold, your kinswoman Elizabeth in her old age has also
conceived a son; and this is the sixth month with her who was
called barren. For with God nothing will be impossible." And Mary
said, "Behold, I am the handmaid of the Lord! Let it be to me
according to your word." And the angel departed from her.'

Saint Luke, the Evangelist, had, according to his own testimony,
'followed all things closely' (Luke 1: 3), and it is very probable
that the first two chapters of his gospel, telling of the circumstances
of the birth and infancy of Christ, are a translation of a primitive
Palestinian narrative; indeed, the Semitic character of the text would
seem to be clear proof of this.[5] We should therefore see in these
narratives of the 'gospel of infancy' at the end of the Old Testament and the beginning of the New, the link which binds the two
times of revelation in one great diptych of the Word of God.

These first pages of St. Luke can also be thought of as the Gospel of Mary, because it is only from her that the first editors of
these narratives could have drawn their information.[6] Saint Luke,
anxious to be faithful to the historic facts (Luke 1: 1–4), twice
gives what is for him the proof of authenticity of his account.
'Mary kept all these things, pondering them in her heart . . . his
mother kept all these things in her heart,' Luke 2: 19 after the
birth; Luke 2: 51 after the return of Jesus from the Passover at
Jerusalem, when He was twelve years old, to the hidden life of
Nazareth. If we would believe the first Palestinian narrators and
the evangelist who made use of them, Mary deliberately preserved
the memory of the marvels of the birth and infancy of Christ, she
meditated on them, and recounted them faithfully. These pages thus
constitute a Gospel of Mary; she too has transmitted to us the
Word of God, the good news of salvation, when it was first being

11

achieved in the world. Thanks to her we know the circumstances of the incarnation of the Son of God, and that knowledge is necessary for our salvation.

Mary has an *apostolic* part to play, not in the sense that like the apostles she was one of the founders and leaders of the Church, but in the sense that she was, like them an eye-witness of the life of Christ, and, like them, proclaims what she has actually seen. Mary shared in the life of Jesus, bore witness to it, and proclaimed also the Word of God to us for our salvation. Unlike the apostles she had no part in the founding and leadership of the Church; but her function, corresponding to her nature as a woman, and one who became the Mother of God Incarnate, was to be a 'type' of the Church, the Mother of the faithful. And the various episodes in the Gospels in which Mary is involved will reveal to us the function of the Church under this symbol. Meditation on the vocation and life of Mary is therefore at one and the same time a meditation also on the vocation and life of the Church; and as a consequence we shall come to understand better our own Christian vocation and life in relation to the Church which is the 'mother of the faithful.'

Chapter I

Daughter of Zion

In the Old Testament the people of Israel, chosen and beloved by God, are frequently personified as a woman. This female personification of God's people is often translated by the title, 'The daughter of Zion.' One could instance numerous references but the most important, because of their relation to the Gospel and the fact that St. Luke makes use of them, are the prophecies of Isaiah, Zephaniah and Zechariah:

'Behold, the Lord has proclaimed to the ends of the earth;
'Say to the daughter of Zion, Behold your salvation comes; . . .'
(Isa. 62: 11)
'Sing aloud, O daughter of Zion! . . .' (Zeph. 3: 14)
'Sing and rejoice, O daughter of Zion: for lo, I come and I will rejoice in the midst of you. . . .' (Zech. 2: 10 and cf. 9: 9) [1]

This usage even passed into liturgical language such as one finds in the Lamentations of Jeremiah.[2] The daughter of Zion appears as a virgin or a mother in travail in certain texts:

'The Lord has trodden as in a wine press the virgin daughter of Judah' (Lam. 1: 15)
'What can I say for you, to what compare you, O daughter of Jerusalem' (Lam. 2: 13)
'The virgin Israel has done a very horrible thing' (Jer. 18: 13)
'For I heard a cry as of a woman in travail, anguish as of one bringing forth her first child,
the cry of the daughter of Zion gasping for breath, stretching out her hands' (Jer. 4: 31)
'Writhe and groan, O daughter of Zion, like a woman in travail' (Mic. 4: 10)

The daughter of Zion is a virgin who belongs to the Lord who will marry her—'For as a young man marries a virgin, so shall your sons marry you, and as the bridegroom rejoices over the bride, so shall your God rejoice over you' (Isa. 62: 5). The daughter of Zion

13

is also a mother who travails in pain, for the Lord will make her pass through the trial of invasion (Jer. 4: 31) and of exile (Micah 4: 10) in order to prepare her, by suffering, for the birth of her deliverance:

> '. . . you shall go to Babylon; there you shall be rescued, there the Lord will redeem you from the hand of your enemies' (Mic. 4: 10)

This suffering of the daughter of Zion, the mother who gives birth with much travail, is as it were a foreshadowing of the Messianic Hope for in the end, if the people of Israel, the daughter of Zion, have to undergo the test of the Exile and the joy of their deliverance this is to teach them that one day the Lord will come, with His Messiah, bringing final deliverance for His people.

The concept of the Daughter of Zion is thus both a mystical and an eschatological one; mystical in that it concerns the union of the Virgin, the daughter of Zion, with the Lord, her husband; eschatological, in the sense that it represents the motherhood of the Daughter of Zion and her painful deliverance of the Messianic Hope or deliverance of the people of God by the coming of the Messiah.[3]

In the account of the Annunciation, in Luke 1: 26–38, the angel Gabriel addresses the Virgin in these words, 'Hail thou, full of grace, the Lord is with thee.' It is essential to set this greeting in its right perspective—the expectation of the Messiah by the daughter of Zion; and four times in the Septuagint, the Greek translation of the Old Testament, this expression $\text{X}\alpha\iota\rho\epsilon$ (chaire), 'Hail thou!' or 'Rejoice' is used (Lam. 4: 21; Joel 2: 21–3; Zeph. 3: 14; Zech. 9: 9). If we except the reference in Lamentations (4: 21) where it is Edom which is being ironically addressed and warned of the evil which is to come, the three other passages are seen to be straightforward prophecies of rejoicing over the messianic deliverance of God's people, and Joel addresses the sons of Zion.

Zephaniah and Zechariah address their greetings to the daughter of Zion herself. These two references link the greeting 'Rejoice' with the proclamation of the messianic deliverance and with the mention of the daughter of Zion. Moreover, this greeting has tremendous import: it is the proclamation made to the daughter of Zion, the figure of the people of God, of the deliverance which will come with the Messiah and this proclamation is to produce in her feelings of joy, happiness and exultation:

'Sing aloud, O daughter of Zion!
(i.e. "Rejoice with vigour"—"chaire sphodra!")
Shout with delight, O Israel!
Rejoice and exult with all your heart,
O daughter of Jerusalem! . . .' (Zeph. 3: 14)

'Rejoice greatly, O daughter of Zion!
(again, "Rejoice with vigour"—"chaire sphodra!")
Shout aloud, O daughter of Jerusalem! . . .' (Zech. 9: 9)

This is the language of joy brimming over, of delight at deliverance and the exultation of the messianic hope! And it is with such greetings and calls to rejoicing, addressed to the Daughter of Zion, the daughter of Jerusalem, the figure of Israel, that the prophets announce the Messiah King who comes in the midst of His people:

'The Lord has taken away the judgements against you,
he has cast out your enemies.
The King of Israel, the Lord, is in your midst;
You shall fear evil no more. . . .' (Zeph. 3: 15)

'Lo, your king comes to you;
triumphant and victorious is he . . .' (Zech. 9: 9)

This then is the way in which Mary is saluted: 'Rejoice thou who art full of grace, the Lord is with thee.' She is saluted as the daughter of Zion, the figure of Israel, to whom deliverance is proclaimed and the coming of the Messiah—the Lord is with thee. This is no cursory greeting but instead the call to messianic rejoicing addressed to the daughter of Zion, 'Rejoice with vigour' (in Hebrew, 'ranni'; in Greek, 'chaire sphodra').[4]

This becomes all the more obvious if you compare the account of the Annunciation with the prophecy of Zephaniah (3: 14–17) taking note of the places where the two texts so clearly agree:

Zeph. 3	*Luke 1*
14. Sing aloud, O daughter of Zion! Shout with delight, O Israel! Rejoice thou, and exult with all your heart, O daughter of Jerusalem!	28. Rejoice thou, full of grace!

15

Zeph. 3	*Luke 1*
15. The Lord has taken away the judgements against you, he has cast out your enemies. The King of Israel, the Lord is in your midst; You shall fear evil no more.	(30. for you have found favour with God.) the Lord is with thee. (33. He will reign over the house of Jacob for ever . . .)
16. On that day it shall be said to Jerusalem: Do not fear, O Zion; let not your hands grow weak.	30. Do not be afraid, Mary; for you have found favour with God.
17. The Lord your God is in your midst, a victorious Saviour. He will rejoice over you with gladness; he will renew you in his love. He will exult over you with loud singing as on a day of festival.	31. Behold, you will conceive in your womb and bear a son and you will call his name JESUS (Yahweh Saviour).

The original Hebrew of the Lucan account would make quite obvious these literary similarities between the messianic proclamation of Zephaniah to the daughter of Zion and the angelic Annunciation to Mary, but even the Greek text makes it clear.[5] We shall return to the significance of these similarities; all that we need to do at the moment is to underline once more the clear connection between the concept of the Daughter of Zion, personifying the people of God, and Mary. The Virgin, the mother of the Messiah, is the personal embodiment of Israel, the daughter of Zion, who was waiting throughout her sad history for the joyous birth of her hope, the promised deliverance of the Lord. Mary, the daughter of Zion, is the 'Incarnation' of Israel.

The angel's announcement contains a curious pleonasm which emphasizes still further the relationship between the Lucan account and the prophecy of Zephaniah, and which directs our consideration towards another symbolic interpretation of the person of Mary. The angel says to Mary, 'Thou shalt conceive "in thy womb" and bear a Son . . . .' The juxtaposition of the verbs 'to conceive' and 'to bear' is quite normal in the Old Testament, but why is there this additional phrase 'in thy womb'?

This pleonasm, 'Thou shalt conceive in thy womb,' indicates the clear contact between the original Hebrew of St. Luke and

Zephaniah's prophecy. Twice Zephaniah, in 3: 15 and 17, speaks of the presence of God in the midst of His people as being 'in thy womb, in thine inwards (bekirēbek).' For Zephaniah, this colourful phrase does not mean 'in the inwards of the Daughter of Zion,' but rather 'in the midst of the temple.' Indeed he says elsewhere:

> 'The Lord within thy breast (bekirēbah) is just,
> He does no wrong;
> Every morning he shows forth his justice,
> Each dawn he does not fail . . . ' (3: 5)

This is a clear allusion to the dwelling of God in the midst of His Temple, where day by day the worship shows forth His faithfulness, and sets forth His law. Other parallels to the messianic prophecy of Zephaniah bear the same allusion, for Joel says:

> 'You shall know that I am *in the midst of* Israel,
> And that I, the Lord, am your God,
> And there is none else!' (2: 27)

And Zechariah proclaims:

> 'Sing and rejoice, O daughter of Zion; for lo, I come and I will *dwell* (shakān) *in the midst of* you. . . .'[6]

> 'Be silent, all flesh, before the Lord; for he has roused himself from his holy *dwelling*.' (2: 10, 13)

The reference here to the Tabernacle and to the Cloud, which were signs of God's dwelling (shekīnah) in the midst of His people, are very plain. When the Temple has been rebuilt God will once more come forth from His heavenly dwelling-place in order to dwell (shakān) in the midst of His people Israel, the daughter of Zion. The Tabernacle or the Temple are the places where God resides at the heart of Israel, in the Ark of the Covenant. 'You shall not be in dread of them; for the Lord your God is *in the midst of you* (bekirēbek), a great and terrible God' (Deut. 7: 21). There are many such texts in the Old Testament which employ this phrase 'in thy womb' as a synonym for 'in the midst of thee,' signifying that God dwells in Israel, in the Tabernacle, the Temple and the Ark of the Covenant.

With the prophets, as with Zephaniah whom we have just been considering, this phrase is also used to describe the rebuilding of the Temple and the coming of the Lord at the end of time according to the messianic expectation. The phrase has an eschatological

17

import. Isaiah expresses this expectation of the return of God in the same way as the text of Deuteronomy which has just been quoted:

'Shout and sing for joy, O inhabitant of Zion, for great *in your midst* (*bekirēbek*) *is the Holy One of Israel*' (Isa. 12: 6; cf. Deut. 7: 21).

If Luke makes use of this particular phrase 'in thy womb' which has become a byword for 'in the midst of thee' and which indicates in particular God's dwelling in His Temple, in the Ark of the Covenant and amongst His people Israel, and if in doing so he gives us a pleonasm by setting it alongside the verb 'to conceive,' then it can only be because such repetition has a purpose. The phrase 'bekirēbek,' 'in thy womb, in the midst of thee,' is reproduced in the Greek with all its original, concrete meaning: 'Behold, thou shalt conceive *in thy womb* ("en gastri") and shalt bear a son.' The significance of this intentional repetition is emphasized a little later in the Gospel when we read, in 2: 21, 'And at the end of eight days, when he was circumcised, he was called Jesus, the name given by the angel before he was conceived "in the womb"' where 'in the womb' is translated as 'en koiliai' which is a more polite way of saying 'en gastri.' Such a pleonasm (his conception in the womb) which is thus repeated can only be intentional and used to recall the words of the angel as well as underlining the connection between these words and the messianic prophecy which proclaimed the coming of God into the midst of His people when the Temple was rebuilt.

This repetition, which has no literary value, underlines very clearly the parallel between the conception of the Messiah in the womb of Mary and the residing of God in the heart of the daughter of Zion, that is to say, in the Temple or the Ark of the Covenant. Mary shall conceive in her womb (en gastri) the awaited Messiah and this is as it were God in the heart of Israel, the daughter of Zion, present in the Temple and the Ark of the Covenant. Jesus will be, as His name suggests, 'Lord and Saviour,' the 'victorious Saviour' of Zephaniah (in 3: 17) and Mary, the daughter of Zion, to whom the angel addresses a messianic salutation (Hail Thou!) will be the new place of God's dwelling, the Ark of the New Covenant. The angel applies the prophecy of Zephaniah to Mary speaking of her as the Daughter of Zion in whose womb the Divine Saviour is to dwell as in a New Ark. After the destruction of Jerusalem in 596 the Ark of the Covenant had disappeared and when the Temple was rebuilt the Holy of Holies was left absolutely empty . . . a kind of symbol that God was to be expected.

St. Luke recognized in the Virgin Mary the Daughter of Zion of the Old Testament, the eschatological Daughter of Zion or 'incarnation' of the faithful 'remnant' of Israel which in its poverty and holiness awaits the joyous coming of God and His Messiah. Mary, the Daughter of Zion, is to be the mother of the Messiah, and following the virgin's conception the Lord will dwell in her womb, as He did in the Ark of the Covenant. Daughter of Zion, mother of the Messiah and her in whom God dwells, such is the title which Mary can bear when seen in the context of the Old Testament as underlined by St. Luke.

Chapter 2

Full of Grace

The similarity between the prophecy of Zephaniah (3: 14) and the angel's announcement to Mary, turns the past participle passage, 'filled with grace,' into a kind of title:

'Hail thou . . .
daughter
Hail thou, full of grace!'

Mary, the daughter of Zion, receives from the angel a new kind of name which characterizes both her vocation and her purpose.

The Hebrew text, at the outset of the account, contained quite recognizably an alliteration which the Greek has rendered very well:

'Ranni muchanah' or 'Ranni chaninah.'

And the Greek text translates with the same kind of sound:

'Chaire kecharitōmenē.'

i.e. 'Hail thou, full of grace.'

If one wanted to render this into English with comparable alliteration one could do so in this way viz.: 'Exult, thou that art exalted in grace!'[1]

This phrase 'full of grace' represents quite clearly a definite title which, because of its alliterative similarity to the messianic salutation which precedes it, emphasizes that the reason for Mary's joy is to be that very grace of God of which she is to be the quite especial object. If Mary is greeted by the messianic form (Chaire), it is because she is the 'Incarnation' of the very Daughter of Zion and she receives therefore a peculiar title (Kecharitōmenē) which indicates the especial grace with which God has endued her.

Mary is the one 'Filled-with-grace,' and she may well rejoice at the joy proclaimed by the prophets to her who should become the Mother of the Messiah, that Daughter of Zion, the symbol of the people who wait for their God, which the Virgin has become by pure grace.

This title which is given her is unique. The verb 'charitoun' from which the perfect participle is taken for this title of Mary, is only found in one place in the New Testament (Ephes. 1: 6). The phrase is therefore quite exceptional.[2] It is worth noting that all the Greek denominative verbs in 'oō' have always this sense of fullness or abundance: 'haimatoō'—to stain with blood, 'thaumoastoō'—to fill with wonder, 'spodoō'—to cover with ashes, are but a few examples.[3] It is this same sense of abundance which we find in this single text in the New Testament, apart from the story of the Annunciation where the verb 'charitoun' is used:

'According to the purpose of his will, to the praise of his glorious grace which he freely (escharitōsen) bestowed on us in the Beloved.'

In Christ, the Beloved, that is to say, in His loving concern for us and in communion with Him, we are filled with the grace of God. Christ is the primary object of this fullness of grace, this perfect love of the Father, which He then in His turn can bestow on those who love Him and dwell in Him. This fullness of grace concerns the Beloved, Jesus Christ, and is able to be shared by Him and through Him with each of the members of the Body of Christ.

Mary, thus receiving the title of 'full-of-grace,' is at the same time placed in a privileged relationship of sharing in this fullness of grace which is found in the Beloved, and united with all Christians who can also find in Christ this same fullness. However, Mary receives this state as a title: that is to say, she becomes as it were a living and sure sign of this fullness of grace which has its origin only in Christ Himself. In the Beloved, in His life, obedience and death, the Father has called the fullness of His love and of His grace to dwell, and every Christian, in communion with Christ, can draw upon this fullness and be filled with it, since Christ has been given for all. Mary, by reason of her vocation as the Mother of the Messiah, has been filled with this grace the fullness of which is in Christ and filled with this fullness of grace which is in the Beloved, even before being the Mother of the Beloved.

One might say that God filled Mary *a priori* with the fullness of grace, the source of which is in the love of Christ for men, in order that every Christian might be filled with this grace *a posteriori,* in living communion with the Lord crucified and risen. But above all, if Mary received the title 'full-of-grace,' it is by reason of her unique vocation as the Mother of the Lord, Mother of the Incarnate Deity, for it is the sign of her destined calling and task which are unique in God's plan, so that this fullness of grace, which every Christian finds in communion with the Beloved, is the normal origin and object of his Christian life, the result of his living attachment to Christ, and not a unique vocation and purpose in the whole plan of salvation. All Christians may find in communion with Christ this same fullness of grace, the source and satisfaction of their Christian life, and Mary also in so far as she is one more Christian amongst us all. But her unique privilege, entirely due to the grace of God, is that of having been the 'One full-of-grace' in view of this vocation and task which belonged only to her: that of being the Mother of God at His Incarnation.

This unique title, 'full-of-grace,' signifies therefore God's predestined purpose that Mary should become the 'Incarnation' of the Daughter of Zion by becoming the Mother of the Messiah, the Son of God. This title which the angel of the Annunciation gives her, or rather this past participle passage which is like a title, glorifies the free gift of divine providence. Before she even realizes that the angel has entered her home to make this marvellous proclamation, she has been, by mysterious design of God, chosen for this unique task, the Mother of the Messiah. It is by His totally free and unsolicited choice that God determined, chose and elected Mary to become what she has become.

Whatever the holiness of Mary may have been amongst that little group of 'the poor of Israel' who awaited the coming of the Messiah with ardour, the Gospel never tells us that it was because of such saintliness that God chose her. The saintliness of Mary is much rather the result of the peculiar providence of which she was the object in the thought of God, before even she had seen the first of her days, if we may use an expression of the psalmist (Ps. 139). From her very conception and birth Mary was predestined to receive this vocation as Mother of Messiah, and to be the Daughter of Zion, 'full-of-grace.' She was prepared mysteriously for this event of the Annunciation, and that is indicated by the title which the angel gives her 'Hail thou, full of grace, the Lord is with thee!' Everything here gives glory to the pure grace and complete liberty of God who chose whom He wished according to the 'good pleasure of his will for the praise and glory of his grace.' This conception of Mary's predestination, according to the free grace of God, and her long preparation for her vocation is one of the constant factors of tradition, and we do not see in what way this can be said to contradict the Gospel. On the contrary, it offers an explanation which is clear from the words of the angel and in the title of the One 'full-of-grace' which Mary receives. This explanation is in perfect accord with many other biblical accounts of particular callings and tasks of the people of God which are planned according to the Lord's eternal design and prepared over long periods in the history of man which is the purpose of His design.

Thus the title of 'full-of-grace' distinguishes Mary as the object of God's predestined plan so far as her messianic motherhood is concerned. It is in a peculiar sense 'in the Beloved,' in Christ and in communion with the Son of God her Saviour and her Son, as well as in anticipation of her unique vocation and task, that Mary is thus predestined to be the one 'full-of-grace,' and is prepared by God for this unique event of the miraculous birth of the Lord amongst men.

That this predestined plan should have affected the life of Mary no one in tradition can possibly doubt: full of grace, Mary has an especial place amongst the saints. The Reformers of the sixteenth century do not all share the same feelings on this point of Mary's sanctity. Calvin, although very cautious in his study of Mary, wished above all to safeguard belief in the full humanity of Christ and the fact that He was born in a very real sense into a world and situation of sin so as to effect its final redemption. The issue of Mary therefore did not interest him in itself. Zwingli, on the other hand, does not see in the assertion of Mary's sanctity any violation of Christ's humanity: 'He who was about to remove our sins but not to make all men holy, must be himself holy. Hence God sanctified his mother: for it was fitting that such a holy Son should have a likewise holy mother.' [4] At the Reformation anything to do with Marian doctrine was considered as being part of free theological opinion, so that Orthodox Christology should not be compromised by this or that opinion. Anti-Marian Protestant polemic had not yet developed as was to be the case later, when it would run parallel with the development of Roman Catholic Marian dogma. Certain of the Calvinist arguments which were developed to safeguard the faith of Christ's true humanity and which were produced in a sinful world are no longer used against Mariology by Luther or Zwingli.

The assertion of Mary's sanctity, by reason of her predestined choice to become the Mother of God at His Incarnation, does not necessarily affect faith in the true humanity of Christ. Indeed one would be able by the same reasoning to assert that Mary's virginity when Christ was conceived, as well as the miraculous birth of Jesus, set Him outside the ordinary conditions of human generation and thus contradict this idea of His total humanity. This would be mean accusing the Evangelist of Docetism, but the sanctity of Mary, like her virginity, is not a contradiction of Christ's humanity. Sanctity does not contradict human nature; indeed, on the contrary, sanctity is the authentic quality of true humanity. Christ would not have been more human if He had been a sinner; nor therefore would He have been more human had He been born of a woman who was a sinner. The Son of God became true man because He was born of a true woman, sharing our human nature and living and dying like a man.

There is even a danger in insisting on a state of sinfulness for Mary, because sanctity then is in danger of appearing as a kind of contradiction of true humanity, and belief in Christ's humanity is altogether compromised since there can be no doubt that He did not know sin in Himself. Sanctity in the Christian life itself bears the risk of appearing as a kind of abstraction outside human nature. It might be asked if the denial of Mary's sanctity, of which the only source is in Christ, is not accompanied by a naturalistic view of the Christian life which would exclude asceticism, contemplation and sanctification since these are seen as achieving greater sanctity in God only by escaping the ordinary conditions of human nature. The anti-ascetic or anti-monastic reaction found in a certain type of protestantism is not altogether removed from the anti-Marian reaction. We are touching here on the importance of a balanced Marian doctrine and trying to keep in sight an authentic evangelical conception of both the Christian life and saintliness.

The idea of Mary's sanctity is, however, also related to our conception of the sanctity of the Church. The Church will no more be 'human' because we may speak of it as sinful. Of course the Church, just in so far as it is a community of human beings, knows full well the presence of sin and its consequences; but in our Creed we still confess that the Church is holy. In so far as it is the Body of Christ, the universal community and spiritual institution founded by the Lord and filled with the spirit, the Church is holy. It is holy in the Word of God which it proclaims, in the sacraments of the

Presence and work of God which are celebrated, in the order of love and unity which it both commands and maintains. Certainly the sinful men who compose it are able despite their being sanctified to introduce sin into the society which the Church constitutes; but the Creed causes us to confess the holiness of the Church all the same. This sanctity is a characteristic of her very belief, being part of her vocation and of her function as the Mother of the Faithful. If one only views the Church as a religious society one does indeed see sinfulness and yet in a certain sense it is no longer the Church that one sees, i.e. the community and institution founded by Christ. The Church is not truly the Church except in so far as she is holy in her vocation and ministry as Mother of the Faithful, ordained for the proclamation of the Word and the celebration of the sacraments, for 'the perfecting of the saints, for the work of the ministry, for the edifying of the Body of Christ' (Ephes. 4: 12).

If we can say of Mary that she is holy, it is because we can see it by faith. As far as the Gospel is concerned Mary does not exist outside her vocation and function as the Mother of the Lord. The Gospel is not interested in Mary as an individual woman but only in so far as she is the Daughter of Zion, 'full-of-grace,' and in the perspective of her messianic motherhood and thus in so far as she is the symbol of the Church, the Mother of the Faithful.

Peter believes, follows, doubts, denies Christ and is then given the ministry of feeding the flock of God. The Gospel reveals to us this man who was the foremost of the apostles both in his nature as the sinner and his calling as a saint. There is nothing parallel in the case of Mary. As far as she is concerned, according to the Gospel, she is the expression of grace in its fullness and of God's infallible and predestined choice which causes His earthly mother to become the symbol of the Church's motherhood. There is nothing further in regard to Mary with which revelation is in the least concerned; we can assert nothing other than this, for this is the most as well as the least that we can state to those who on the one hand would wish to speak of Mary as if she were sinful or on the other as separated from our condition as human creatures. We do not see how either the one or the other can be legitimately proved from the Gospel. Mary, full of grace, Daughter of Zion, the Mother of God Incarnate, the symbol of Mother Church is holy because in her the Gospel sees the living sign of a unique and pre-destined choice of the Lord, the response of faith from a perfectly human creature, but one who was also totally obedient.

25

Chapter 3

Poor Virgin

The clear and precise record of St. Matthew (1: 18–25) and of St. Luke (1: 27, 34–5), as well as the apparently even more coherent version of St. John (1: 13), compel an authentic Christian creed to confess Mary's virginity before Christ was born. Denials of her virginity have most often been the result of non-theological causes, and Protestant theologians who have from time to time cast doubt on Mary's virginity at the time when Jesus was conceived will find it difficult to refer on this point to the traditional Reformed faithfulness to Holy Scripture. How, moreover, can they, if they are unfaithful to sacred Scripture in this particular, reproach theologians of other churches for their unfaithfulness in regard to other matters. If every one is to draw from Scripture only what pleases or agrees with his own system then any reference to given revelation becomes altogether impossible. What really divides Christians is not their various interpretations of a total objective scriptural revelation, but the arbitrary choice with which they approach what is given, having once taken up their entrenched positions on subjective and non-theological grounds; or as a result of having been born into this or that church, rather than into any other. On such premises it is of course impossible to see how our lost unity ever can be re-established.[1]

Mary's virginity is an undoubted objective and given fact of revelation in the New Testament. But what is the significance which ought to be given to the title of 'Virgin,' which St. Luke is pleased to underline in his account of the Annunciation?

We must note first of all that in the Old Testament this title of 'Virgin' often has a pejorative sense. The daughter of Jephthah bewails her virginity (Judges 11: 38): that is to say, she bewails the fact of having to die without having been able to know the honourable state of marriage and of motherhood. The title of 'Virgin' given to the Daughter of Zion, the symbol of the people of

26

Israel, frequently shares this sense of opprobrium (Joel 1: 8; Amos 5: 2; Lam. 1: 15; 2: 13). In these texts the virginity of the Daughter of Zion is the symbol of Israel awaiting the birth of the Messiah which has not yet occurred, and is a burden to her for she dreads death before she has known motherhood, especially the birth of the Messiah who must deliver her for ever from shame and suffering.

Now Mary, the Daughter of Zion, also a virgin, herself receives the promise of the long expected motherhood of God's Messiah, but in an unheard of fashion. Her virginity, which once more points her out as indeed the Daughter of Zion, is now, however, no longer a matter of shame, since she is to be fruitful and give birth to the Son of God.

If virginity, without hope of marriage and motherhood, was a sad thing for Israel the state was, however, considered honourable for individuals and made possible one's engagement in religious functions, in the same way as continence (Lev. 21: 7, 13; Ezek. 44: 22). Just prior to the Christian era the concept of virginity had begun to take on a mystical character. In the writings of Qumrān, we see that in the course of the War of the Last Days, the camp of the 'Sons of Light' is forbidden to the women. The 'Sons of Light' are associated with the Heavenly Host; they are close to God and hence live an angelic life.[2]

One finds a trace of this concept of a relationship between virginity or continence and proximity to God in Rabbinic literature. In this tradition it is affirmed that Moses was separated from his wife, Zipporah, after the vision of the burning bush: '. . . this Moses of flesh and blood separated himself from his wife on the day that thou didst appear to him in the bush.'[3]

The Rabbinic tradition has clearly no regulative character for us but it is able to clarify the thought of the period.[4] It might be thought, therefore, that we find in the Epistle to the Galatians a tradition according to which Sarah conceived Isaac in a miraculous fashion (4: 22-3). Isaiah's prophecy (54: 1) concerning the Daughter of Zion is applied to Sarah and then to the Church. 'Jerusalem, our mother, which is on high':
> 'For it is written, Rejoice thou barren that bearest not; break forth and cry, thou that travailest not: for the desolate hath many more children than she which hath an husband' (Gal. 4: 27).

Later it is a question of 'The child according to the flesh' (Ishmael) and of 'The child according to the spirit' (Isaac), who are compared with Israel according to the flesh and Israel according to the spirit, which is the Church.[5]

It is clear that the tradition which surrounded the birth of Christ was rich in this idea that proximity to God carries with it virginity and continence for the heroes of the Faith. This Judaic tradition, though non-canonical, enables us to understand how virginity was thought of in the time of Christ's birth, and how the Gospels of Luke and Matthew were certainly able to give Mary's virginity its full spiritual significance.

The Virgin Mary who gives birth to the Messiah is the Daughter of Zion, but her virginity is no longer a matter of shame since she has become fruitful by the operation of the Spirit. On the contrary, indeed, this virginity is the sign of the intimacy between God and Mary. Further than that, according to Judaic tradition of the time, she is in the line of Sarah who gave birth 'according to the Spirit,' of Moses and Zipporah, separated by the unique calling of God at the burning bush, and of the 'Sons of Light' associated with the angels in the conflict of the last days. . . .

Jesus also reveals this relationship between continence and 'the angelic life,' when He answers the Sadducees' question concerning resurrection in regard to the woman who had married seven brothers: 'And Jesus answering said unto them, The children of this world marry and are given in marriage; but they which shall be accounted worthy to obtain the world to come and the resurrection from the dead, neither marry, nor are given in marriage: Neither can they die any more for they are equal unto the angels; and are the children of God, being the children of the resurrection' (Luke 20: 34–6). It is moreover curious to note that this mysterious reply is followed by a reference to the burning bush which is first used to prove that Moses also received the assurance of resurrection. One obviously cannot press too closely the sense of this relationship but might there not have been in the mind of Christ a secret link between the revelation of the burning bush to Moses, his continence and resurrection of such a kind that they all pour out together in the same breath? This passage does not make of virginity a privileged status in relation to marriage in the light of the resurrection; but there is certainly an echo of that Judaic thought to which we have referred above according to which closeness to God does involve both virginity and continence.

In the same way we have to interpret Christ's reply to Peter: 'Truly I say unto you, there is no one who has left home, wife, brethren, parents or children, for the sake of the kingdom of God, who will not receive even more at this time, and in the time to come life eternal' (Luke 18: 29–30; Matt. 19: 27–9; Mark 10: 28–30). The call of Christ to follow Him is able to imply such a complete separation as the renunciation of marriage 'for the sake of the kingdom of God'; and this separation is, to whosoever accepts it, worth a hundredfold in this world and life eternal.[6] There is here, in a new way, a close relation between the intimacy of the kingdom and the renunciation of marriage. Virginity and continence become a sign that a new world has begun, that the order of creation and nature is not a final and unalterable order, that the new order of the Kingdom has emerged on earth, overturning our already existing conceptions, our already unchangeable institutions, our unalterable tradition, and opening up a breech for life eternal by which the light of the angelic world may shine forth. Here, then, is affirmed the relationship between virginity or continence and life lived in the intimacy and proximity of God. There is here no judgment of a moral kind concerning virginity nor a derogatory one concerning marriage. All here is in the nature of symbol: but we will return to this delicate matter later.

Similarly we find in the book of Revelation an allusion to virginity as the sign of unique communion with God. It arises in connection with the 144,000 who represent the unnumbered crowd of the elect: 'These are they which were not defiled with women, for they are virgins. These are they which follow the Lamb whithersoever he goeth. These were redeemed from among men, being the firstfruits unto God and to the Lamb. And in their mouth there was found no guile, for they are without fault before the throne of God' (Rev. 14: 4–5). We are here in the field of metaphor. It is not a question of a group set apart, but of the host of the redeemed. Lust indicates idolatry: and the redeemed have not rendered worship to the Beast. Lying indicates prayer to false gods: and the redeemed have not prayed to the Beast; they have been sanctified by the name of Christ and they are spotless. They follow the Lamb, as Israel followed God in the desert; there they will celebrate their eternal marriage: they are virgin and belong only to Christ Himself. Virginity, taken here in a metaphorical sense, indicates the intimacy of the redeemed with the Lamb, who is Christ glorified: they are wholly given over to Him and united with Him for life eternal. We rediscover here in a metaphorical sense this idea of virginity as the sign of proximity: readiness to accept His will, intimate union with Him, and total and unique consecration to Him who is all in all.

The title of virgin given by St. Luke to Mary thus points her out, in the surroundings of her time and of her religious life, as a being set apart, chosen by God in a privileged sense, for a particular vocation and a unique task. As a virgin, Mary entered into a peculiar relationship with God in order to encompass His plan for His Incarnation. Mary's virginity indicates her exceptional intimacy with God: 'The Lord is with thee, the angel said to her.' The Annunciation is for Mary like the burning bush, where she realizes that the God of Israel has chosen and determined to be in a relationship with her such as had never hitherto been experienced. He is to become His Son in Jesus Christ. Her virginity is the sign of this exceptional and miraculous relationship.

One cannot fully grasp the significance of this title of Virgin simply by placing it in direct relationship with Mary's sanctity. Mary is not virgin because she is holy; nor is she holy because she is a virgin. It is essential to distinguish between these two titles lest we devalue Christian marriage which is also holy.[7]

We need to see the sanctity and virginity of Mary as two distinct results of her predestined choice by God. Because she is the One 'full-of-grace,' the object of God's special choice made valid in the fullness of His grace, Mary is both holy and a virgin. The fullness of grace, of which she is the object, produces a unique sanctity within her and sets her in so unique a relation with God that no other can come and fill her; her virginity is the sign of this fully sufficient love of God for her and she has nothing else to expect but the marvellous presence of the Lord in a miraculous conception. Mary lives in sanctity in her virginity; she is, as one often speaks of her, the Holy Virgin; but it is important to distinguish sanctity and virginity in order to understand properly their real significance and their direct dependence on that fullness of grace which gave validity to her election.

Mary's virginity gives her a 'consecrated character': she is set apart in order to become in a miraculous fashion the mother of the Messiah. Her unique relation with the Spirit sets her in such close proximity to God that she must remain alone in order to point out to our eyes this unique choice of her Lord. According to a Rabbinic text when Zipporah, the wife whom Moses left, learnt that the spirit was fallen upon Eldad and Medad (Num. 11: 26ff.), she cried out 'How sad for the wives of those men,' because for her their intimacy with God must mean their renunciation of marriage.[8]

It is against this Judaic background that we have to see the real significance of Mary's virginity. She is a virgin, set apart and consecrated because she is predestined by her Lord for a unique task: the Holy Spirit is to come upon her, and the power of the most Holy is to overshadow her; the cloud of light is to embrace her as it did Moses upon the Mount Sinai (Exod. 24: 16–18), as it did the tent of the tabernacle in the desert (Exod. 40: 34f.), and as it did Christ, Moses and Elijah at the Transfiguration (Luke 9: 34). Even more, she is to receive God Himself as the Son in His Incarnation: she is to become the dwelling-place of God 'which the glory of the Lord shall fill' (Exod. 40: 35). This unique event in the history of salvation gives Mary a sacred character which sets her apart and of which virginity is the sign. Though she is to remain fully human and a creature, she is 'blessed among women,' occupying a special place in God's plan, and virginity is the sign of this extraordinary mystery: Mary is alone with God in order to receive Him in order that the fullness of the Lord may dwell in her and nothing other might be able to fill her. It is essential that this fullness should be received without any other human help, and in the poverty of the Virgin of Israel, the Daughter of Zion, the One 'full-of-grace.' Here virginity appears at one and the same time as a sign of consecration and a sign of solitary powerlessness which gives glory to the fullness and power of God: 'the power of the most High shall overshadow thee.' Following the sacred character of Mary's virginity we come now to its 'character of poverty.' Mary's virginity is also a sign of poverty, of humility, and of waiting upon God who alone in the fullness of His power can fill those whom He chooses. Virginity is a sign of emptiness and of total trust in God who makes rich such poor creatures as we are. Further it is also a call to contemplation which must and can only be satisfied in those who turn from man and expect all of God.

31

Mary's virginity is the absence of human love, like 'Eros,' which, according to the order of creation, is essential to bring forth a new being to life. Human love is man's possession and a power of creation. In order to indicate that the Son of God has truly come from the Father, and that from the very moment of His conception that salvation is not the fruit of human endeavour the Lord chose a virgin to give birth in our midst. The most coherent portion of the prologue of St. John's Gospel makes clear the significance of her virginity as a sign of human poverty: 'He (that is, the Christ), was born not of blood, nor of the will of the flesh, nor of the will of man but of God' (John 1: 13). Whatever position might be taken in regard to this less normal but perfectly plausible reading it expresses exactly the sense of Mary's virginity. Mary is a virgin in order to indicate that it is God who has given birth to Christ, that the Saviour is not superman, the fruit of human endeavour seeking deliverance. Neither blood, that is to say human heredity, nor the will of the flesh, that is to say the effort of a sinful creature, nor the will of man, that is to say the decision of a human father, are the origin of our eternal salvation, but only God in his eternal plan who predestines the Virgin Mary to give birth within herself and bring forth her only Son, the Saviour of the World. All is of God and it is by Him that this first act of the Incarnation comes about.

Mary's virginity is therefore a real sign of man's poverty and his inability to work out his own salvation, to bring into being that perfect One who can save him.

In her canticle 'The Magnificat,' Mary confesses her dependence before the fullness of God: 'He hath regarded the low estate of his handmaiden' (Luke 1: 48). This is not a confession of sin but Mary's simple assertion, in her humility as a 'poor one of Israel,' that she is dependent for all upon her Lord and His fullness. Her virginity is the sign of her humility and her attendance upon God, the sign that she is a humble creature who depends for all upon her Creator. The Lord is with her, and the Holy Spirit comes upon her, the power of the Most High covers her with the cloud of light, as it covered the Ark of the Covenant, to make in her His dwelling. As Virgin, she revealed that all that she is comes from the Most High and that she has not been party to any human effort in order to give salvation place. Full of grace, all is of grace in her, the pure gift of love which only comes from God Himself.

It is necessary also to reconcile with this character of poverty, which her virginity signified, the fact that this will be at first a burden of shame for her: the doubt in Joseph's mind when he 'resolved to put her away quietly' before the angel reassured him (Matt. 1: 18–25), and the possible surprise of her family . . . these (this doubt of her husband and the astonishment of her family), Mary must accept as a type of her poverty and humility and service of the Creator who had desired this virginity in order to magnify His glory and all-powerfulness in His redeeming work, which is to be His work done by Himself alone, the work of a God who descends to us in order to be God-with-us, Emmanuel.

Mary's virginity, the sign of her poverty and humility as one who waits upon the Lord, who is her fullness, is also a state in which the creature may lovingly contemplate his Creator. Because Mary in view of the Messiah's birth, does not know any other love than that of God, and her unique communion with Him, she is entirely turned toward Him and waiting readily for His response. Alone as she is in this love and intimacy with the Lord, she has only to love Him with pure contemplation. It is all His support, His joy, His waiting upon Him, His defence and His justification. Her virginity thus predisposes her to a life of contemplation in the peace of waiting on the Creator who will become her Son, whom she is going to bear and give birth to for the salvation and joy of the whole world. There is, in this virginity, a contemplative solitariness about Mary which will break forth before Elizabeth when she will give vent to the 'Magnificat.' Many times in the Gospel we shall rediscover discreet reminders of Mary's life of contemplation which add to the mystery of the marvellous incarnation of God, the son of a virgin, in order that His glory and His power might be made manifest, the pure gift of His love for men whose humble destiny He comes to share.

At last, suiting her consecrated and independent character, the virginity of Mary carries with it a 'character of novelty.' Mary's virginity is the sign that God is going to accomplish a quite new act, that Time is approaching its end and the Kingdom is at hand.

Many times in the Gospel celibacy, continence or virginity are set in relation to the coming of the Kingdom (Matt. 19: 12, 29; Mark 10: 29; Luke 18: 29; 20: 35; and see also 1 Cor. 7: 29). The fact of free renunciation of marriage points out that from the

C

coming of Christ the creative order is not necessarily unavoidable; the law of creation can be broken by the new order of the Kingdom. In following Christ, and in order to point out the proximity of the Kingdom of God in which the law of marriage will have no more sway, certain within the Church will receive a call to renounce marriage and family: 'He that is able to receive it, let him receive it,' says Christ (Matt. 19: 12).

To the question posed to Him by the Sadducees, in which they asked to whom of seven successive husbands a woman would remain the wife in the future life, Jesus replied (Luke 20: 34–6, Mark 12: 25; Matt. 22: 30): ' . . . they neither marry nor are given in marriage; but are as the angels which are in heaven.' Celibacy is a sign of the resurrection, for in the Kingdom there is no marrying or giving in marriage. Celibacy in the Church thus recalls the new order of the Gospel, whilst marriage is still a witness to the old order. In the Kingdom of God, the fullness of love will be such that one will no longer feel the need for a limited kind of intimacy. On the contrary it will appear as a limitation of love. Thus, Christians who maintain celibacy are an open sign of the fullness of love which will be experienced in the Kingdom. On the other side celibacy has a distinct relation with resurrection from the dead; it is a sign of eternity, incorruptibility and life. Indeed marriage has as its natural end the procreation of children. It ensures the continuity of human life by the generation of new creatures because men are destined to die and they need successors. But at the resurrection of the dead those who have been judged worthy of it will know death no more. 'They will no more be able to die for they will be like the angels and will be the sons of God, being sons of the resurrection.' It will be no more necessary in the other world to ensure a succession since we shall be immortal. Further, in the Kingdom of God there is only One Father since all, like the angels, are to be called sons of God. Because of its relationship with the resurrection of the dead, with eternity and the angels, the state of Christian celibacy is an open sign of the world to come.[9]

Hence, Mary's virginity, at the very moment when the Son of God becomes Incarnate, that Son of God who is to bring in the new age, is a sign that, with the Kingdom of God which is approaching, and of which the order is already making its appearance in the world, the old order of creation is no longer an absolute necessity. Other signs, such as the miracles of Christ, will also indicate this overturning of the world's pattern due to the eruption of God in our midst, by the invasion of this new order of God's Kingdom into the order of natural creation. Mary's virginity troubles and astonishes and challenges natural man who is thereby brought face to face with the complete novelty of the Kingdom which is about to be installed by the Incarnation of the Son of God. A similar concern, astonishment and even challenge are created by the monastic life in the Church's tradition, and those who live that life have the task of orientating men towards a contemplation of all that is essential: the fullness of the love of God who one day will fill all in all.

The Virgin Mary thus introduces into this world, in which marriage has become a universal law according to natural creation, the novelty of the Kingdom of God which makes its appearance with Christ.

Thus the virginity of Mary is a triple sign: a sign of consecration as being set aside for the exclusive service of God; a sign of poverty as one who is called to accept only God's fullness; and a sign of the novelty of the Kingdom which is coming to overturn the laws of natural creation.

Monasticism in the Church will in its turn provide the evidence of these three characteristics of virginity or chastity. Monastic celibacy is a sign of consecrated obedience, contemplative poverty and eschatological newness.

The monk, in the Church, responds to a particular call which is embodied in concrete form in the three classic commitments of chastity in celibacy, poverty within the community of goods, and obedience by the acceptance of a recognized authority.[10] Each of these three commitments is in its turn a sign of consecrated obedience, contemplative poverty, and eschatological newness. Here we have only to concern ourselves with the first: the chastity of celibacy.

By his engagement to the chastity of celibacy a monk is called to become a sign of consecrated obedience. Christian celibacy sets him apart and consecrates him exclusively for Christ's service and his neighbour's. This is not to say that the Christian who marries is not able to realize a similar consecration or obedience, but his married state obliges him, according to the will of God, to meet certain necessary obligations in order that he may discharge his very real duties towards his wife and family (1 Cor. 7: 32–5). The monk by the nature of his commitment is committed to an obedience which *à priori* knows no limit: a dedicated obedience wholly in the service of Christ, the Church and his neighbour. We must not here interpolate moral judgments about which is the superior or inferior status: a monk in spite of his status may be faithless, disobedient or but little dedicated; a married man in his status which legitimately binds him may equally be very obedient to the service of Christ, the Church and his neighbour. St. Augustine showed that very clearly.[11] It is not a question here of considering personalities with their qualities or their faults, but their status in relation to their vocation in which they seem either to be limited in their availability, because of their marriage according to God's will itself, or to have a consecrated availability without reserve in the service of the Lord by their monastic life. Monastic celibacy has therefore this primary sense of consecration to God with the greatest availability possible, without at all falling into a fussy kind of piety, and, recognizing Mary in her peculiar function as an example in the Church, monks are able to live out their chastity in celibacy by regarding her, in her fullness of consecration and obedience to the work of God, as one whose virginity had been something set aside, a consecration and a total availability for the work of God in her and through her.

By this commitment in celibacy, the monk is called to become a sign of contemplative poverty. His celibacy, as a sign of poverty and human deprivation, is a summons to the love and intimacy of God. Without a life of intense prayer, the monk would be in the spiritual misery of a solitary human life. But his solitude with God is a poverty which leads him at one and the same time not only to a life of contemplation but to the giving of himself in charity for all. Alone in a human sense he is 'all for all' in his availability for fraternal love. Alone with Christ, he is yet directed, by his status, into frequent dialogue with God, in prayer and meditation, and in liturgical worship of the Lord in the daily office and the Eucharist. And the poverty which his celibacy marks enables all his time to be given to the praise and intercession of God, to charity and sacrificial service for men who are his brothers.

By the commitment to the chastity of celibacy the monk is summoned also to become the sign of eschatological newness. He manifests in his status the coming of the Kingdom in which married and human lives are taken up into the love of Christ, into the eschatological wedding feast of the Lamb: God will become all in all, bonds of human affection will be surpassed by universal and eternal love. A monk manifests therefore in his status the over-turning of the natural creative order by revealing God's invasion in the world and the necessary separation from the things only *of* the earth in order that the fullness of the life in God might have full sway: all is new in creation and human life for the Lord has come, or because He comes. The monk is the living symbol of the ancient liturgical cry: 'Maranatha, the Lord is coming!'

The whole Church is also living in this consecrated submissive-ness, contemplative poverty and this eschatological newness, sym-bolized by Mary's virginity. The Church, as the Bride of Christ and the Mother of the Faithful, is to know in her faithfulness this state of spiritual virginity. She is all for her Lord without any other love save that for Him and the men for whom He died. 'Husbands love your wives, even as Christ also loved the Church, and gave himself for it; That he might sanctify and cleanse it with the washing of water by the word; That he might present it to himself a glorious Church, not having spot or wrinkle, or any such thing; but that it should be holy and without blemish' (Ephes. 5: 25-7). She is like Mary of Bethany, 'sitting at the feet of the Lord, listening to his word' (Luke 10: 39), in the voluntary surrender of this world's power. She is resplendent with the freshness of the Kingdom which she had within herself and on which she awaits the glorious mani-festation: 'The spirit and the bride say: come!' (Rev. 22: 17). Later we shall return to this connection between Mary and the Church, signified by their common virginal motherhood.[12]

A very ancient tradition of the Church affirms a perpetual virginity of Mary; and the Reformers of the sixteenth century themselves confessed 'Mariam semper virginem.' This ancient belief is founded on three meanings which we have given to Mary's virginity. Firstly, the consecration and submissiveness of Mary, as one entirely given over to her only Lord, were not only to serve her purpose as the means for the Incarnation. The gifts of God are irremovable; and Mary remained entirely devoted to her God, as her God had wished, and this vocation of total consecration is wit-nessed to as her perpetual virginity. Secondly, Christ was the full-ness of Mary, and nothing after the Incarnation could any more

37

satisfy her: her perpetual virginity indicates that she had received all when the Son of God became her Son, and that she could no longer concern herself with any other thing than to exult with joy at the contemplation at such an act of grace. And thirdly, if the virginity of Mary is the sign of eschatological newness or novelty inaugurated by the Incarnation and the Coming of the Kingdom, then it is a sign which is perpetual like celibacy which is 'for the sake of the kingdom of heaven,' of which Christ has spoken (Matt. 19: 12).

It does not seem possible to affirm in any absolute way that the text of the New Testament treats with undoubted clarity the perpetual virginity of Mary, although certain commentators believe that they are able to perceive a 'theme of virginity' on Mary's part in the account of the Annunciation.[13] What we have said concerning Judaic opinion of the time, and concerning Moses in particular, seems in every case to give a valid coherence to such a doctrine of perpetual virginity. The prophetess Anna, a widow after seven years of marriage, who 'did not leave the Temple but served God day and night in fasting and prayer' (Luke 2: 36–7), is such an example of a life of such chastity given over to the contemplation of God. We must also refer to the ideal of the Essenes who strongly affected the era in which Mary lived and who 'renounced marriage for themselves.' [14] It is not unthinkable that a Jew, contemporary with the virgin, should have been able to conceive the possibility of a perfect male or female chastity.[15] There is in every case, if not unquestionable textual evidence, at least a valid coherence in the doctrine of Mary's perpetual virginity. One is not able to attest against this doctrine the reference to Jesus' brothers and sisters (Matt. 12: 46ff.; 13: 55), because they could well have been children of a former marriage of Joseph's, or, allowing for the elasticity of terms describing relationship in Judaism, could have been simply His cousins, male or female. The study of names does not lead us to any conclusions which support these brothers as being indeed His true brothers. Called 'brethren' by Jesus (Matt. 13: 55), James and Joseph are indicated as sons of another Mary, at the foot of the Cross (Matt. 27: 56; Mark 15: 40). There is no argument to be drawn from this text then that can affirm that Mary had other children than Jesus.

The entire tradition of the Church has held to the perpetual virginity of Mary as a sign of her dedication and of the fullness of

God's gift of which she was the object. The Reformers themselves respected this belief.

Luther preached the perpetual virginity of Mary throughout his life. On February 2, 1546, on the Feast of the Presentation of Christ in the Temple, he said: '. . . A virgin before the conception and birth, she remained a virgin also at the birth and after it.' [16]

Zwingli also was completely in agreement. He often speaks of Mary's perpetual virginity. In January 1528, he declared in Berne: 'I speak of this in the holy Church of Zurich and in all my writings: I recognize Mary as ever virgin and holy.' [17]

Finally, Calvin condemned those who would assert that Mary had other children besides Jesus. Helvidius had maintained at the end of the fourth century that the Virgin Mary, after the miraculous birth of Jesus, had had several children of Joseph, namely those who are referred to as the brethren and sisters of the Lord in the gospels. St. Jerome answered him in his treatise *De perpetua virginitate beatae Mariae adversus Helvidium.*[18] As far as Matt. 13: 55 was concerned Calvin equally opposed Helvidius: 'We have already said in another place that according to the custom of the Hebrews all relatives were called "brethren." Still Helvidius has shown himself to be ignorant of this by stating that Mary had many children just because in several places they are spoken of as "brethren" of Christ.' [19] In his commentary on St. Matthew's gospel: 1: 25 Calvin writes as follows: 'Concerning what has happened since this birth the writer of the gospel says nothing . . . certainly it is a matter about which no one will cause dispute unless he is somewhat curious; on the contrary there never was a man who would contradict this in obstinacy unless he were a pig-headed and fatuous person.'[20]

Lastly Calvin's thought is made even more clear in a sermon on Matt. 1: 22–5, which was published in 1562 in the shorthand notes of Denys Ragueneau: 'There have been certain strange folk who have wished to suggest from this passage (Matt. 1: 25) that the Virgin Mary had other children than the Son of God, and that Joseph had then dwelt with her later; but what folly this is! for the gospel writer did not wish to record what happened afterwards; he simply wished to make clear Joseph's obedience and to show also that Joseph had been well and truly assured that it was God who had sent his angel to Mary. He had therefore never dwelt with her nor had he shared her company. There we see that he had never known her person for he was separated from his wife. He could marry another all the more because he could not enjoy the woman to whom he was betrothed; but he rather desired to forfeit his rights and abstain from marriage, being yet always married: he preferred, I say, to remain thus in the service of God rather than to consider what he might still feel that he could come to. He had forsaken everything in order that he might subject himself fully to the will of God.

'And besides this, our Lord Jesus Christ is called the first-born. This is not because there was a second or a third, but because the gospel writer is paying regard to the precedence. Scripture speaks thus of naming the first-born whether or no there was any question of the second. Thus we see the intention of the Holy Spirit. This is why to lend ourselves to foolish subtleties would be to abuse Holy Scripture, which is, as St. Paul says, "to be used for our edification." ' [21]

For Calvin and the other Reformers accept the traditional view that Mary had only one son, the Son of God, who had been to her the fullness of grace and joy.[22]

In this same attitude of respect for the mystery of the divine predestination in regard to Mary, we are able to concede that the traditional doctrine of perpetual virginity is for the monk consonant with the unique vocation which is Mary's, in that she is entirely dedicated to the work of God, exceptionally fulfilled with God's grace, totally directed towards the Kingdom of God. Mary is in her virginity the sign of the preacher who is set apart and dedicated by the Lord, is filled with all the fullness of God, and has nothing more to await than the final completion when the Kingdom of God should be revealed, of which she already, in a hidden and anticipatory way, sees the fulfilment. She is the sign of the Holy Church which only awaits and looks for the return of Jesus Christ.

In a lovely 'Prayer and Meditation on the incarnation and birth of Our Lord and Saviour Jesus Christ,' the Reformed Pastor, Charles Drelancourt, in the middle of the seventeenth century wrote: 'O Almighty God, who, by thine infinite and incomprehensible power didst draw from man (Adam) the mother of the living (Eve) without the aid of woman, according to the rich treasures of thine inexhaustible wisdom, thou hast thought it fitting to fashion the Prince of Life in the substance of a woman without any work of man. A woman had borne for us the fruit of death and here we behold another who presents us with the fruit of life and immortality.

'O Lord, whose will it was to be born of a virgin, but of a virgin betrothed, to honour thy one same act with both virginity and marriage, and to obtain for thy mother both a support and a witness and innocence. . . .

'There, O Lord, by a handful of virgin earth, thou didst form Adam in thy image and likeness and didst clothe him with justice and holiness, but here with virgin blood thou hast formed the new Adam, who is thy living image, the splendour of thy glory, and the graven record of thy person.'

Chapter 4

Dwelling of God

The places where the event of the Annunciation to Mary and that of the Annunciation to Zachariah occurred must be compared, and this comparison will make obvious useful differences for a proper understanding of Mary's rôle.

Zachariah, when he received the vision announcing the birth of John the Baptist, was in Jerusalem, the holy and glorious city, the place of pilgrimage for the Jews. Mary was in Nazareth, an obscure little country place, from which it was thought that nothing good could come out of her (John 1: 46), *and* in Galilee, a cosmopolitan district so peopled with foreigners that one describes it as 'the district of foreigners' or 'Galilee of the Gentiles.' Isaiah prophesied: 'In the latter time he will make glorious the way of the sea, the land beyond the Jordan, Galilee of the nations . . . the people who walked in darkness have seen a great light: . . . for unto us a child is born, unto us a son is given' (Isa. 9: 1, 6; see also 1 Maccabees 5: 15: 'Galilee of the Gentiles'). Zachariah is engaged in prayer in the Temple of Jerusalem in the very midst of the chosen people, whereas Mary is amongst the strangers to the Covenant in a tiny Galilean village. Zachariah is reminded continually in the solemn liturgy of the hope of Israel; he awaits the Messiah and the forerunner is announced to him. He will be the father of the greatest of the prophets: John the Baptist. Mary too, in her humble poverty, is involved in this hope of Israel, and she too is engaged in the birth of that Christian universalism which will ultimately touch all nations; she awaits the Messiah and the Son of God is announced to her; she will be the Mother of God Himself, Jesus Christ. In this first comparison Mary appears as the initial sign of Christian 'universalism.' Zachariah is still bound up with and limited by the Jewish race when the angel appears to him promising him a son. Mary, however, is already in the midst of, and open to, the entire world when the angel makes known to her the promise of the Son of God.

42

Zachariah is in the Temple, 'that he might enter into the sanctuary of the Lord and burn incense there,' a liturgical act which crowned his priestly career. Since the appointment to this liturgical function could apparently be assumed only once in the life of any priest [1] the account underlines very thoroughly the priestly ancestry of John the Baptist, son of Zachariah, the priest, in the course of Abia, and of Elizabeth who is a descendent of Aaron. The context of the annunciation to Zachariah is thus strictly a priestly and liturgical one, having the sanctuary of God as its setting and probably appearing on the sabbath day when the people were gathered together.[2] For Mary, on the contrary, the setting of her annunciation has nothing priestly or liturgical about it, or rather she herself becomes the place in which the priesthood and liturgy of Israel are all summed-up in an unforeseen fashion. We shall see, indeed, liturgical allusion in the words of the angel, yet there is no Temple but only a simple dwelling far from Jerusalem; it is the angel who 'comes in unto her' to speak with her whilst Zachariah 'entered into the sanctuary' to find God there. The simplicity of this visit of God to a humble dwelling, contrasting with the splendour of the encounter of Zachariah with the Lord in the sanctuary of the Temple, is very marked; Mary has no priestly ancestry, but is a simple young woman betrothed to a man of the House of David. The mystery of Mary's origin underlines still more the mystery of her divine motherhood. It cannot indeed be explained at all, save by the unique predestination of God and the superabundance of His grace, whereas for Zachariah and Elizabeth their priestly descent and their religion seemed to play a particular part in the choice of God: 'And they were both righteous in the eyes of God walking in all the commandments and ordinances blameless' (Luke 1: 6). Zachariah, a just priest beyond reproach, is set within the religious order of Israel where God responds by His grace to prayer and the offerings of sacrifice. Mary, a young woman whose origin and saintliness remain a secret, is set within the charismatic order of the Church in which God pours out His grace in the Beloved (Ephes. 1: 6), in this step of descending and incarnation which alone enables true prayer and the sacrifice of the action of grace to be a real response. It is a sign of the completion of the sacrificial and privileged priesthood of the Old Covenant.

It is after the solemn liturgy of the burning of incense that the people who gathered there understand, as they see Zachariah made dumb, that he had had some vision in the sanctuary. For Mary there is no solemnity of worship nor influence of people in prayer who might be witnesses of her annunciation. For her all is done in the 'simplicity' and solitude of her home whereas for Zachariah the solemn rites and the crowd of worshippers occupy his view. The angel tells Zachariah that 'his prayer has been heard,' whereas the angel immediately salutes Mary as the one who is 'full-of-grace.' [1] Zachariah receives the promise as a result of his faithful prayer, but Mary has been filled with grace by the mystery of divine predestination. Mary is the sign of the total generosity of God's love which does not wait for the entry of His servant into the sanctuary but comes to where His servant is, having already been heard in the fullness of grace, which she could hardly have assumed, and still less demanded.

Zachariah has a vision of the angel of the Lord standing at the right of the altar of incense; he sees him with that solemn objectivity of his appearing, as had been the case for so many other holy men of the old covenant. In the account of the annunciation to Mary there is no question of an external objective vision, though this is not to say that the angel was not visible to the virgin; but Mary, the witness of the account, did not believe that she had to be precise about the vision: the angel enters, speaks and leaves her. All here centres on the Word of God itself, without the vision seeming to play anything like the important rôle it does for Zachariah. It is in the 'inwardness' of her being that Mary truly encounters her God. His Word alone is important and not the visible appearing of His messenger.

One might well be able perhaps to continue making these comparisons, but we have said enough to indicate the special character of Mary's annunciation and the indication which it provides for a relation with the old covenant which thus comes to an end, and of the relationship with the new which it inaugurates. These differences between the two accounts not only indicate the end of the Jewish religion, but show that the fulfilment of Israel's hope, symbolized in its worship, is made in the person of Mary.

If God, whose only sanctuary was in Jerusalem, visits Mary by His angel in the humble village of Nazareth, then it is surely because Mary is the Daughter of Zion: where she is, there the 'symbol of Jerusalem' is, with all the promises attached to that Holy City. Mary may be in the midst of a cosmopolitan people, in

Galilee of the Gentiles, alone in her dwelling, but it is the whole of her faithful race whom God encounters in her, since by grace she is the 'symbol of the people of Israel.' Thus, in Mary, Daughter of Zion, in the midst of a mixed people, the Lord meets His chosen race, already present and open to the entire world, for a universal mission. In Mary, Judaism becomes universal by the arrival of the Messiah, Jesus of Nazareth, the Galilean. Jesus is a Jew, but He is the Son of God who becomes incarnate amongst the nations in the midst of Jews blended with Gentiles. Mary, Daughter of Zion, in Nazareth of Galilee, the district of the nations, becomes the 'expression of a Judæo-Christian universalism' which will ultimately reach the end of the earth.

If God, who attached the promise of His Presence and Revelation to the Temple of Jerusalem alone, and more particularly the Holy of Holies enters the dwelling-place of Mary to accomplish the act of His Presence and Revelation in its most extraordinary form, the Incarnation, then surely it is because Mary really is at that moment both Temple and Holy of Holies, the dwelling of God and the Ark of the Covenant. Later Christ, and then the Church, and then each Christian, will be called 'Temples of God' (John 2: 21; 1 Cor. 3: 16; 6: 19), but at the moment of the Annunciation and the Immaculate Conception Mary is the dwelling of God. We shall see that the words of the angel describe her as such. God here has no longer any need for the traditional priesthood, the sacrificial worship of the Temple, of the Holy of Holies, or the Ark of the Covenant. He has chosen, in order to manifest the generosity and freshness of His love for men, a young woman, ineligible for the priesthood, whom He fills with grace without awaiting her prayer and who is the symbol of the Temple, the Holy of Holies and the Ark of the Covenant, a 'sign of the end of the priesthood' in its sacrificial and privileged form as found in the Old Testament.

The context of Mary's annunciation, in relation to the vision of Zachariah in the solemn setting in the liturgy, makes of the virgin as we have seen 'a sign of the simplicity, the generosity and the inwardness' of God. The Lord descends in the humility of Mary's dwelling, in order to announce to her the generosity of His promise of salvation and in order to make her hear His Word more in the depth of her heart than in any outward manifestation and appearance.

The response of the angel to Mary, who is astounded by her divine motherhood since she is a virgin, is going to make clearer, by references to the Old Testament, the fact that she actually is the place at that moment of the Ark of the Covenant and the dwelling-place of God: 'The Holy Spirit will come upon thee, and the power of the Most High will overshadow thee (*ēpiskiasei*); that is why he who shall be born will be called the Son of God . . . ' (Luke 1: 35).

The parallelism of this text with that of the book of Exodus (40: 35) has been indicated by many commentators, both Catholic and Protestant [3]: 'The cloud covered the tent of meeting and the glory of the Lord (kabod, doxa) filled the tabernacle. And Moses was not able to enter the tent of meeting because the cloud abode upon it (shakān, ēpeskiazen), and the glory of the Lord filled the Tabernacle' (Exod. 40: 35). The verbal resemblance of these two accounts relates them and underlines afresh the plan of Luke, in the two first chapters of his gospel, by which, whilst describing the event of the Incarnation, he also sets it in relation to an event of the Old Testament, with the intention of revealing the continuity of the two Testaments. Here it is the fact that Mary can be in some way assimilated to the dwelling-place of God, and hence Jesus is truly the Son of God ('*therefore* the child to be born —of thee—will be called Holy, the Son of God'). The conception by Mary is set in relation to the manifestation of God in the tent of meeting.[4]

It is necessary to underline the two fundamental factors in this manifestation of God. The luminous 'cloud' envelops and covers with its shadow the tent of meeting, and rests in some fashion both above and beyond it so that the glory of the Lord fills the dwelling. It is the same verb, 'covering with its shadow' (shakān, ēpiskiazein) which is used in the account of the Annunciation, a word whose 'liturgical' connotation is just right for signifying the Word of God *upon* His dwelling in order that He might *fill* it with His glory. The Holy Spirit will come *upon* Mary and the power of the Most High will *overshadow her*. The luminous cloud of the Old Testament, a symbol of the Presence of God, is here made personal and is called the 'Holy Spirit' or 'the power of the Most High.' The Holy Spirit, the Power of God, will come upon Mary in order to cover her under its shadow, as the luminous cloud came upon the tent of meeting in the desert in order to cover that under its shadow: it is the mystery of the 'Shekīnah,' of the adumbration of the cloud, a symbol of the supreme presence of God in the midst of His people, a supernatural event well known in the Old Testament. And the consequence of this mystery of the 'Shekīnah' upon the dwelling of God, is that it is the dwelling-place itself for the glory which comes to fill it. Following this same theme of the cloud which covers and the glory which fills the dwelling, the account of Luke continues: '. . . therefore he who shall be born (of thee) will be called holy, the Son of God.' For Mary, as for the dwelling of God in the desert, the consequence of the Presence of God in the 'Shekīnah,' the luminous and enveloping cloud, is that God's glory, which comes to fill her, is present. Like the glory of God which filled the dwelling covered by the shadow of the luminous cloud, the Holy Son of God is going to come and dwell in the Virgin Mary, covered as she is by the shadow of the power of God or the Holy Spirit which rests upon her.

The account of the Transfiguration of Jesus produces these same elements of the Presence of God revealing itself in the midst of His people (Luke 9: 28–36).

Peter, James and John are present at the Transfiguration of Christ and they 'see his glory' in the midst of Moses and Elijah who also appear in 'glory.' Jesus is there revealed as the glory of God Himself, dwelling in the midst of His own people. Christ appears here as the glory of God such as filled the tent of meeting where the Ark of the Covenant reposed. The second Epistle of Peter recalls the event thus: 'For when he received honour and glory from God the Father and the voice spoke to him from the majestic glory, "This is my beloved Son with whom I am well pleased," we heard this voice borne from Heaven for we were with Him on the holy mountain' (2 Pet. 1: 17–18). There is here an allusion to Sinai, the holy mountain; there also, the cloud covered the mountain and the glory of the Lord covered Mount Sinai under its shadow (Greek: 'descended upon'), and continued thus for six days (Exod. 24: 15, 16). Peter sets the Transfiguration in relation to the relevation of Sinai, and Luke (and the other Evangelist) in relation to God's appearing upon the tent of meeting. In the two cases Christ is the glory of God, that is to say the Beloved Son, in whom dwells the whole love of the Father.

Peter, in the Gospel account, shows the link between the glory of God manifested and the tent of meeting; he wishes to cover this glory and give it a dwelling-place: ' . . . let us therefore make three tabernacles, one for thee, one for Moses and one for Elijah.' The glory of God is present on the earth in the presence of the one who is transfigured and the two who are glorified; the cloud then intervenes as a sign of the Presence of God above them all: 'Whilst he spake there came a cloud and it covered them under its shadow (ēpiskiazen) and, when they entered into the cloud, the disciples were seized with fear, and a voice came forth from the cloud saying: 'This is my beloved Son; hear him' (Luke 9: 34, 35). It is the same verb, 'to cover under his shadow' (ēpiskiazein) which is used in the book of Exodus, for the tent of meeting as the dwelling-place of the glory (Exod. 40: 35). In the account of the Annunciation of Mary, the dwelling of the glory, the Son of God, and in the account of the Transfiguration of Christ, the glory of God that Peter would like to put under a tent, thus revealing himself as a Jew eager to respect the law of Moses, the luminous cloud is the sign of the presence of the Father who speaks from on high of His beloved Son, whom He has chosen to be the glory present upon the earth.

It is therefore the same theme which we find in the three accounts of the Exodus, of the Annunciation, and of the Transfiguration, the cloud, the symbol of God's revealed presence which covers with His shadow, and the glory, the symbol of the presence of God, which fills, inhabits and transfigures the place or the being in whom He is.[5] In the first, the glory comes to fill the dwelling-place of God, the tent of meeting; in the second, the holy Son of God comes to inhabit Mary, the new dwelling-place of glory; and in the third the glory reveals itself on the mountain to the eyes of the disciples from without: it has no need of a dwelling-place ('Peter did not understand what he was saying' in his desire to set it under a tabernacle, as was the case with the Ark in the desert). It is at once the Temple and the God who inhabits it, the Son of God who is manifested to the eyes of all, the 'full revelation' of His Presence, and the total 'unveiling' of the glory. The veil of the Temple will be torn asunder when Christ is crucified to signify the definite emergence of the glory from the Holy of Holies by the resurrection which will bring back Christ for all the world.

'The Word became flesh,' wrote St. John, 'and became "tabernacled" amongst us, and we have seen his "glory," the glory as of the only Son of the Father, "full" of grace and truth' (John 1: 14).

This text once more echoes the classical words of the revealing of God in the Old Testament, in the Annunciation, and in the Transfiguration. The flesh which the Son of God takes at His Incarnation is the new tent, or tabernacle, which the glory is to inhabit, the fullness of grace and truth in our midst. God is truly in the midst of men without any other temple than His Body which radiates His glory, and which His disciples have seen. There is no longer a veil apart from the veil of His flesh which the eye of faith can pierce in order to adore the glory.

In the account of the Transfiguration, as in that of the Annunciation, the cloud or the power of the Most High which overshadows either Christ or Mary, signifies the transcendent character of God who reveals Himself whilst still remaining 'above' the place of His manifestation; the glory which is the Beloved Son in its fullness, signifies the real Presence of God who comes to dwell in the 'midst of us.' As in the revelation in the tent of meeting in the desert, the cloud overshadows the Holy Place, whilst it is also above it, and the glory fills it because it is within (Exod. 40: 35). The power of the Most High will overshadow Mary, the dwelling-place of God, and she 'will conceive in herself' a son who is the Holy Son of God. At the Transfiguration, the cloud will be the sign of the Father who speaks from on high of His glory revealed which will be His beloved Son. God reveals Himself as transcendent and also as imminent, as the Most High and the Incarnate, as the Father and the Son, as the luminous cloud above His dwelling-place and the glory within that dwelling-place.

In the light of these scriptural parallels, Mary therefore appears at the time of her conception of the Messiah as the new dwelling-place of God, as the tent of meeting or the Holy of Holies, the sacred heart of the people of Israel upon whom the luminous cloud will come, the Holy Spirit or the power of the Most High, that is, God transcendent to His creatures, so that He might cause to dwell in her the glory, His one and only beloved Son, full of grace and truth, the Word who is made flesh and tabernacled amongst us, God present to His creatures.

One might further relate the account of Mary's visitation to Elizabeth with the account of the bearing of the Ark of the covenant by David.[6] This relationship would be in the true line of the literary style of the first two chapters of St. Luke's gospel. The

49

D

history of Christ's childhood is unfolded in constant reference to the events of the Old Testament which clarifies the meaning of the gospel. 'And David arose and went with all the people who were with him from Baal-Judah to bring up from there the Ark of God which is called by the name of the Lord of Hosts and sits enthroned on the cherubim' (cf. 2 Sam. 6: 1–23).

'In those days, Mary arose and made haste to the hill country to a town of Judah' (cf. Luke 1: 39–56).

The bearing of the Ark, the seat of God's presence, stimulated the joy of the people and caused David to give his joyous leaps, dancing before the Lord; the arrival of Mary stimulated the joy of Elizabeth, and caused the babe, John the Baptist, to leap within his mother's womb. The verb 'skirtan' (Luke 1: 41, 44) indicates the leaps of joy which accompany the coming of the Lord:
'The mountains skipped like rams, and the little hills like young sheep' (Ps. 114: 4, 6).
'Like lambs they leapt in praising thee, O Lord, their liberator' (Wisdom 19: 9).
'But for you who fear my name the sun of righteousness shall rise with healing in his wings. You shall go forth, leaping like calves from the stall' (Mal. 4: 2).

Thus, this verb, 'to leap'—'skirtan,' used twice in the visitation, serves to express thrice the exultant delight before the Lord who liberates, in the Greek version of the Old Testament.[7] St. Luke employs the word yet once more, after the Beatitudes: 'Rejoice thou this day and leap with joy, for thus your reward will be great in heaven' (Luke 6: 23). It is, especially, that eschatological joy in the presence of the Lord who frees which is expressed by this verb, 'to leap.' One can equally note in the two accounts the cry of the people and the cry of Elizabeth: 'phonē' and 'kraugē' (2 Sam. 6: 15; Luke 1: 42). The verb 'anaphōnein—to make a sound, reverberate' is not used in the New Testament except in the account of the Visitation, and in the Old Testament the Septuagint only uses it five times, and always in order to describe a liturgical acclamation, and particularly in the presence of the Ark (1 Chron. 15: 28; 16: 4, 5, 42; 2 Chron. 5: 13): 'Moreover David appointed certain of the Levites as ministers before the Ark of the Lord, to invoke, to thank, and to praise the Lord God of Israel' (1 Chron. 16: 4). Thus Elizabeth, struck by Mary's salutation, feels the babe leap within her, filled with the Holy Spirit as she finds herself at once in the presence of God Himself, realizing this marvellous presence and thus echoing the acclamation which this revelation of God calls forth: like David and the people of Israel, or the Levites, before the Ark which bore the presence of Yahveh, she gives vent to a cry before Mary who bears the Son of God, a joyous acclaim which was the fruit of grace and praise to God alone. She has seen Mary the one who bears the Holy Presence, and she cannot withold the great cry of ecstasy which characterized the appearance of the Ark as the place of the Lord's Presence.

Mary, the Daughter of Zion, the virgin of Israel, the Dwelling of God, and the Ark of the Covenant! These titles serve to indicate that Mary is the place where God's final visitation of His people is taking place. Already the prophet had united the symbols of the woman and the dwelling in speaking of Israel whom God would visit and dwell in:

'The Lord appeared to him from afar. I have loved you with an everlasting love; therefore I have continued my faithfulness to you. Again I will build you, and you shall be built, O virgin Israel! . . . and there shall be a day when watchmen shall call from the hill-country of Ephraim: arise and let us go unto Zion, to the Lord our God' (Jer. 31: 3-6).

'For as a young man marries a virgin, so shall your son marry you . . .' (Isa. 62: 5).

'Say to the daughter of Zion: behold thy Saviour comes . . . and one shall call thee "sought out," a city not forsaken' (Isa. 62: 11, 12).

The fusion of these two images, the Daughter of Zion and the Dwelling of God, used by the messianic prophet is complete in the symbolism relating to the Church in the last time, when the people of God (of whom Mary is the type) shall be renewed: 'And I saw the holy city, new Jerusalem, coming down from God out of heaven, prepared as a bride adorned for her husband; and I heard a great voice from the throne saying "Behold the dwelling (skēnē) of God is with men. He will dwell with them (skēnōsei); and they shall be his people, and God himself will be with them" ' (Rev. 21: 2, 3). The new Jerusalem, the transfigured Church, is thus indicated at the same time by these images of the city, the young woman betrothed, the Tabernacle, and the Holy Tent which sheltered the divine Presence in the desert. Moreover, in the book of Revelation our vision is directed to the double symbol of the Temple and the Woman, the dwelling-place of God our Saviour: 'Then God's temple in heaven was opened and the ark of the covenant was seen within his temple . . . and a great portent appeared in heaven, a woman clothed with the sun . . . ' (Rev. 11: 19–12: 1).

Thus from the prophetic vision of the people of God awaiting the Messiah under the form of the Daughter of Zion and the Woman and the Tabernacle, up to the final vision of the Temple with the Ark and the Woman clothed with the Sun, it is the same symbolism which one encounters. Mary, on the occasion of the Incarnation, thus gathers up in herself the whole people of Israel in their expectation and symbolizes in herself the whole mystery of the Church in its fulfilment. Mary is thus the Daughter of Zion, the Woman who is to bear the Messiah, the Temple of God, and the Ark who bears the Presence of Yahveh

These 'types' of the Ark, the Temple, and the Tabernacle are very ancient and very frequent in the Marian symbolism of tradition.[8] The Latin Litanies of the Virgin call Mary, 'the Ark of the Covenant, "foederis arca." ' It is by a kind of intuition, linked with their faith in the divine motherhood of Mary, that the Fathers have attributed these titles to the virgin; it is possible to-day to understand these images in the light of profound meditation on the opening of the gospel according to St. Luke.

As we have just seen in regard to the text of the book of Revelation, Mary is a symbolic figure representing the transition from Israel to the Church. As the Daughter of Zion, the Woman who bears the Messiah, and the Dwelling of God, or the Ark who bears the Presence of the Lord, Mary sums up the expectation of Israel and symbolizes the mystery of the Church, the Mother of the faithful and the Temple of the Spirit.

When Mary will have brought the Messiah into the world she will remain, on account of her motherhood, a type of the Church, but the symbolism of the new Temple will describe either Christ Himself, the Church or each Christian. The physical Body of Christ, and then His mystical Body the Church, and last of all, the Body of each faithful member of the Church which is the Body of Christ, will be in turn described as the new Dwelling of the Lord. 'Destroy this Temple, said Jesus, and in three days I will raise it up. . . . He spoke of the Temple of his Body . . . ' (John 2: 19–22).

'Do you not know that you are the Temple of God, and that the Spirit of God dwells in you . . . in Christ the whole structure is joined together and grows into a holy temple in the Lord; you also are built into it for a dwelling-place of God in the Spirit' (1 Cor. 3: 16; Ephes. 2: 21–2).

'Do you not know that your body is the temple of the Holy Spirit which is in you and which you have from God . . . ' (1 Cor. 6: 19).

Mary, who is the embodiment of the Church, the Daughter of Zion and the Dwelling of God on the day of the Incarnation, will take her place once more in the heart of the people of God, and after having been the Ark of the covenant by bearing the Son of God, she will be like any member of the mystical Body of His Son, the Church, the Dwelling of God, who bears Him spiritually in her heart. But, because of her unique vocation as the Mother of God, she will remain the privileged type of the Church, the symbol of a virginal motherhood which the Church will have to re-live without ceasing in its ministry as Mother of the Faithful.

Christ spoke prophetically of His resurrection when speaking of the destruction of His physical Body by death, and the building again of this same temple in three days. 'When therefore Jesus was raised from the dead, his disciples remembered that he had said this, and they remembered the scripture and the Word that he had spoken.' In speaking this mysterious word about the destruction and building of the Temple in three days 'Jesus spoke of the temple of his Body' (John 2: 21, 22). Thus the new Temple, the place where the glory of God dwells, is the Body of the Risen Christ. Just in so far as the Church is assimilated to this resurrection body, and each of the faithful becomes a member of the Risen Christ by Baptism, this new Dwelling of God will arise, made of living stones, in which the true worship will be offered in Spirit and in truth. On the day of the Annunciation, the Lord left the Temple of Jerusalem to make His Dwelling in the humble dwelling of His servant Mary and of Nazareth in Galilee of the Gentiles. From that time onwards the Dwelling of God becomes universal, the Lord erects His Holy Tabernacle, or tent, amongst the men of all the earth: and Christ will be able to say later to the Samaritan woman that the hour is coming when neither in Mount Gerezim nor in Jerusalem will the Father be worshipped but the true worshippers will worship the Father in Spirit and in truth. God indeed is Spirit and everywhere that the power of the spirit and of truth are revealed there will be the Temple of the Lord and true worship; that is to say that everywhere that the Body of the Risen Christ is present by the power of the Holy Spirit, with the Church, the Word and the Sacraments, there will be the Temple and true worship, since there God will be present in His glory in the midst of men (John 4: 21–4).

The new Temple is therefore the universal Church, the Body of the Risen Christ, indwelt by the Holy Spirit. The Church therefore becomes, after Mary, and like her, the Dwelling-place of God in the Spirit (Ephes. 2: 22). Mary has borne in her own body the Son of God, just as the Ark of Covenant bore the Presence of the Lord of Hosts. The Church bears in herself the Holy Spirit, by which she is built up into a Holy Temple; she is the mystical Body of Christ, and even, in the Eucharist, bears the sacramental Body of Christ so as to give food to the faithful. On the last day she will appear 'in the heavens' as the temple, the Woman clothed with the sun, victorious over the powers of evil (Rev. 11: 19–12: 1).

By his attachment to the Body of Christ in Baptism and Eucharist every Christian becomes in his turn a temple of the Holy Spirit: 'Your body is a temple of the Holy Spirit which is in you and which you have from God' (1 Cor. 6: 19). Thus, like Mary, and like the Church, every Christian belongs no longer to himself but is indwelt by God, having been redeemed by God to become His permanent dwelling: 'You do not belong to yourself; you have been bought with a price' (1 Cor. 6: 19, 20). A Christian can therefore only live, like Mary, in purity of heart and body: 'Your bodies are members of Christ . . . ; he who is united to the Lord becomes one spirit with him' (1 Cor. 6: 15, 17). As with Mary and as with the Church, the Christian must therefore glorify God in his body: 'Glorify God therefore in your body' (1 Cor. 6: 20). To glorify God in one's body is to be aware of this dwelling of the Holy Spirit in His temple, of this dwelling of the glory of God in the sanctified body of each Christian as it once dwelt in the Tabernacle, the Temple and the Ark of the Covenant. It is for the Christian to be aware, like Mary, that he bears Christ in order to offer Him to others.[9] St. Paul will go so far as to say: 'It is not I that lives but Christ who lives in me' (Gal. 2: 20).

Thus Mary, the Mother of the Lord, who has borne the physical body of Christ and is the dwelling of God and the Ark of the Covenant, remains the figure of motherhood for the Church; as a spiritual mother, the Holy Church gives birth to the members of the Body of Christ, the faithful, by her own life, by the Word of God and the Sacraments of His Presence. And they in their turn become temples of the Holy Spirit, and find in Mary the example which encourages them in that purity of heart and of body which, having been redeemed, belong henceforth only to God: they bear God with them and witness to His glory which dwells in them in its fullness.

Chapter 5

Handmaid in the Faith

Though Daughter of Zion, Full of Grace, Poor Virgin, Dwelling of God, Mary yet experienced her unique election in the perfect humility of the handmaid of the Lord. If the various titles of Mary which we have underlined are indicated or suggested by the account of St. Luke, the words of the angel, and those of Elizabeth, Mary herself assumes only one which occurs twice: 'handmaid of the Lord' (Luke 1: 38, 48). If the other titles express her predestination, her election, her vocation and her task in God's plan, that of 'handmaid' describes her humanity, her nature and her obedience. We have seen and we shall see again that her predestination and her task place Mary in a unique and privileged position in the Church; and one hardly knows how to emphasize enough the greatness of her choice and vocation. But this unique place of Mary in God's plan strikes one all the more in that she receives it in the humility of her humanity, in her submission as a handmaid of the Lord. It is God and God alone whom she glorifies in her humanity, describing herself as the humble handmaid of her Lord.

'Mary said: Behold the handmaid of the Lord: be it unto me according to thy Word. . . . The Lord has regarded the lowliness of his handmaid . . . '

In these two references to the handmaid and her lowliness, we see not only a reference to the particular character of Mary. It is still as Daughter of Zion, as the symbol of the people of God awaiting their Messiah, that Mary is handmaid and humble. As the people are often called 'the servant' in the Old Testament, Mary here is called 'the handmaid.' One can compare with these words a text of the fourth book of Esdras (9: 45) which applies the title of 'handmaid in humility' to the daughter of Zion, who is, in her suffering, likened to a sterile woman: 'God has heard his handmaid, he has noted my humility . . . and has given me a son.' As the handmaid of the Lord Mary is again the personification of Israel the servant.

The poverty of Mary links her with the group known as 'the poor of Yahveh' who await in humility, with faith and devotion, the coming of the Messiah and the Saviour. The 'poor of Yahveh' are Israel according to the Spirit who do not seek salvation by any other means than a humble waiting in faith and prayer: such are Zachariah, Elizabeth, Simeon, Anna, and Joseph. . . . God loves these poor ones who rely upon nothing except Him, and Mary, the personification of this Israel according to the Spirit because of her poverty and extreme humility, will be the object of the most amazing grace: the motherhood of the Messiah. Thus, as handmaid and poor one, Mary is again the true Daughter of Zion whom God loves and whom He will fulfil even in her poverty: 'He has regarded the lowliness of his handmaiden: henceforth all generations shall call me blessed' (Luke 1: 48). Christ will say later to His disciples: 'Blessed are the poor, for theirs is the kingdom of God' (Luke 6: 20). In the order of the Israel according to the Spirit, in the new time of Christ, it is poverty which inherits the Kingdom of Heaven, the poverty of the handmaid of the Lord, who is full of grace: and it is poverty which receives the supreme grace of becoming the Mother of God when He is incarnate. But if the title of handmaid and the belonging to the group of the poor ones denotes Mary as the Daughter of Zion, her humility is no less a personal attribute, the fruit of God's predestined grace. Because Mary is truly poor according to the Spirit, because she has the spirit of a handmaid of the Lord, she has her part in this Israel according to the spirit, this community of the poor ones of Yahveh, and she can, according to the divine predestination, become the personification of them and thus embody all Israel both as handmaid of the Lord and Mother of the Messiah.

The poverty of Mary, living out her unseen, humble and quite ordinary existence and sharing life with common humanity in an insignificant little village, is altogether the sign of the grace and glory of the Lord's greatness. God chose the feeble things of this world to make known His power. All human power is a veil concealing the unique power of God. If God predestines Mary to become His Mother in His incarnation, He would have her poor, humble and unknown, in order that He might manifest the better the splendour of His grace. Because in Mary all is poverty, humility and the hidden life, all that comes from God in her will appear as the grace and glory of God alone. Nothing in Mary masks or veils the peculiar power of God. All shines forth as God's grace alone

in Mary because she is wholly poor according to the spirit. All that
shines through her is the power of God because she is truly frail in
her humanity. All that reveals itself in her is the pure gift of God
because she is truly attentive and receptive in her faith. Everything
in her glorifies the Lord because it is only the predestination of
God which has filled her with grace.

Mary, on the threshold of the new age of redemption, is, in her
poverty, the formal negation of every success of the power of man,
the final end of every philosophy that believes that man can reach
God by his own efforts, the abolition of every religion of works
which would seek to put its confidence in human virtue that
would obey the divine law. The Virgin Mary, in her poverty, is a
sign of the power, the grace, and the love of God who alone can
save us, whilst descending to the depth of our humanity, in order
to share it totally and lead us with Him, by His special help, to the
glory of His kingdom. Mary is thus a living proclamation of the
mystery of the grace of God which always predestines us, precedes
and prevents us, before anything good can emerge from our hearts.
Mary, in her humble poverty and unique election, is the most perfect expression of the all-powerful and full sufficiency of that grace.
Everything in her sings 'soli Deo gloria, to God alone be the glory!'

Mary, as the handmaid of the Lord, is a type of the Church. The
Church is essentially the handmaid of the Lord in its ministry of
praise, of proclamation and of charity. The holiness and mission of
the Church cannot in any way authorize her to impose herself to
rule or to control.

Like Mary the faithful and holy Church is beloved of God for
her poverty. The Church is, above all, the Church of the poor in
spirit, as Christ was the friend of the poor. The Church, in the
greatness of its mission and the reality of its saintliness, remains the
place where humility is loved because it glorifies God, who is alone
great and powerful. The Church prefers a hidden life. In her our
life is hidden away with Christ, in God. The holy and faithful
Church does not seek to make a fuss, to be noticed or to be paid
honour. The Church lives out its holiness and faithfulness in the
ordinary existence of men and women; she does not seek to be
distinguished, to be pointed out or to be separated from men; she
lives in the midst of them in the ordinary circumstance of their life.
The only things which should distinguish her from the world are

the truth which she bears in herself, the holiness of her life, and her charity which she spreads abroad. The Church does not seek for the company of the great of this world, but is pleased to share the love of those whom one calls falsely, the 'little men.' Just as Christ was willing to share a meal in the home of Zacchaeus, and just as He loved the company and the food of publicans, the Church has in her heart a privileged place for ordinary men, the common folk, who are without fame, greatness or riches. With Mary the Church loves the dwelling of a simple house in an unknown village. It is the spirit of the hidden life of Nazareth which must distinguish most the spirituality of the Church. This is not to contradict or deny the beauty of her liturgy or the forthrightness of her preaching. The liturgy is for the glory of God and is a sign of the Kingdom of Heaven and it is right that the Church should present it with beauty and grandeur. Preaching is for the salvation of men and the Church must not fear to be in the public eye. But the liturgy will glorify the Lord all the more, and preaching will be all the more effective when the daily life of the Church, her members, her ministry and her institutions, resembles more the life of the Virgin Mary at Nazareth. Her poverty and her humility as a handmaid, will be, as for Mary, a sign of the grace and the glory of the greatness of the Lord. For God has chosen the weak things of the world in order to make known His power. The power of the Church might be a veil over the unique power of God. If the Church is truly poor and servant-like, all that God does will shine through her as grace and glory from Him alone; if the Church is, in her poverty, truly ready to receive all He offers then that too will be made manifest in what she is and in what she does, as the pure gift of God alone.

It is essential that the Church, like Mary, should be, in her status of a humble handmaid, the denial of all the efforts of man's power, and the sign of the pure grace of God who seeks us out in the humility of our human condition in order to lead us to the glory of His kingdom.

Full of grace in her poverty, Mary is willing to be the handmaid of the Lord. The grace of God which has filled her evokes in her faith in the truth of the angel's promise. After an understandable hesitation before the mystery of her virginal motherhood which is announced to her, she submits totally, in an act of pure faith, to the Word of the Lord. Grace has predestined her, predisposed and prepared her for this act of faith. The sign of the motherhood of Elizabeth who bears a child in her old age, in spite of her sterility, and the word of the angel: 'Nothing is impossible with God,' lead on immediately to her act of faith which expresses itself in the form of a surrender in obedience and trust: 'Behold the handmaid of the Lord; be it done unto me according to thy word.'

The faith of Mary is first of all an act of submission: 'Here I am!' Since it is all the grace of God it is natural that she renders all thanks to God in the offering of her entire being. This movement is one of marvellous purity. The sobriety of her words makes clear once more the glory of grace in her. The faith of Mary is thence an act of obedience: 'I am the handmaid of the Lord.' Mary enters into God's plan, accepts the formidable vocation of the Daughter of Zion, and the revolutionary task of being the Mother of the Messiah. She does not accept this vocation as in any sense being one of glory for herself, but as a task for God. With this magnificent service she also accepts the distress of an abnormal situation of being a Virgin Mother who will have to bear the possible criticism of her immediate relatives, the certain scorn of Joseph, her affianced husband. All this is weighed, accepted and received in perfect obedience to the service of God. The handmaid of the Lord does not discuss it but commits it to her master.

Mary's faith is finally an act of trust: 'Let it be unto me according to thy word.' After a moment of confusion at the greeting of the angel, Mary has from the start accepted her messianic motherhood; she has never doubted the words of the angel, but has simply raised the question of how this motherhood can be since she has never known a man. Then, at last, when the angel reveals to her that it will be as it was with the Ark under the luminous cloud, when the power of the Most High will overshadow her, and that Elizabeth in her motherhood is a sign of the all-powerfulness of God, she acquiesces completely and places herself in the Lord's service. The movement of Mary's faith is of great simplicity and purity: there is astonishment before the mystery, the acceptance of her motherhood and a query concerning the fashion of it, but faith and obedience to the Word of God. She reproduces in herself the typical progress of a Christian faith accepted as the fruit of the pure grace of God. When grace touches the conscience of a man it first arouses there astonishment of a natural kind; holding on to the development of grace, man then asks great questions about faith; until, enlightened by the Word of God and the Holy Spirit, he enters the life of faith and places himself in the service of God, putting his trust in the truth of the Gospel. Elizabeth at the Visitation will recognize in Mary one who believes *par excellence:* 'Blessed is she who believed that there would be a fulfilment of what was spoken to her from the Lord' (Luke 1: 45). Mary's faith is the fruit of pure grace and the Word of God. She is bound with all her trust to the truth of the Lord's promises.

Mary appears here as the first who, in the new order of Christ, fulfils the authentic progress of faith. Zachariah, himself, remained sceptical and demanded a sign after his vision in the Temple: 'How shall I know this, for I am an old man and my wife is advanced in years' (Luke 1: 18). In spite of the vision and the word of the angel Zachariah doubted, whereas Mary accepts, and puts her trust in the promise only raising the question of 'how,' but never demanding a sign. The comparison of these two annunciations reveals very clearly the purity of Mary's faith. Zachariah will be made dumb because of his unbelief: 'And behold you will be silent and unable to speak until the day when these things come to pass, because you did not believe my words which will be fulfilled in their time' (Luke 1: 20). Elizabeth, the wife of Zachariah, who has been a direct witness of this muteness of her unbelieving husband, recognizes with all the more admiration the determined faith of Mary: 'Blessed is she who hast believed . . .' (Luke 1: 45). Zachariah remains then a character of the Old covenant, with a heart slow to believe, the object of a miracle of God which is worked out in spite of his poverty of faith. Mary is truly the first Christian woman, the true believer who, predestined by God's pure grace, enters into His plan by the total offering of her whole personality, by joyous obedience, and peaceful trust in the Word of the Lord. It is not in spite of Mary and her poverty that the Lord acts, but in her and with her, establishing in her by grace the possibility of believing and acquiescing with a pure faith in the truth of the Good News.

Mary is because of that the blessed Believer (she who has believed), the first Christian woman, the Mother of believers, in the sense that Abraham is called the Father of believers. Abraham inaugurated the old covenant by an act of faith which recalls that of Mary at the dawn of the New Testament. God promises Abraham a posterity when he is old and his wife is sterile, 'Abraham believed in God, who counted it to him as righteousness' (Gen. 15: 6). 'In hope he believed against hope that he should become the father of many nations . . . : no distrust made him waver concerning the promise of God, but he grew strong in his faith as he gave glory to God fully convinced that God was able to do what he had promised' (Rom. 4: 18–21). Abraham was for Israel the example of faith *par excellence*.

When the angel announces to Mary the maternity of Elizabeth, so old and sterile as Sarah had been, a sign of the all-powerfulness of God, He is placing the virgin before a typical case in Israel, the case of the miracle of God in Abraham and Sarah, which had been at the outset of the old covenant. Mary is thus clearly invited to repeat the act of faith, such as that of Abraham, the father of believers. God who had reconciled sterility and motherhood in Sarah and now in Elizabeth, can reconcile in Mary both virginity and motherhood. 'Nothing is impossible with God' (literally, 'no word will be impossible on God's side,' Luke 1: 37). This word of the angels to the Virgin Mary echoes the Word of God in the apparition of the three angels at the oak of Mamre (Gen. 18: 1–15). Sarah laughed, saying to herself, 'Truly, can I bare a son?' God then said to Abraham who had fervently believed in the promise of a posterity: 'Is anything too hard for the Lord? At the appointed time I will return to you, and next year, in the spring, Sarah shall have a son' (Gen. 18: 14). The text of the Septuagint recalls that of St. Luke: 'Mē adūnatei para toi theoi rēma?' (Gen. 18: 14) 'Ouk adūnatesei para tou theou pan rēma' (Luke 1: 37). This text, well known by Mary, sets her in the same context as Abraham's faith, and she is urged by faith in the Word of God to fulfil Abraham's act of faith: 'Let it be done unto me according to thy word ("kata to rēma sou")!' The play on words between the statement: 'Nothing is impossible with God (no *Word* will be impossible on God's part),' and the acceptance of Mary: 'Let it be done unto me according to thy *Word*,' which twice employs the word 'rēma,' perhaps invites a further reflection. It is true that this word has a somewhat general meaning, but it does seem to play a particular part in St. Luke in the Gospel narrative of the childhood of Jesus ('rēma' occurs eight times in the first two chapters, as opposed to a dozen times in the whole gospel). The Word signifies the 'word-events' announced by God or His angels as 'messianic promises': there are the words spoken to Mary which she will keep in her heart (1: 38; 2: 19, 51), to the shepherds on Christmas Eve (2: 15, 17), to the old man Simeon (2: 29), and the events occurring at the time of the birth of John the Baptist (1: 65). The word of the angel, quoting the text in Genesis (18: 14), which records the miracle of the birth of Isaac, the seed promised to Abraham in his faithfulness, seems indeed to have a direct allusion to this ancient promise: 'Every word and promise ("rēma") on God's part is possible.' Abraham experienced the miraculous event of Sarah's motherhood, though she was old and barren, and Mary is also able to experience the same, becoming a mother even in her virginity. And when Mary replied: 'Let it be done unto me according to thy word and promise ("rēma"),' one may well believe that she was remembering this word and promise of God which Abraham received because of his pure faith, and which had just been repeated in connection with herself by the mouth of the angel. Like Abraham, the father of the believers, she too can receive this word-promise-event of a messianic kind by an act of pure faith: she is the first believer of the New Testament, the mother and example of all believers in the Church, even as Abraham was the father and example of the believers of the old Israel, and which he is also for all Christians.

The end of the 'Magnificat,' to which we shall return, also refers to this link between Abraham and Mary:
'He has helped his servant Israel, in remembrance of his mercy, as he spoke to our fathers, to Abraham and his posterity for ever' (Luke 1: 54–5).

Israel is here personified as the servant, just as Mary is the Handmaid. The deliverance brought to the world by Mary, the Handmaid of the Lord, by the Incarnation of the Son of God, is to help Israel, the servant of Yahveh. It is also the fulfilment of the word and promise given to the Fathers of the Old Testament, and to Abraham at the beginning and through him to his posterity for ever.

In the beginning, Abraham, the Father of believers, embodied all Israel in himself: he received God's promise for Israel and effected the initial act of faith which set in train the succession of blessings in the New Testament as far as Mary. At the Annunciation a new embodiment of Israel, a servant of Yahveh, took place in Mary, the Handmaid of the Lord: she received the promise of God for the

63

new Israel, the Church, and fulfilled the initial act of faith which was to set in train the event of the Incarnation for the redemption of the world. Abraham is the original personification of Israel, whereas Mary is the eschatological personification. It is one and the same promise of God which re-echoes in the mystery of a quite impossible natural situation (barrenness or virginity *and* motherhood), and which has as its object the birth of a son who will incarnate the hope of God's people; it is one and the same act of sheer faith which responds to this word and promise: 'Abraham believed in the Lord, and this was reckoned to him for righteousness . . . let it be done to me according to thy word! . . . blessed is she who believes, for there will be a fulfilment to the words which have been spoken unto her by God!'

Mary's whole heart is thus arrested by the Word of God, which had just echoed in her ears, and which recalls for her the promise made to Abraham: with all her faith, the fruit of the grace with which she alone was filled, like Abraham 'hoping against all hope,' she believed; like him, in the presence of God's promise, even incredulity did not cause her to hesitate; but her faith filled her with power and she gave glory to God in the conviction that what He had once promised, He was powerful enough to accomplish once more (cf. Rom. 4: 18–22).

Mary, by her faith which unites her to Abraham, is able to be described as the Mother of believers in the New Testament, that is to say, she who at the first believed in the Incarnation of the Son of God our Saviour has remained for all Christians an example of a pure act of faith, causing them to reproduce, in the Church, and in themselves, this life of faith founded on the sole grace and Word of God.

Mary, the Mother of believers, is the figure of the Church; she shows the Church the way of faith, the fruit of grace received in her poverty, expressed in an act of offering, obedience and trust in God.

The Church can only live by faith and with faith, or else she will appear as a religious society with more or less temporal power to support her claim to authority. And the faith of the Church is to be, like that of Mary, offering, obedience and trust. The faith of the Church is expressed in her liturgical and ministerial offering:

the Church is the bride of Christ, and adores Him in her worship in Spirit and in Truth; the Church is the Handmaid of men, and loves them in her charity and compassion. The faith of the Church is obedience to God and not to men: the Church is free in regard to human philosophy and power; she is only the Handmaid of the Truth revealed in Jesus Christ, of the love and justice made manifest in Him; she is to permit no obstacle to the spirit or body which will impede her in proclaiming the Gospel or in maintaining brotherhood and justice amongst men. She is to defend the wholeness of the Word of God and at the same time she is to maintain liberty and goodwill amongst all mankind Faith in the Church is trust in the Word and promise of God. She knows that the gates of hell will not prevail against her for she is the Body of Christ, bearing within herself the Word of God and the Sacrament of His Presence, in particular the Body and Blood of the Risen Lord in order that they may be given as food to believers. In her human poverty, she is rich toward God, and she can walk in full confidence amidst the obstacles of history, its treasons, infidelities and persecutions.

E

Chapter 6

Mother of the Lord

'And Mary arose in those days, and went with haste into the hill country into a city of Judah. And entered into the house of Zacharias, and saluted Elizabeth. And it came to pass that when Elizabeth heard the salutation of Mary, the babe leaped in her womb; and Elizabeth was filled with the Holy Ghost: and she spake out with a loud voice, and said, Blessed art thou among women, and blessed is the fruit of thy womb. And whence is this to me, that the Mother of my Lord should come to me? For, lo, as soon as the voice of thy salutation sounded in mine ears, the babe leaped in my womb for joy. And blessed is she that believed: for there shall be a performance of those things which were told her from the Lord' (Luke 1: 39–45).

The account of the angel's annunciation to Mary makes clear the titles of Daughter of Zion, Full of Grace, Poor Virgin, Dwelling of God, Handmaid of the Lord, whether it does so explicitly or by reference to the Old Testament. The account of the visitation by Mary to Elizabeth, brings out rather the titles of Mother of the Lord and of the Blessed Believer.

The Visit to Elizabeth

Mary, bearing the sacred Presence, like the Ark of the Covenant, journeys to Judæa to pay a visit to the house of Zachariah which was to last three months. The Son of God who is within her and the Holy Spirit which overshadows her, like the glory and the cloud which indwelt and overshadowed the sanctuary, drive her with haste to her kinswoman Elizabeth. The Virgin is consumed with the desire to communicate to her relatives, who are also the poor of Yahveh, the Good News of the messianic greeting. The text of the prophet Isaiah floods into her mind in the presence of this vision:

'How beautiful upon the mountains are the feet of him who brings good tidings, who publishes peace, who brings good tidings of good, who publishes salvation, who says to Zion, "your God reigns"' (Isa. 52: 7).

St. Paul applies this text to the preacher of the Gospel (Rom. 10: 15), but may we not see in Mary the first bearer of the Gospel of the Incarnation and Redemption? With speed, she bears the good news to the hill country, as it were to Zion, to Zachariah and to Elizabeth—the news that God reigns according to the very word of the angel: 'The Lord God will give to Jesus the throne of David his father; he shall reign over the house of Jacob for ever and his rule shall never end' (Luke 1: 32f.). Mary carries to Judæa the news of peace, goodwill and salvation. This haste and this joy of Mary well illustrate the mission of the Apostles and the Church after her. Indwelt by the Holy Spirit, bearing the Word and the Body of Christ, the Church has only one desire and one joy and that is to transmit them to all men that they may share peace, goodwill and salvation by a proclamation of God's rule.

The entry of Mary into the house of Zachariah and the greeting which she directs to Elizabeth appear as a revelation of God Himself, like some miraculous epiphany. Mary's greeting echoed in the ears of Elizabeth like a voice coming from God and gives rise in her to a sense of miraculous wonder. John the Baptist, in her womb, leaps with joy, according to the messianic prophecy: 'But for you who fear my name the Sun of righteousness shall rise with healing in his wings. You shall go forth leaping like calves from the stall' (Malachi 4: 2). John the Baptist is like David who danced and leapt with joy before the Ark of the Covenant at the entering-in of Jerusalem (2 Sam. 6: 16; 1 Chron. 15: 29). The Son of God in Mary produces in her a kind of messianic exaltation, even as the sacred Presence in the Ark calls King David to dance and tumble with joy. 'And Elizabeth was filled with the Holy Spirit.' The word of Mary is heard as the Word of God; John the Baptist, the Forerunner, in spite of his unborn state, trembled with joy; Elizabeth had been filled with the Holy Spirit. The word of Mary, on account of the Messiah whom she bears, is made one with the very Word of God, producing the miracle of the awakening of the Forerunner by messianic rejoicing and the gift to his mother of the spirit in abundance. Mary here appears for the first time as one intimately linked with the mission of the Son of God; she is indeed the Mother of the Lord. Mother and Son are made one; the word of the mother conveys the Word of the Son, she transmits the Spirit of God, and produces a divine miracle in Elizabeth. This unity of Mother and Son emphasizes very strongly the reality of the incarnation: God has truly taken flesh in the Virgin Mary, *is* the Son of Mary, and Mary is the Mother of God.

It is this reality of the incarnation which is affirmed by Mary's title of 'Mother of God—"theotokos,"' which the Council of Ephesus was to pronounce in A.D. 431. In order to comprehend in all its depth and breadth the mystery of the incarnation, one must acknowledge this unity of Mother and Son, of Mary and Jesus, at the time of the incarnation and confess Mary to be 'Mother of God.'

The Church spiritually bears within her the Word of God as Mary does both physically and spiritually. Her mission, fulfilled in the urgency and joy of the last time, is to bear to the world peace, goodwill and salvation by the proclamation of the reign of God. The Church is to cause the greeting of God to be made known before men: 'The Lord be with you!' That is *all* her preaching. The Church enters the world fraternally in order to bring her, in the sweetness of love, the joy of her deliverance: peace, goodwill and salvation. On account of the Word of God which she bears within herself, and the words of which she finds in scripture, always newly understood and deepened in her tradition, the word of the Church is the Word of God: 'He who hears you, hears me' (Luke 10: 16); 'praedicātio Verbī divīnī est Verbum divīnum,' that is to say, the preaching of the Word of God *is* the Word of God, according to the certainty of the Reformers.

This word of the Church, which conveys the Word of God, awakens in the heart of men the prevenient signs of faith. All that in a man speaks to him already of Christ because grace has predestined and prepared him, all that, by His very nature, remains an echo of His whole creative being, all that there is of human value that Christ wishes to draw to Himself in order to sanctify, begins to be awakened and made to tremble, even as the Forerunner in the womb of Elizabeth. The sweet and joyous greeting of the Church to the world, like that of Mary, knows neither harshness, nor violence, but imprints itself in peace and love. The Church does not clamorously seek to break down the doors of the world, but takes her place humbly at the table of the poor. She does not force men's consciences by her reason and self-justification, but she is to speak peaceably of the Truth which she experiences in the deepest recesses of her being because this Truth is Christ Himself who dwells in her and of which she is the body. The Church respects the secret preparatory work of the Spirit in the hearts of men, in those echoes of the whole creation and human values which Christ embodies in order to sanctify them. The Church waits patiently for the time when God will achieve His victories.

But the Church is sure that by her word, that conveys the Word of God, the Holy Spirit is spread abroad in human beings in order to fill them as Elizabeth was filled. She knows, with the prophet, that the Word of God is always efficacious even when one neither can nor should be measuring its effect. 'For as the rain and the snow come down from heaven, and return not thither but water the earth, making it bring forth and sprout, giving seed to the sower and bread to the eater, so shall my word be that goes forth from my mouth; it shall not return to me empty, but it shall accomplish that which I purpose, and prosper in the thing for which I sent it' (Isa. 55: 10f.).

The word of Mary who bears the Word of God produced the miracle of awakening the Forerunner with the messianic joy and filling his mother with the Holy Spirit. Thus the word of the Church, which bears the Word of God, produces the miracle of awakening prevenient signs of salvation, and filling men with the Holy Spirit, that one day they may lead the fullness of life in Christ.

Elizabeth, full of the spirit, thus gives vent to a great acclamation, like those who celebrated the praise of God before the Ark of His Presence in the sanctuary. The Holy Spirit naturally draws the heart of man to praise. He can do no more than express himself with vigour concerning this act of grace. This eschatological outburst of Elizabeth, in the presence of the revelation in Mary of men's final deliverance, recalls the long expectation of the Messiah's coming:

'Sing, O barren one, who did not bear, break forth into singing and cry aloud, you who have not been in travail! For the children of the desolate one will be more than the children of her that is married, says the Lord' (Isa. 54: 1).

Here, Elizabeth, the barren one, and Mary the Virgin, are united by this common rejoicing of the Daughter of Zion, the people of Israel, who awaited, through the suffering of history, for the final deliverance which the Messiah would bring them. Elizabeth, the barren, feeling the child move within her and realizing that Mary, the Virgin, is Mother of the promised Messiah, understands that the prophecy of the Daughter of Zion, has been fulfilled, and that the sons of the barren and of the Virgin are to be the foundation of the immense family of the new Israel.

She thus pronounces the benediction which is dictated to her by the spirit which fills her:
'Thou art blessed amongst women and blessed be the fruit of thy womb!'

This greeting of Elizabeth must be understood in the biblical sense of benediction. In speaking of Mary and Jesus as 'Blessed, eulogĕmĕnĕ, or eulogĕmĕnos' Elizabeth is stating that they are the object of God's 'blessing,' and she proclaims the 'act of grace' of which they are the subject before God. She proclaims them 'blessed by God' and she 'blesses God' in regard to them. Following biblical thought indeed, God's blessing is the matter of an act of grace by God.

Thus Mary and Jesus are proclaimed 'Blest of God': they share in the blessing of the Lord belonging to His plan of salvation, and in a particular relationship to Him. On Palm Sunday the crowd greet Jesus as the Messiah and King using the same title:
'Blessed (eulogĕmĕnos) is he who comes in the name of the Lord' . . .
'Blessed is he who comes, the King, in the name of the Lord' . . .
'Blessed be the kingdom (eulogĕmĕnĕ) which comes from David our Father' . . .
'Blessed is he who comes in the name of the Lord, the King of Israel!' (Matt. 21: 9; Luke 19: 38; Mark 11: 10; John 12: 13).

Jesus Himself, in another place, will apply this greeting to His glorious coming again at the end of time: 'For I tell you, you will not see me again, until you say, Blessed is he who cometh in the name of the Lord' (Matt. 23: 39). These references show that the blessing of Elizabeth has a truly messianic and eschatological character. She greets Mary as 'the Blessed one' and He who is in her is 'the Blessed,' who comes in the name of the Lord; she greets Mary as the Mother of the Messiah King whose kingdom is coming.

It is necessary to recall here that the title of 'blessed, eulogētos,' was used by the Jews to indicate God, whose name they dare not pronounce: Yahveh. It is thus that Zachariah begins his canticle by using this title which at once denominates the name of God and the praise of which He is the end and object: 'Blessed be the Lord God of Israel . . . ' (Luke 1: 68). During the trial of Jesus the High Priest asks of Him: 'Art thou the Christ, the Son of the blessed?' (Mark 14: 61). St. Paul several times refers to this title in passages of doxology in the Epistles where there seems to be quoting of a liturgical type: ' . . . the Creator, who is blessed throughout all ages. Amen!' (Rom. 1: 25; 9: 5; 2 Cor. 1: 3; 11: 31; Ephes. 1: 3; and see also 1 Peter 1: 3). Some have thought to see a difference between 'eulogētos,' which would refer to God the Blessed, and 'eulogēmĕnos' which would refer to man blest by Him. Now the Hebrew root of this word ('baruk') knows no such distinction as the Greek. In the blessing of Abraham by Melchisedek (Gen. 14: 19f.), it is the same word ('baruk') which is used for both the blessing of the patriarch and of God: 'Blessed be Abram . . . and blessed is God most High. . . .' The Greek tradition of the Septuagint itself makes the distinction between 'eulogēmĕnos' and 'eulogētos.' The Rabbis were scandalized by this same Hebrew word being applied first to Abraham and then to God. According to them this error of protocol had caused Melchisedek to lose the priesthood in preference to Levi! But in the book of Judith, a blessing certainly inspired by that of Melchisedek (Gen. 14: 19f.) in fact reverses the Greek word, which shows their similar meaning (one sees, for instance, 'eulogētos' in Judith 13: 17 and 'eulogēmĕnos' in 13: 18, when referring to God; 'eulogēte' in 13: 18 and 'eulogēmĕnē' in 14: 7 and 15: 10 when referring to Judith).

The parallelism speaks for itself. Mary is blest like Judith and Abraham, and the fruit of her womb is blest like the Lord God, the Most High, who has created Heaven and earth.

Gen. 14: 19–20	Judith 13: 18	Luke 1: 42
Blessed, Abram	Blessed art thou, O daughter	Blessed art thou (Mary)
(baruk, eulogēmĕnos)	(Eulogētĕ)	(Eulogēmĕnē)
By God Most High	By God Most High	
Who has made heaven and earth		
	Amongst all the Women of the earth	Amongst women.

Gen. 14: 19–20	*Judith 13: 18*	*Luke 1: 42*
And blessed	And blessed	And blessed
(baruk eulogētes),	(eulogēmĕnos),	(eulogēmĕnos).
Be God most High,	The Lord God,	The fruit of thy womb;
	Who created heaven and earth	
Who has delivered thine enemies	Who has led thee	
Into thy hands.	To cut off the head.	
	Of the chief of your enemies.	

At the same time this greeting which recognizes the Mother of the Messiah King and the approaching kingdom, the blessing which rests upon the Mother and the Son, is an act of grace by God, for the one who, in His Mother, comes in the name of Yahveh. Recognition of the Messiah King and the act of grace by Him and His Mother are made one in the greeting of Elizabeth.

Mary is proclaimed 'blessed among women.' She is the woman chosen amongst all others, above all others, as the first of women, the blessed one. None before her had received so great a blessing, and none after her will be able to receive quite the same; no one in time can be the object of an act of grace by God so joyous and so tremendous. Mary, the Daughter of Zion, the Virgin Mother of the Messiah is the most perfectly blest and happy mother of all time, and because of that is worthy of the most perfect and joyous act of grace by God.

The same title 'Blessed . . . Blessed . . . ' unites both Mother and Son. In the period which precedes the nativity, Mary is closely linked with Jesus in the blessing of God, and in the act of grace by God. She becomes one with the fruit of her womb. They are both taken into the same blessing and the same act of grace. Here still we can notice the physical and spiritual unity of Mary and God, which emphasizes the full reality of the Incarnation. We find a second time the truth and the sense of the dogma of Ephesus: Mary is Mother of God, 'theotokos.' Mary is not simply an impersonal instrument which enables God to come amongst us and which one can really ignore. Her human and real person, her nature and history are linked with the incarnation of God. And it is this which the double and parallel greeting of Elizabeth points out: 'Thou art blest. . . . He is blest . . . !' The divine motherhood of

72

Mary is a truly human motherhood in the deep sense of the unity of mother and son, the human mother of God and the Son of God made man. 'A purely physical conception without any conception by the spirit would not only have been meaningless, but truly frightening; and it is not possible that redemption for men should end with the destruction of her who should be first to share in it. Mary only became the mother of this Son without peer because she could embody that motherhood in a personal sense.'[1] To do that would in the end be to lessen faith in the true humanity of Christ, and not to consider Mary as a mother in any real sense, as physical and yet also psychological and spiritual as well. Hence the title of 'Mother of God' emphasizes all the more the humanity, as well as the true divinity, of Christ. Mary is 'Mother' of God: that means to say that God is truly one who became her son, a son in the human sense of fully man. Mary is the Mother of 'God': that means to say that, as from her miraculous conception, her son was the Son of God, God Himself in His Incarnate Presence. Thus the Council of Ephesus (A.D. 431) which gave Mary the title 'Mother of God' and that of Chalcedon (A.D. 451) which asserted the two natures of Christ in one person, are in the end saying the same thing and expressing very well the mystery of Christ who is truly God and truly man, as the Gospel states.

'And why is this granted me that the Mother of my Lord should come to me?' Elizabeth, filled with the Holy Spirit, has discerned the messianic motherhood of Mary. She is the Mother of the Messiah who has been awaited so long. The title of Lord (Kyrios) which Elizabeth gives to the Messiah emphasizes His divine character. It cannot be said that in the mind of Elizabeth there is a clear awareness of having recognized the Mother of God in the sense that the Council of Ephesus would understand this title. And yet there can be no doubt that her greeting is more far-reaching in a sense than the knowledge which we would expect her to have of the Messiah King: 'The mother of my Lord!' A little later she recalls what has been said to Mary 'by the Lord,' and there the title very clearly indicates Yahveh, the God of Israel. In Psalm 110, on the Priesthood of the Messiah, the psalmist writes: 'The Lord (Yahveh) says to my Lord (adonai): sit at my right hand till I make your enemies my footstool.'[2] It is clear that for him the Messiah designated by the title of 'my Lord' is distinct and subordinated to Yahveh, the God of Israel. And yet Christ is to use this very quotation as being interpreted in applying to Himself, the Son of God, aware of His Divinity, with the title of 'My Lord' (Matt. 22: 44). A word which surpassed the knowledge that the psalmist could have of it discovers its full significance in the mouth of Christ: 'Yahveh said to my Lord,' that means to say: 'God the Father said to God the Son: . . . ,' hence, the word of Elizabeth which surely surpasses the awareness that she can have had of it, finds in the account of St. Luke its real significance. It is necessary to recall here, in particular, his references to the Ark of the Covenant which Mary represents. St. Luke gives to the title of 'Kyrios' its divine significance. Christ is Lord, for He is God. The Council of Ephesus, following in the line of tradition this understanding of the title of 'mother of the Lord' given by Elizabeth to Mary and interpreted by the Gospel writer according to the plan of revelation, as the title of messianic divine motherhood, therefore names Mary 'Mother of God.' This would be the faithful interpretation of the word of Elizabeth, 'mother of my Lord' and of St. Luke's text. Indeed the Council of Ephesus faced a doctrinal situation that St. Luke does not envisage, but the same content of dogma is there under the two expressions of Mary's motherhood. 'The mother of the Lord' of Elizabeth is 'mother of God,' truly the human mother of God who is true God and true man.

Mary, Mother of God

When the old Latin liturgy calls Mary the 'Mother of our Lord Jesus Christ' [3] and when the Council of Ephesus talks of her as 'theotokos, Mother of God,' tradition is here only uncovering the real meaning of the Gospel and in particular the words of Elizabeth, 'the mother of my Lord.'

The Ephesian dogma has an essentially Christological import. Mary is not called Mother of God in order that her person may be glorified, but for the sake of Christ, in order that the truth about Christ's person should be plainly and clearly understood. For Mary is still the handmaid of the Lord, and the dogma which concerns her to subordinate to the truth concerning her Son, the Lord; the Council of Ephesus in speaking of her as Mother of God, is defining Christ as having two natures, divine and human, but as being one person only; it thus recognizes the truth of the incarnation from the time of the miraculous conception of the Son of God in the Virgin Mary.

The doctrinal background of the period explains the Council's

definition. The theological school of Antioch had been led to conceive the distinction of the divine and human natures in Christ as
a distinction of two persons. Nestorius, who was a product of
this school, had been, since A.D. 428, Bishop of Constantinople
where he had spread this teaching. A priest, Anastasius, denied in
his preaching that Mary could be called 'Theotokos, mother of
God': for him, she was only the mother of Christ the man
'Christotokos'; and the second person of the Trinity was united to
the man Christ who had been conceived in Mary. For 'Nestorianism' a true human nature could only be a human person. In order
to be fully man Christ must be a human person distinct from the
divine person who was united with Him. There was therefore no
unity of the two natures, divine and human, in a single person of
Christ but there was between the two persons, Christ the man and
the Word of God, a relation of special grace. What the Gospel tells
us about Christ concerns at one stage His human person and at
another His divine person. One can see the ultimate conclusion to
which this error leads: Mary being only the mother of Christ the
man is simply a channel by which God can give Himself humanity;
God does not take upon Himself flesh in the sense that He would
be truly born as a man but is united with a man who would pre-
exist such a union. In this line of thought there is therefore for
God no true Incarnation implying a truly human birth, and therefore a true mother, but rather a particular kind of union, between
God and a man, Christ, of two distinct persons. The idea of some
merit of Christ the man by which He could be raised to the dignity
of this union flows naturally from this line of thinking.

One sees that the 'unity' of Christ, the 'reality' of the incarnation and the total 'free gift' of redemption are here made matters
of debate.

Cyril, Bishop of Alexandria, became the centre of the reaction against Nestorius and his school. It is the second letter of Cyril
to Nestorius which was recognized by the Council of Ephesus in
A.D. 431, after its first session, as expressing the truly orthodox view
of the Church. He wrote for example: 'Although the natures,
united by a true unity, are different from them both there results
only one Christ and one Son; not that the union suppressed the
difference between these natures, but because divinity and humanity
have constituted, for us, by this inexpressible and mysterious
encounter in one unity, one only Lord, Christ and Son. . . . It is not

75

that first of all an ordinary man was born of the holy Virgin and then upon him the Word descended, but we say that from the mother's womb and united with her flesh he accepted a carnal birth as his very own . . . thus the holy fathers did not hesitate to call the holy Virgin "Mother of God".' [4] Twelve anathemas of St. Cyril were then read before the Council, but we do not know if they were approved. The first expressed in other terms the relationship between the title of Mary 'Mother of God' and the reality of the incarnation—'If anyone does not confess that the Emmanuel is truly God and that for this reason the holy Virgin is Mother of God (for she has borne according to the flesh the Word of God made flesh), let him be anathema.' [5]

At the Reformation Luther and Zwingli are to have the same great respect for this definition of the Council of Ephesus. Luther wrote in 1539 in a treatise entitled, *Of Councils and Churches:* 'Hence this council (of Ephesus) did not establish anything new in the faith, but defended the ancient faith against the new vagueness of Nestorius. Indeed the article according to which Mary is Mother of God has been in the Church from the beginning and has not been newly produced by the council but on the contrary contained in the gospel or in Holy Scripture. For in St. Luke (1: 32) we find that the angel Gabriel announces to the Virgin that she must bear the Son of the Most High and Elizabeth says: "whence comes it that the Mother of the Lord should come to me?" And the angels at Christmas together sing: "unto us is born this day a Saviour which is Christ the Lord." In the same way St. Paul (Gal. 4: 4): "God has sent his Son, born of a woman." These words which I hold to be true surely support quite strongly that Mary is the Mother of God.' [6] Zwingli had printed in 1524 a sermon on 'Mary, ever virgin, mother of God.' [7] He here freely employs the title Mother of God. In a passage where he defends himself against the accusations of men of ill will, who have declared that they had heard Mary spoken of by him as a sinner like any other creature, he says, 'I have never thought, still less taught, or declared publicly, anything concerning the subject of the ever Virgin Mary, Mother of our salvation, which could be considered dishonourable, impious, unworthy or evil. . . . I hope this is sufficient to have made plain to pious and simple Christians my clear conviction on the matter of the Mother of God: "I believe with all my heart according to the word of holy gospel that this pure virgin bore for us the Son of God and that she remained, in the birth and after it, a pure and unsullied virgin, for eternity." '

Let us take note in passing how much this Marian doctrine of the most humanist, most 'protestant' amongst the Reformers, can over-throw the established opinions on the subject of the 'Reformed Tradition.' Whatever may be the position theologically that one may take to-day on the subject of Mariology, one is not able to call to one's aid 'reformed tradition' unless one does it with the greatest care . . . the Marian doctrine of the Reformers is consonant with the great tradition of the Church in all the essentials and with that of the Fathers of the first centuries in particular.[8]

Calvin is rather more hesitant in the presence of this title 'Mother of God' which has been given to Mary. One is astounded to read from the pen of this Reformer, who is so full of respect for the first four councils, remarks that would seem to point to a certain kind of Nestorianism in his Christology. He writes in one place: 'In this regard we willingly receive the ancient councils like Nicea, Constantinople, the first Council of Ephesus, Chalcedon and the like which were held to condemn the errors and evil opinions of heretics. We bear them, I repeat, in honour and respect, in so far as they hold to the articles which we have here defined, for these councils do not contain anything but a pure and natural interpreta-tion of Holy Writ, which the holy Fathers with great prudence have employed to overthrow the enemies of Christianity.'[9] Yet on the other side, in a letter to the French community in London on September 27, 1552: 'Concerning the other points which they have discussed (the two parties of the community, those who were more catholic and those who were "more conservative"), I have no doubt that there has been some ignorance in that they have reproved this fashion of speaking of the Virgin Mary as the mother of God, and because of their ignorance it is likely that they have assumed a temerity and brashness which is too great as we are reminded by the old proverb which says that the more ignorant people are the more courageous they tend to be. However to con-tinue in fraternal friendship with you I am not able to disguise the fact that I find it wrong to have this title ordinarily attributed in sermons about the Virgin, and for my own part I would not think that such language was good or proper or convenient. If it should be done by all sorts of level-headed people I am not able to be per-suaded by that that there should be such a usage in your Church for that would be tantamount to speaking of the blood, head, and the death of God. You know that scripture accustoms us to a rather different manner of speaking, but there is worse in this in that it could give scandal, for to speak of the Mother of God instead of the Virgin Mary can only serve to harden the ignorant in their superstition. And he who is content with that shows quite clearly that he does not know what it is to edify the Church.' [10]

Whilst admitting the definitions of the Council of Ephesus, Calvin thus shows himself hesitant in regard to the title, 'Mother of God.' He shows an anti-monophysite, not to say Nestorian, attitude (the monophysites confounded the human and divine natures in Christ, the Nestorians on the contrary separated them).

Bullinger, Zwingli's successor, who represents the second generation of the Reformation and a kind of stabilization of Reformed doctrine, writes: 'Nestorius, the heretic, recognized two natures in Christ, and he understood them as being two persons. Indeed he taught that the Word had not been united in one person with the flesh, but had only been its habitation in the flesh: that is why he would not admit that the Blessed Virgin Mary was called "theotokos" (Gottesgebärerin) or Mother of God (Mutter Gottes).' [11] Thus Bullinger, for Christological reasons, described Mary as 'the mother of God.' [12]

The French pastor, Charles Drelincourt, wrote in 1633: 'On account of this close and unaccountable union (of the natures of Christ), what belonged to one of those natures can be attributed generally to the person. Hence just as the Apostle, St. Paul, said that the Jews crucified the Lord of Glory (1 Cor. 2) . . ., we find no difficulty in saying with the Ancients, that the Virgin Mary is the Mother of God; for he whom she bore is God above all else, eternally blest (Rom. 9).' [13] This Calvinist pastor here takes a different position from that of Calvin quoted above. He does not hesitate to speak of the Mother of God since St. Paul speaks of the crucified Lord of Glory. The acceptance of the title is in close relationship to the view that one has of the union of the natures of Christ in one person. It is a test of faith in the reality of the incarnation.

If God has truly taken flesh in the Virgin Mary, and if the two natures of Christ are really united in one person, Mary cannot be only the mother of the humanity of Christ as if that could be separated from His divinity. She is the mother of one single person, the Mother of God made man, of the Only Christ, true God and true man. On the other side, if Christ's humanity is real He has, as a unique person, a true mother, who demands a relationship of mother to son in the full sense, physical, psychological, and spiritual. There is in the reality of the incarnation of God and in the reality of the humanity of Christ a fundamental need for Mary to be called Mother of God, and that she should be a truly human mother and not only an instrument to permit God's appearing on earth.[14] Because God was in Christ He had in Mary a Mother who was thence Mother of God; because He is truly man He has in Mary a true, human mother. The human unity of Mary, Mother of God, and of Jesus, Son of God, appears very clearly in the account of the visitation as we have seen in many respects.

Mary and the Incarnation

To take seriously the incarnation and humanity of the Son of God, as so clearly set forth by this title Mother of God, now leads us to consider the anthropological, psychological and spiritual implications of the maternal and filial relationship between Mary and Christ, since it is clear that this motherhood of the virgin is not only a corporeal phenomenon as Nestorianism would affirm.

We are not here concerned with a purely psychological and spiritual kind of meditation which would give free rein to the subject of Mary, on the pretext that never enough could be said about her. Such a meditation would run the risk of removing us from a healthy theological consideration of the mystery of the incarnation. It is not forbidden to permit one's meditation to benefit from a use of the imagination provided that such imagination is concerned with images which have a direct relation with Christian teaching, and are not decorations which just embroider the truth which can really gain nothing from it. We shall not go as far as Luther, whom it is perhaps good to quote here, so as to reverse a little more the opinions so well established on the Marian doctrine of the Reformation: 'She, the Lady above heaven and earth, must forget her goods, have a heart so humble that she might have no shame in washing the swaddling clothes or preparing a bath for John the Baptist like a servant girl (in the house of Elizabeth). What humility! it would surely have been more just to have arranged for her a golden coach, pulled by 4,000 horses and to cry and proclaim as the carriage proceeded: "Here passes the woman who is raised far above all women, indeed above the whole human race" . . . but no, she makes her long journey on foot, first one mile, then twenty,

79

then more and yet she is already the Mother of God! It would have been more just surely that all the hills should leap and dance!' (at the Feast of the Visitation, July 2, 1532) [15]; and then on another Feast of the Visitation, July 2, 1537, Luther said: 'When the Virgin received the acclamation of Elizabeth as being the blessed Mother of God, because she had believed and because all was coming to pass as the angel had spoken, she was not filled with pride by this praise which no other woman had ever yet spoken to her—this immense praise: "No woman is like unto thee! you are more than an empress or a queen! you are more than Eve or Sarah; blessed above all nobility, wisdom or saintliness!" No, she was not filled with pride by this lofty, excellent and super-abundant praise . . .' [16]

To take seriously the mystery of the Incarnation of God and His true humanity makes legitimate, and even demands a consideration of, what this extraordinary motherhood meant for Mary. On account of the sober quality of the Gospel, we may well hesitate sometimes to make such a meditation but then we run the risk of neglecting the person of Mary and the greatness of her divine motherhood. We are in danger of thinking of her simply as an impersonal tool of the Incarnation and thus of minimizing the very reality of the Incarnation, and making of him, unconsciously perhaps, only an appearance of God despite the truly human conditions of His Presence, i.e. the humble birth, the humble motherhood of Mary, the human childhood of Christ, in a family and in a human situation. The completely human character, both of Mary's motherhood and of Christ's childhood, is an essential element in the fact of the Incarnation. To take seriously the human conditions in the domestic, social and religious sense of the life of Christ is necessary for a true belief in the Incarnation. God truly and completely became man.[17] The dogma of the divine motherhood of Mary is part of seeing clearly the humanity of Christ. To call Mary the 'Mother of God' is to recognize that God became incarnate so completely and so really in our human flesh that He had a truly human mother and was a truly human son in a human family.

In this perspective we have the right and even the duty to try and estimate what this motherhood must have meant to Mary. To do this it is not necessary to assume that Mary had a perfect understanding of the mystery from the outset. Mary's perfection consists not so much in a total knowledge and understanding of the mystery

with which she lived, but in her complete faith that this mystery
was that of God Himself. By the Annunciation and the Visitation,
Mary understood in faith that God was coming to make in her His
Dwelling-place in a unique and ineffable manner, and His Son was
the Messiah King, the Saviour Jesus, the Son of the Most High, the
Son of God, the Blessed, Kyrios—the Lord. It does not add anything to Mary's perfection to assert her full awareness of the
mystery of the Incarnation in the sense that the Church later would
plumb it. Mary has an immediate awareness and understanding of
the mystery of the Incarnation, that God is in Jesus in a unique
fashion and that Jesus is truly the Son whom she bears and whom
she must bring up as a true mother should; Mary has a direct
awareness and understanding of the mystery of the Son of God
made man; and this awareness and understanding, which are immediate and from the very outset, will increase in so far as Mary sees
Jesus goes out on His mission. The meditation of Mary on the
mystery which affects her appears twice in the Gospel concerning
marriage. All here is in the nature of symbol. But we will return to
this delicate matter later.

We can imagine the feelings of joy which Mary must have shared
in the upbringing of this divine Son. What questions she must have
been faced with in the presence of this unique being whose mother
she was. How much she must have admired Him and how great
must have been the desire to worship Him. This close relationship
between God and His human mother could only draw Mary the
more into a life of faith, piety and unique love. To hold in her
arms the Son of God, and live and eat with Him and to enjoy His
company for many years could do no other than deeply mark the
life of Mary. On the other side, if Christ truly became man like
ourselves He was a child and thus had to be brought up and
educated like us. The Apocryphal Gospels have tried to present the
childhood of Christ as being shot through with the 'marvellous.'
The Canonical Gospels offer no place for these legendary stories.
On the contrary indeed the occasion of the Passover visit of Jesus,
Mary and Joseph to Jerusalem shows us the Christ child as the
object of very special care on the part of His parents. His mother
even has occasion to reproach Him. Certainly His reply already
reveals His supernatural task, just as the debate which He has just
held with the doctors does the same. However the account tells us
that His parents did not understand the import of His reply, which
clearly shows that they were not accustomed to this 'marvellous'

F

side in their child (Luke 2: 41–50). If Mary was acquainted with the divine character of her Son and had been in faith sanctified by Him, nothing openly seems to have been shown of this in the behaviour of Jesus at Nazareth, prior to this conversation with the doctors in the Temple at the age of twelve.

The Gospel tells us that 'the Child grew and increased in wisdom' and that 'the grace of God rested upon him' (Luke 2: 40). This reference reveals at one and the same time the reality of the divine nature in Jesus and also the discreet manner of its appearance. Was it not said also of John the Baptist with practically the same words 'the child grew and increased in spirit' (Luke 1: 80)? In the course of this first period of Christ's childhood, Mary lived by faith in the promises of God from the time of the conception and birth of Jesus, and not in the permanent company of an infant prodigy who was for ever revealing Himself as God. But this faith was 'the assurance of things hoped for, the certainty of things not seen' (Heb. 11: 1). Without the miraculous sign which had marked the conception and birth of Christ, whilst yet keeping and meditating on them in her heart, Mary lived in the faith that one day there would be revealed the Messiah of whom she knew herself to be the mother. If Jesus had constantly been revealed in His divine nature during His childhood, Mary would have had no need of faith nor would she have been surprised at the reply of her son at the age of twelve: 'Why did you seek me? Did you not know that I must be about my Father's business?' (Luke 2: 49). She knows that He is the Son of God, but she also knows that she must live in the hope of faith, until He enters upon His supernatural mission as the Messiah. At the age of twelve it seems to her that she must still be His cautious mother and that the humanity of the Son of God still demands her quite human mothering. She does not seek to hasten the time of fulfilment as she will at Cana. She remains always the happy believer, she who lives above all by faith. Mary also, as a human creature, is saved by faith and not by sight. As Luther was to write of her: 'She not only has the glory of being Mother and Virgin, of being the Mother of the Son of God, but she has also eternal salvation by faith; she does not obtain this salvation because she is Mother and Virgin, Mother of the Son of God. It was always possible for her to fall but she is the eternal dwelling-place of the Holy Spirit and she remains perpetually holy, and blessed Mother for eternity' (July 2, 1533).[18]

After this occasion at Jerusalem, Jesus 'returned with them and came to Nazareth; and he was submissive to them; but his mother kept all these words in her heart; as for Jesus he grew in wisdom, in stature and in grace before God and man' (Luke 2: 51-2). This Passover journey marked a turning point. The relationship of Jesus with the Temple, the Word of God, and with 'his Father's business' are revealed. His messianic mission is awakened and this is, after the first shock, a new matter for meditation in Mary's heart. The refrain concerning the growth of the Child is repeated: 'He grew in stature and wisdom; he grew in the grace of God,' and this not only in the mysterious relationship with the Father, not only 'before God' but also 'before men.' It seems that with the passing years Christ's wisdom and grace are revealed in a new way to the eyes of those around Him, and particularly to Mary, who little by little sees that the words spoken to her by the Lord at the Annunciation, by Elizabeth at the Visitation, and by Simeon and Anna at the Presentation, are coming true: she is indeed the Mother of the Son of God, of the Saviour and the Messiah King.

However, Jesus remained in submission to His parents. In this reference there is revealed all the humanity which continues in His relation as a Son with His mother. At one and the same time Mary assumes a new awareness of her divine motherhood and Jesus submits Himself voluntarily to her human motherhood. Joseph, a man of faith, and one respectful of the mystery of which he himself has had a revelation, protects them both; and Jesus is also in submission to him as a father, to him whose true Father is in Heaven. This willingness to submit reveals very clearly the real humanity of Christ; and how very much Mary must have been edified about humility in seeing her Lord thus submit to her authority as a mother! One can here imagine the continual exchanges of mother and Son, in the loving demands of a mother and a child, of authority and obedience, of foresight and recognition. Mary lives with God who is her Son; Jesus submits to Mary who is His mother and of whom He is the Creator and Saviour! This insoluble mystery and on which one could meditate for ever, reveals the Incarnation of the Son of God, the reality of His human nature.

To call Mary 'the Mother of God' is to express in the only way which is adequate the mystery of the Incarnation of God who became man.

Chapter 7

Mother of the Messiah King

The Joy of Mary : the Magnificat

After the marvellous encounter between Mary and Elizabeth we are given a canticle which expresses the messianic joy of Mary and echoes the eschatological greeting of Elizabeth. And Mary then says:

'My soul doth magnify the Lord,
   And my spirit hath rejoiced in God my Saviour.
For he hath regarded the low estate of his handmaiden: for, behold from henceforth all generations shall call me blessed.
For he that is mighty hath done to me great things; and holy is his name.
And his mercy is on them that fear him from generation to generation.
He hath shewed strength with his arm; he hath scattered the proud in the imagination of their hearts.
He hath put down the mighty from their seats, and exalted them of low degree.
He hath filled the hungry with good things; and the rich he hath sent empty away.
He hath holpen his servant Israel, in remembrance of his mercy;
As he spake to our fathers, to Abraham and his seed for ever' (Luke 1: 46–55).

This canticle of the Virgin Mary is shot through with biblical references. As with the account of the Annunciation and Visitation, we can note here a constant use of the images and words of the Old Testament. Mary is, in this canticle again, the true Daughter of Zion, the fulfilment of the messianic hope of Israel. She appears as one living in close contact with the history of her people, with the scripture with which she is so familiar that she expresses her joy in the very words of the prophets.[1] The first verses, in the first person, are those which recall texts referring to Israel as a people; here Mary again does not rejoice and sing as an individual but as one linked with the whole people of God; as the Handmaid of the Lord she represents, as the Daughter of Zion, the Israel which is the servant of Yahveh.

The very development of the 'Magnificat' shows Mary as the eschatological personification of Israel:

' . . . for he has regarded the lowliness of his handmaiden. . . . He has helped his servant Israel . . . in remembrance of his mercy to Abraham . . . '

If we retrace our steps through the 'Magnificat' in an historical sense we see first Abraham who symbolizes the whole of Israel, then, in this sacred history, the entire people who are the servants of Yahveh and finally at the outset Mary, the Handmaid of the Lord, who symbolizes the whole people and particularly the poor of the Lord, as they await the coming of the Messiah and share the joy of His appearing.[2]

The whole meaning of the 'Magnificat' may be summed up in this single theme: God loves the poor, the Messiah King wills to be born of a poor Virgin and the Glory will be manifested in humility.

The most obvious link between this canticle of Mary and the Old Testament is its close resemblance to the canticle of Hannah (1 Sam. 2: 1-10). Mary appears as one who has transferred to her life the very situation of Samuel's mother. Hannah, humbled by her barrenness, had addressed this prayer to God: 'O Lord of Sabaoth, if thou would'st consider the poverty ('ani, tapeinōsis) of thy servant, remember me, and do not forget thy servant but give her a little child and then I will give him to Yahveh for his life long . . . ' (1 Sam. 1: 11). Mary will sing in her song: 'He has regarded the poverty (tapeinōsis) of his servant . . . ' Then Hannah, having been heard and now the mother of a son whom she has consecrated to the Lord, prays in a manner which bears a close resemblance to Mary's song; we set down here the principal parallels:

Hannah	*Mary*
My hearts exalts in the Lord	My soul magnifies the Lord
My strength is exalted in the Lord . . .	and my spirit rejoices in God my Saviour
there is none holy like the Lord . . .	holy is his Name . . .
those who were hungry have ceased to hunger . . .	He has filled the hungry with good things . . .
The Lord makes poor and makes rich	the rich he hath sent empty away . . .
He brings low (tapeinoi) and he also exalts . . .	He has exalted those of low degree (tapeinous) . . .

This canticle of Hannah is a messianic song which expresses the hope of the poor. It ends with the mention of the Messiah King:

> 'The Lord will judge the ends of the earth; he will give strength to his kings, and exalt the power of his anointed' (1 Sam. 2: 10).

This hymn of messianic expectation of the poor of the Lord, placed in the mouth of Hannah, the poor barren handmaid who had become a mother, was very fitting as a prototype for the canticle of Mary, the poor one, the Handmaid of the Lord, the Virgin who has become Mother of the Messiah. The fundamental theme of both these canticles is the love of God for the poor, and His glory which is revealed in the victory of the humble.

The 'Magnificat' in its style and the images it employs similarly reflects this messianic song of Isaiah (61: 10–11):

> 'I will greatly rejoice in the Lord, my soul shall exalt in my God; for he hath clothed me in the garments of salvation, he has covered me with the robe of righteousness, as a bridegroom decks himself with a garland, and as a bride adorns herself with her jewels. For as the earth brings forth its shoots, and as a garden causes what is grown in it to spring up, so the Lord God will cause righteousness and praise to spring forth before all the nations.'

This outburst of joy, which speaks of salvation put on as a garment and of hope in the seed which will cause the praise of God to break forth, proclaims the joy of Mary who, being overshadowed by the luminous cloud of the Most High, the Holy Spirit, miraculously conceived the Son of God, and who, about to give birth to justice, sets forth her praise before all nations: 'Behold from henceforth all generations shall call me blessed.'

It is above all else the joy of Mary which, at the outset of her song, breaks out into such an immense acknowledgment and act of grace to the Lord. All her being, her soul, spirit and voice offer glory to God alone; she keeps nothing for herself; she recognizes that all is but by the grace of God in her, the one 'full-of-grace.' The supernatural events which thus affect her are not for her own glory, but for God's glory alone; it reveals the unique greatness of God; her soul magnifies the Lord.

The sole source of her joy is God her Saviour. The exultation which she expresses is the same as that of Elizabeth: it is the delight of the last days, the great longing of joy in Israel which at last sees, for itself and all creation, the arrival of the final deliverer. As with John the Baptist and Elizabeth in the name of all Israel which waits, and in the name of all creation which longs for deliverance, Mary quivers with this ineffable delight in the presence of God who comes at last to inhabit the earth in order to save men. She also pre-figures the eschatological delight of the Church which, with all the creation, will one day behold the return in glory of the Risen Lord.

The ecstatic joy of Mary comes from God alone, her Saviour. It is not, however, merely the joy of human motherhood which gives her cause for rejoicing, but that she is to be the Mother of the Messiah, her Saviour. The child whom she bears is her God and Saviour. There is in the expression of this delight at one and the same time an objectivity and yet a profound intimacy: Mary humbles herself before the mystery of this salvation which her motherhood is to assist and she calls God 'her Saviour.' Like every other creature she needs Him: it is He who, foreseeing her divine motherhood, has prepared her for that 'yes' which she has been able to speak so simply; it is He who, during the whole of His earthly life, on the Cross, at the Resurrection and the Ascension, by His intercession before the Father and by the gift of the Holy Spirit at Pentecost, is going to support her in that faith and fidelity which will secure for her eternal salvation: her spirit rejoices in God her Saviour. Mary thus calls forth the event of the Annunciation by which God has made known to her her own personal salvation and that of all mankind. The Lord of all glory has been willing indeed to consider the poorest and most insignificant of His creatures in order to make of her His Handmaid. Here occurs this principal theme of that poverty which receives glory. It is because

Mary has nothing with which to establish her own claim, because she is scarcely more than a child and a virgin and because she is poor and dwells in an unknown village and has neither pride nor power nor riches—it is because of all these things that God loves her and chose her in order that He might do great things in her, and make of her the Dwelling of God, the Mother of God. The glory of the Lord here enters into the world through the porchway of humility and poverty.

It is because of this very separation between the glory of the Master and the poverty of the Handmaid who can make no other claim whatever to her divine splendour that Mary will be proclaimed blessed by all nations. This proclamation will never be able to turn away the hearts of men from their love and adoration of the Lord so long as Mary will remain in the Church the humble Handmaid whose task, despite her poverty, is precisely to set men on the way to the glory of God. She can speak in all humility of how all ages will call her blessed, for she knows that this blessing of which she will be the object, in so far as she will represent the poverty of the handmaid whom she is willing to be, will only lead up to God, and never remain fixed upon herself. How can the poverty of the hand-maid in any sense fit the glory of the Lord? It is because she is the Mother of God that she will be able to be proclaimed thus blessed; all that she is is of God, by God and for God; she is in the poor status of a handmaid, the Ark which the presence of God inhabits, the Mother whose son is God. Her poverty as a handmaid is her pure receptivity, transparence, detachment and direction towards God: she can only welcome God, she can only let Him make His appearance, as if through herself and she can only detach men from herself in order to point them to their only Saviour. The praise of Mary is only true if it is praise to God for Mary the poor hand-maid of the Lord and the blessed Mother of God.

Luther wrote in his commentary on the 'Magnificat': 'We are able to learn there what is the true honour with which we can venerate and serve her. How are we to address her? Consider her words and then she will teach you what to say: "O blessed virgin and Mother of God, how hast thou been able to be considered as nothing, and disdained as of little consequence and yet God has none the less regarded thee with all his grace and all his riches, and accomplished in thee such mighty things? You have deserved nothing, but beyond and above thy merit, there is the grace of God in thee, rich and overflowing. Yes, you are blest from this hour and unto all eternity, thou who hast found such a God ... " ' [3] Bullinger, the balanced Reformer, wrote: 'What pre-eminence in the eyes of God the Virgin Mary had on account of her piety, her faith, her purity, her saintliness and all her virtues, so that she can hardly be compared with any of the other saints, but should by rights be rather elevated above all of them, appears very clearly in the first chapters of the gospels of St. Matthew and St. Luke, and particularly in her "Magnificat." . . . If Mary really is the Mother of the Lord, as the blessed Elizabeth, filled with the Holy Spirit, so explicitly named her, then it is altogether just that she should be named by the Fathers of the Church "theotokos," that is to say Mother of God (Gottesgebärerin or Muttergottes). Nestorius denied that in the most infamous manner. All the same, if women of the Old Testament like Sarah, Rebecca, Leah, Rachel, Deborah, Hannah, Abigail, Esther, Susannah, Judith and others were notable and excellent women how much more notable and worthy of praise is she who surpasses with distinction all women, the blessed Virgin Mother! ' [4]

Let us once more refer to the Reformer Charles Drelincourt: 'We do not simply believe that God has favoured the holy and blessed Virgin more than all the Patriarchs and the Prophets, but also that He has exalted her above all Seraphim. The angels can only qualify as servants of the Son of God, the creatures and workmanship of His hands; but the holy Virgin is not only the servant and the creature but also the Mother of this great and living God.' [5] And finally Karl Barth: 'Behold from henceforth all generations shall call me blessed. What unspeakable grandeur there is in this encounter: the quite simple fact, without any show, that it was sufficient for God with one look only to pour out the fullness of grace and on the other side the power and immense import of this event: "All generations shall call me blessed." All the angels in the whole of heaven now regard only this place where Mary was, this young girl, to whom however nothing has happened save that God turned upon her lowliness his simple regard. This short instant in time is full of eternity, of an eternity ever new. There is nothing greater in heaven or earth. If ever in the history of the world anything of great importance has taken place it is this "regard." We speak of Mary but this is properly to speak at the same time of the Church and in a sense of ourselves also. There is nothing here which resembles those touching symbols which one gives to children at the moment of their Confirmation. We are not like a little girl bearing a candle in the night which at any moment a breath of wind can extinguish and which she must protect with her hand. No: "Behold from henceforth all generations shall call me blessed." Here there is no hesitation, no fear, no light which runs the risk of being extinguished but rather certitude: victory has already been won. All the history of the world from its beginning, in its course and in its end considers this unique moment which is Christ. Our calling is to be on the side of Mary. For this joy and this revelation of the soul can also be at any instant our joy. We have only one thing to do, like Mary: to let God act. Let it be unto me as thou hast said.' [6]

This word of Mary: 'All generations shall call me blessed,' establishes and legitimizes the presence of the Mother of the Lord in the liturgy and the preaching of the Church. How else could she be 'called blessed' than by the ordinary means of the preaching of the Word of God by the Church: worship and preaching?

Mary is with the Church and in the Church in order to sing her song, in order to make known the praises of Him who has called us from darkness into His glorious light. It is clear that the Magnificat renders all glory to God for the great things which He has just accomplished in the Incarnation of her Son. The Virgin Mary does not claim for herself any merit or any glory; that would be contrary to her spirit of poverty and humility. However, we have just seen because of this very poverty which cannot screen the glory of the Lord, and because she is not just an impersonal though pure instrument in the event of the Incarnation, but the Mother of God, chosen as a person to say yes to her motherhood, that Mary can prophesy in all humility that all generations shall call her blessed. And now, reciting the great things which God has done and that all the glory is to return to Him, she says that the Almighty accomplishes them for her and in her (moi). Her personality is not disintegrated by the great things which God accomplishes: it is for her and in her, in Mary, that the Lord comes to be incarnate in order that He may enter the world and save it. This reference to Mary, who plays a personal and motherly rôle in the Incarnation, excludes every idea that she could only be an impersonal tool and is finally of no account whatever.

The Incarnation is a truly human event. God in becoming

incarnate does not simply use the human person as a neutral instrument, He gives it worth and dignifies the human person by becoming the truly human Son of a truly human Mother, who plays a personal rôle in the Incarnation. The 'moi' of the Virgin Mary, in her canticle, is one more sign of the reality of the Incarnation and the truth of the humanity of Christ. The salvation which He comes to effect in humanity, God wishes to bring about through a human person, who freely responds, in the plan of her pre-destination, to this supernatural Motherhood which is the means of the Incarnation of the Son, true God and true man. The person of Mary is therefore a sign of the true humanity of God in His Incarnation. There is here no suspicion of any trace of monophysitism, according to which Mary would represent the humanity of Christ who Himself would only share the divine nature. The humanity of the person of Mary conditions the humanity of Christ who is true God *and* true man.

Mary, as a faithful Jewess, does not speak of God by His name but by His attributes—she calls Him the Almighty, the Holy.

God is powerful and holy, He is the God of justice who inspires religious fear in His people, but He is also, and above all else, for Mary the God of mercy, the Lord who extends His love and His compassion from one generation to another. He always remembers His mercy, and always comes to the help of Israel, His Servant, and through Israel to the help of all mankind. Here, Mary, the Handmaid of the Lord, taking the place of Israel the Servant, becomes the symbolic being in whom is revealed the greatest love, the hitherto unheard-of mercy and the final help of God. By her and through her the great compassion of the Creator for all His creatures is to pass and extend to all generations who shall know the Christ, Saviour and Mediator. Mary is the unique sign of the mercy of God at the moment of the Incarnation, in which is concentrated the love of the Lord for Israel, His Servant, and from which is to be shed abroad the fullness of the love of God for all the world, in Jesus Christ, the God of Love, who gives His life for all men. In the beginning Abraham had been the sign of the mercy of God who must extend himself to all Israel; in the fulfilment Mary is the sign of this same mercy which is going to be extended to all the world in Christ and His Body, the Church.

The mercy of the Creator, the God of Love, the Holy and all-powerful, which is extended from Abraham, the Father of Believers, to all his seed throughout the centuries, through the Fathers, Israel the Servant, and then the poor ones, finds in Mary, the poor and blessed Handmaid, a point of introduction on the day of the Incarnation in order that love shall be born among men, Christ the Saviour who will establish the Church in the Holy Spirit, in the sight of the Kingdom of God. This mercy, this compassion for all men, is a strong love which does not contradict but rather implies the holiness and power of God. This love of God, the Holy and Powerful, is to be described by Mary in terms which might seem revolutionary for a too tender and facile sensibility. In this second part of her canticle the Virgin appears as the strong woman who defends the right of God and sings of the love of Him who is named Holy and Almighty.

Mary here recalls some of those female heroes of the Old Testament who stood in defence of the justice and glory of God and the honour of His people, like Deborah, prophetess and judge, a mother in Israel (Judges 4: 4), or Judith, the glory of Jerusalem, who walked uprightly before God (Judith 13: 20; 15: 9). Hannah herself, the humble and barren one, sang by God's grace about her motherhood: 'The bows of the mighty are broken, but the feeble gird on strength' (1 Sam. 2: 4). . . . Mary also is going to sing of the great mercy of God in expressing the victory of the poor, who had been heard in their expectation, by the coming of the Messiah King in poverty. It is the fulfilment of the song of Hannah and of Psalm 113:

> 'He raises the poor from the dust, and lifts the needy from the ash-heap, to make them sit with princes, the princes of his people. He gives the barren woman a home, making her the joyous mother of children' (vv. 7, 8 and 9).

For the Virgin Mary, the love of God reveals His holiness and His justice; the mercy of the Lord is made concrete in precise acts of justice among men. Here we must relate the Church to Mary in order that one may constantly instruct the other afresh in the fact that the love of the Lord is not a platonic feeling but a compassion which makes Him suffer with those who suffer and which calls forth their deliverance. Has the Church always experienced this teaching of the mercy of God such as Mary outlines in her song? Are we not troubled in our conscience, as persons or as a Church, by the strong words of the Mother of God?

For the Virgin the signs of the mercy of the Lord are the putting down of the proud and the powerful and the exalting of those of low degree, the sending away empty of the rich, so that the hungry might be filled with good things. She could have enumerated other signs but these two are sufficient to reveal that the love of God takes a concrete human social form and is not simply an interior spiritual consolation. Pride, power and human riches screen the almightiness of God, offend His holiness and contradict His love. God deploys the strength of His arm, He parts the veil which hides His power, His holiness and His love, He scatters the proud, puts down the mighty from their throne and sends the rich empty away. His Incarnation, which is the coming of His Glory in the poverty of His Handmaid, implies a reversal of the human situation and a revaluation of the order of the world. It is truly the invasion by the Kingdom of God of the order of fallen creation in which the proud, the powerful and the rich always have the last word. This invasion of the Glory of the Lord in the poverty of His Handmaid brings in its train the scattering of the proud, the putting down of thrones and of riches which no longer count in the kingdom of the poor who are raised up and the hungry who are fed. Political and social justice, equality of rights and community of goods, are the signs of the mercy of the Messiah King sung by His Mother and His Handmaid. It is thus that the gospel of eternal salvation also becomes the gospel of liberation.

Mary, the first Christian woman, is also the first revolutionary of the new order. The Church, of which the Virgin is the type, cannot proclaim the good news of salvation without at the same time making the love of God concrete by the defence of justice for the poor and needy. The Church is the Handmaid of the Lord, like Mary, when she is poor like her, when she finds her joy amongst the poor and when she shares with them their search for their deliverance. For it is the will of the Lord, His promise and His new order which demand it. No more than Mary herself the Church cannot please herself amongst the proud, the powerful, and the rich of this world. Like Mary, the Church loves the poor and the needy, and she rejoices that in His mercy the Lord scatters the proud, overturns the powerful from their seats and sends the rich empty away; for then these proud, powerful and rich people will know in their turn the poverty which His love and His glory will bring; then they will know in their turn the poverty which can be raised up and the hunger which can be satisfied by the one and only Mighty, the one and only rich, Lord of Glory.

The Virgin Mary is here preparing us for the entry of Christ into the Temple to overturn the tables of the money-changers; she is providing a prelude for the Sermon on the Mount in which Jesus will proclaim blessed the poor, the gentle, the afflicted and the needy . . . for they can be given consolation and their needs met in the Kingdom which belongs to them (Matt. 5: 3–11); she prepares the way for the grave indictment of Christ against the rich who already have their human reward; they are filled now but they will hunger one day (Luke 6: 25), but then, in that hunger, they will perhaps find salvation in God who will come to them. 'It will be difficult for the rich to enter the kingdom of heaven,' says Christ (Matt. 19: 23). This is a constant theme in the Gospel; it finds an echo in this first canticle of joy and victory which Mary chanted to glorify the poverty which alone enabled God to come. St. James will pronounce terrible words on the rich who have not heard the call of the Gospel and have not been willing to be poor in order to receive the riches of God: 'Go to now, ye rich men, weep and howl for your miseries that shall come upon you. Your riches are corrupted and your garments are moth eaten. Your gold and silver is cankered; and the rust of them shall be a witness against you, and shall eat your flesh as it were fire. Ye have reaped treasure together for the last days. Behold, the hire of the labourers who have reaped in your fields, which is of you kept back by fraud, crieth: and the cries of them which have reaped are entered into the ears of the Lord of Sabaoth. Ye have lived in pleasure on the earth, and been wanton, ye have nourished your hearts, as in a day of slaughter. Ye have condemned and killed the just; and he doth not resist you' (Jas. 5: 1–6).

The Church, with Mary, with Christ and the Apostles, loves the poor and cannot really be pleased with the company of the proud, the powerful and the rich. The Church, with Mary, proclaims the scattering of the proud; she believes in the overturning of the powerful from their seats and in the sending of the rich empty away, whether as a sign of the very victory of God, as a sign of His mercy for the poor and needy whom He loves or as a sign of His love for the powerful and the rich whom He can only love in His humility and poverty, for there only are they able to reach Him in truth and truly to receive Him, the Mighty One who gives true riches.

Thus Mary sang of her joy in God her Saviour, who shows mercy to all men on condition that they are willing to become poor and needy since then alone can they receive the certainty of being filled by Him. It is this love which, coming from the Lord, extends from age to age, from Abraham who left all to follow the search for God; it is this love which is extended through the poor of Israel, passing through Mary, the poor and blessed handmaid, and finding its fulfilment in Christ who had neither place to lay His head and who for the rich became poor in order that He might enrich us by His poverty; it is this love which is extended through the Church of the poor in order to reach its fulfilment in the Kingdom of God, which belongs to the poor, the meek, the afflicted, the needy, and to those who show mercy, to the pure, to the peaceful and to the persecuted.

Thus Mary believed and sang; and thus the Church believes and sings as she proclaims the Poor Virgin, Full-of-Grace, the Servant, the Handmaid of the Lord, the Dwelling of God, the Blessed Believer and Mother of God.

Chapter 8

Mother of the Suffering Servant

The Suffering of Mary : the Sword

Forty days after the birth of Jesus, following His Presentation in the Temple, Mary hears a prophecy of Simeon which is to make clear another side of her life as Mother of the Messiah. 'And Joseph and his mother marvelled at those things which were spoken of him. And Simeon blessed them, and said unto Mary his mother, Behold this child is set for the fall and rising again of many in Israel, and for a sign which shall be spoken against; (Yea, a sword shall pierce through thy own soul also) and the thoughts of many hearts shall be revealed' (Luke 2: 33-5).

The going up to Bethlehem, before the birth of Christ, appears as a second stage of the ascent of the Messiah towards His place, the Temple of Jerusalem, the first stage, following the symbolism of Mary as the Ark of the Covenant, having been, as we have seen, the visit of three months which she paid to Elizabeth in the land of Judah. The movement of the first chapters of St. Luke is indeed really this ascent of the Messiah to the historic dwelling-place of God in Jerusalem. The Lord has revealed the universality and the simplicity of the messianic mission of His son, by choosing Mary of Nazareth as the new and temporary dwelling, far from the Temple of Jerusalem and its liturgical ceremonies. But it is necessary that the Messiah should reveal Himself in the place where the glory of Yahveh rests, the House of His Father. Joseph and Mary therefore present themselves first of all at Bethlehem in order to be enrolled for the great re-taxing, and thus indicate the legal connection of Christ with the line of David, King of Israel. This second journey of Christ to the land of Judah is not, like the first, shot through exclusively with messianic joy. Mary begins to endure the suffering which she must bear in her divine motherhood. Her son will not be able to be born in the home surroundings of Nazareth. She is not a mother like others who can enjoy their children for themselves. Mary, the Mother of the Messiah, must follow the destiny and the mission of the Son of God which will entail for her suffering mixed with joy. We can imagine the hardships of the journey from Nazareth to Bethlehem and the suffering which Mary would have to bear, being obliged to bear the child in a stable, in the disturbed atmosphere of a displaced population which does not even permit her to find a place at the inn. And she is not able to bear her child, the Son of God, save in the manger used by the animals. What inward conflicts this must have meant for her who had heard the promise of the angel: 'He shall be great, and he shall be called Son of the Most High'! What faith not to doubt these words but to understand anew that the Glory of God wills to inhabit such complete and utter poverty. Certainly God's goodness will bring her some consolation when she sees the shepherds running up to tell of their vision of the angels in the field.

Her motherhood is therefore now to bear spoliation, renunciation and sacrifice. The Son of God who has left the Father, in order to be incarnate in Mary, already begins His return to the Father in which He leads men who follow Him to their salvation. But for Mary this return involves detachment and suffering. She must obey her Son who is also her Creator. Her human motherhood will only be mortified despite the joys, and the wonders, which her divine motherhood will involve for her.

'And when the days of her purification were accomplished according to the law of Moses they took him to Jerusalem to present him to the Lord, as it is written in the Law of the Lord: "every male that openeth the womb shall be called holy to the Lord," and to offer sacrifice according to that which is said in the Law of the Lord, a pair of turtle doves and two young pigeons' (Luke 2: 22–4).

After the birth of a boy, a woman, according to the law, must observe forty days of purification, during which she was not permitted to touch anything consecrated or to enter the sanctuary. This purification was in regard to 'religious' purity, which we must distinguish from 'moral' purity. Mary did not consider that she was excused from the law of religious purity which concerned the holiness of God and all the things which are to do with His worship. Religious impurity, even contracted in acts which were perfectly pure in a moral sense, prevented certain religious acts, and this limitation underlined the sacred character of God's dwelling-place

97

and *not* the moral sin of one who, for a time, might find himself
'religiously impure.' [1] To argue from this reference to Mary's purification therefore that she was *morally* impure and underwent the
purification for some moral sin, is to ignore the real significance of
the laws of religious purity at that time. It is equally vain to desire
to show that for her this purification had another sense than
purification had for other Jewish women because she could not
have contracted such religious impurity. One would then have to
assert that she did not carry out the washings before meals which
were also considered as an act of external purification (Mark 7:
1–13).

Christ will make plain in His teaching the uselessness of these
external Jewish lustrations by showing that they can become hypo-
critical and He will emphasize the prime necessity of moral purity.
Mary, as a faithful Jewess, would not wish to avoid the practice of
the law, and she thus reveals, as St. Paul was to say of her, that
'God sent his Son, born of a woman, subject to the law in order
that he might redeem those under the law' (Gal. 4: 4–5). Mary and
Joseph were ready to fulfil the law with regard to Jesus because for
them it would have been a moral sin not to have carried out an
order of legal purification.[2] On the other hand the Gospel speaks
of *their* purification, as opposed to the law which only recognizes
the purification of a woman ('*Her* purification,' Lev. 12: 6). Does
the use of this plural mean that both Joseph and Mary are
involved? That would appear strange since the man in this instance
did not contract any impurity according to the law. Was it then a
case of Mary and Jesus? The same difficulty arises. It seems more
likely that the Gospel here refers rather to the whole religious law
of purification to which men submit out of respect for the holiness
of God and His demands, than the case of one or two people in
particular, Mary and Joseph or Jesus. It is the whole age of law
which is here referred to, and the religious act of the ascent to the
Temple for the Presentation and Sacrifice.

Here appears the second religious act involved in the birth of a
first-born. The law said, 'The firstborn of man amongst thy sons
thou shalt redeem, and it shall be when thy son asketh thee in time
to come, saying, "What is this?" that thou shalt say unto him, "By
strength of hand the Lord brought us out of Egypt from the house
of bondage." And it came to pass that when Pharaoh would hardly
let us go that the Lord slew all the firstborn of man and the first-

born of beast in the land of Egypt: therefore I sacrifice to the Lord all that openeth the womb being male, but all the firstborn of my children I redeem. And it shall be for a token upon thy hand, and for frontlets between thine eyes, for by strength of hand the Lord brought us forth out of Egypt' (Exod. 13: 13–16). The first-born were thus considered as belonging especially to God, in memory of the deliverance of Israel. Like the ceremony of unleavened bread, the 'azyme' ('the bread of tribulation'), which was a memorial of the Exodus 'in haste' from the land of slavery (Deut. 16: 3), and like the Passover Feast with the Lamb slain, which is a memorial of the 'saving blood' on the doors of the Israelites during the night of their deliverance from Egypt, the ransom of the first-born was a memorial of the 'salvation of the children' of Israel when the angel struck the first-born of the Egyptians. These three ceremonies had in the law the same significance; it is the same explanation which describes them; they are a memorial, a sign of the passing of Israel from slavery to deliverance (Exod. 13: 9; 12: 14; 13: 16). Just as every year the days of unleavened bread and the passover feast made present and active the historical deliverance of the People of God as a kind of sacrament making present the salvation of God, the ransom and the consecration of the first-born made present and living this same deliverance. This first-born was in a way a permanent sign of the salvation of Israel in a family and a permanent memorial of the Passover. It recalled for the family God's sparing of the first-born of the people in the night of their deliverance; it was the daily and domestic memorial of this salvation which Israel kept each year in the Passover Feast.

The members of the tribe of Levi were alone consecrated to the liturgical service and they replaced in worship all the first-born of the other tribes whose consecration did not involve a liturgical function in the Temple, but who remained in their families as a sacred sign and memorial of salvation (Num. 3: 12, 13): they belonged to God, like the Levites, but not on account of their liturgical function. The first-born who therefore belonged to God, belonged *de jure* to the Temple and the liturgical duties there, but *de facto* they were replaced by the Levites and for this reason must be ransomed by the priest. Yahveh had said to Aaron, the priest, that he must ransom the first-born of men by paying for him five shekels of silver (Num. 18: 16).

Mary and Joseph thus conformed here to the law but St. Luke

99

underlined the inner character of the rite not by speaking of the ransom but of the presentation of Jesus. What matters here is the sense of the rite which is the consecration to God of the first-born and the recognition that he belongs wholly to the Lord. One could be quit of the ransom in any place so long as the appointed son was given to the priest. Now Mary and Joseph fulfil the journey to the Temple which quite clearly underlines the profound meaning of the ransom: they go to the Temple to consecrate Jesus to God, and to reveal the Lord's right to their child.

We here reach the third and decisive stage of the ascent of the Messiah to the Temple and of the Son of God to the House of the Father. Mary on this occasion of the Presentation appears in all the starkness and detachment of her human motherhood. Joseph and Mary are the poor; they can only offer the two birds ordered by the law for the poor (Lev. 12: 8); but they are poorer still than any parents in Israel: their first-born son is the Messiah, the Son of God; His consecration as a first-born to the Lord bears its total significance; it is not only a ceremony of ransom but a total sacrifice of their son to the Lord; a total abandonment of their parental rights. Mary has not a Son just of her own even when consecrated to the Lord, but she is the Mother of the Son of God who only belongs to God, who is God, and from whom she will have to detach herself little by little in order that He may undertake completely His messianic task.

The ceremony fulfilled is therefore fundamentally an act of consecration and sacrifice, a gift to God and a renunciation of self, a surrender to God and a stripping of self. This presentation recalls the surrender of Samuel by Hannah in the service of the Temple of Yahveh at Shiloh (1 Sam. 2: 24-8). The barren woman who longed so much for a child, and was once heard, fulfilled her vow: 'I give him to the Lord: all the days of his life he is given to the Lord.' Mary, in just the same way, filled with joy by her messianic motherhood, knows that her Son is wholly God's and she gives Him to the Lord at the Presentation in the Temple, stripping herself totally of her human claims as a mother.

The verb 'to present'—'paristanein,' which sums up the act of ransom for St. Luke, clearly indicates this sacrificial act of Mary as a memorial of the deliverance of the People of God. In the Epistles of St. Paul this word 'to present' has a clearly sacrificial significance (Rom. 6: 13–19; 12: 1; 1 Cor. 8: 8; 2 Cor. 4: 14; 11: 2; Ephes. 5: 27; Col. 1: 22, 28). 'Even so now yield your members' servants to righteousness unto holiness . . . even so present your bodies a living sacrifice, holy, acceptable unto God . . . for I have espoused you to one husband, that I may present you as a chaste virgin to Christ . . . ' (Rom. 6: 19; 12: 1; 2 Cor. 11: 2). The context of this verb 'to present' is always a liturgical context, implying the offering of a being in order that it might be consecrated to God and the corresponding spoliation on the part of the one who makes the offering: it implies the two senses of the word sacrifice which is at one and the same time an offering and a renunciation. Mary, in presenting Jesus for this rite of redemption and consecration of a first-born, offers Him to God, first recognizing the right of the Lord's total claim on the Messiah, whilst she herself is despoiled, thus renouncing her right to a human motherly claim on her son.

This presentation and offering of Jesus, the first-born, is, as we have seen, a sign and memorial of the historic deliverance of Israel. . . . In thus presenting their son, according to the law, Mary and Joseph fulfil a memorial of the Passover: they recall in fact that the Lord has spared His people and delivered them from slavery in Egypt. This first-born who is redeemed will be, as in every Israelitish family, though here *par excellence*, a living sign of salvation, a daily memorial of the passover, which He will one day fulfil in the sacrifice of the Cross. Thus, Jesus, who will offer Himself one day as the Passover Lamb, perfect and eternal, on the Cross and who will institute the Passover meal of the new covenant in the Eucharist, in which He is present as the lamb offered, is already found in a state of offering on the day of the Presentation in the Temple, as a sign and memorial of the deliverance of Israel whom He will lead to its fulfilment in the sacrifice of the Cross. And it is Mary, with Joseph, who carries and presents Jesus, the new born, as a sign and memorial of this deliverance. She is here, truly, the type of Mother Church who one day, and for ever, will be called to bear and present the Body of Christ in the Eucharist, as the sign and memorial of the Redemption and Resurrection. This Presentation of the Eucharistic Body of Christ, before God in the act of grace and in intercession, and before men as food and communion, will mean for the Church as for Mary a movement of offering and consecration at the same time as it means an act of renunciation and despoiling.[3] The presentation of Christ, by Mary and by the Church, is an act of consecrating grace and a recognition of poverty.

101

Mary can only offer to God what He has given her in the fullness and free gift of His love. And the Church, in the same way, will say in her Eucharistic liturgy: 'Offerimus . . . de tuis donis ac datis . . . all comes of thee, and our only offering is to recall thy wonders and thy gifts.' [4] The hands of Mary and of the Church are empty: it is God alone who will fill them with Christ; their only possible offering which is valid, the sole act of grace and the only intercession which they can present to God being Christ Himself, their Saviour, Mediator and Intercessor.

This act of presentation and offering of Christ who has filled their poverty thus implies for the Church and Mary an attitude of sacrifice, of self-stripping and detachment. Mary and the Church are called to decrease so that Christ may increase; they are called to practise detachment in order that they may allow Him to fulfil His mission, and to experience spoliation in order that all glory may return only to Him.

The ceremony of ransom and of Presentation is completed by the offering, as sacrifice, of 'a pair of turtle doves or two small pigeons.' Joseph and Mary have chosen these two birds of the poor for sacrifice, for they have not the means of offering a lamb or the larger turtle doves which are ordinarily prescribed (Lev. 12: 8). This sacrifice has a double significance. The first bird which replaces the lamb is offered as a holocaust in order to symbolize the total gift of those who offer; it is a sign of total consecration to the Lord, and we have seen what that signifies for Jesus and, in consequence, for Mary. The second bird is offered as a sacrifice for sin, that is to say as a sign of legal purification for Mary; we have also seen what this purification means. In every way, like the ceremony of ransom, this symbolic sacrifice seems to be dominated by the act of presentation, the consecration of Jesus the first-born to the Lord. This consecration is the profound meaning of the legal observance of Joseph and Mary (by the ransom and sacrifice of a bird). The presentation is summed up in this recognition by Joseph and Mary that their Son belongs to God, that He is the sign and memorial of the deliverance and that they must themselves be stripped and become detached in order that He may be permitted to perform His messianic task.

This mission Simeon is to recall for them in his inspired canticle. This just and pious member of the poor, who awaits the consolation of Israel, and on whom the Holy Spirit rests, who knows by revelation of the spirit that death will not overtake him till he has seen Christ the Lord, thus comes into the Temple, urged by the Spirit, to receive the Messiah into his arms. In this short account one finds three times a mention of the Holy Spirit who causes Simeon to appear as a man whose only existence is in God; and it is as an icon of the Father that he receives Jesus into his arms; he is there to greet Mary and Joseph with their offering, to receive in the name of the Father Him whom they come to consecrate to Him, *and* hand back to Him. He blesses God in his canticle. He can now die for his eyes have at last seen the salvation of God, prepared before the face of all people, a light to lighten the Gentiles and to be the glory of the people, Israel (Luke 2: 29–32). This song rings out, like the prophecy which follows it, before Joseph and Mary have fulfilled what is required by the law of the Lord (Luke 2: 39). The ritual act which they are to fulfil must first find its meaning in Simeon's revelation of the glorious coming of the Messiah and the suffering which it will entail for Jesus and for Mary (a sign to be spoken against and a sword). The Presentation and consecration of Jesus to God by Mary and Joseph, as their sacrifice, are both prepared for in the prophecy of Simeon. It is like a liturgy of the Word which prepares for and explains some liturgy of sacrifice. The canticle and prophecy of Simeon draw out the two aspects of Christ's mission, and, in consequence, two aspects of the Presentation: the first, salvation, light and glory in the messianic mission of Jesus which the sacrifice of the act of grace and the joyous surrender of Mary call forth; and secondly, a sign to be spoken against and a sword, present in this mission, which call forth the sacrifice of the despoiling and detachment of the Virgin.

In his canticle Simeon says that he has seen in Jesus the Salvation prepared by God before the face of all people. The Saviour whom he holds in his arms will not only be the inheritor of the throne of David, the King of Israel, the Messiah of the people of God. Following the Angel Gabriel, who had revealed the royal character of the Messiah 'over the house of Jacob—and for ever,' the Christmas angels had already proclaimed the universal outreach of this messianic kingdom: 'Glory be to God in the highest, and on earth peace to men of goodwill!' However, this promise could still be interpreted as referring to the Jews scattered all over the earth and chosen by God's love. Simeon clearly reveals to Joseph and Mary that the Saviour has been prepared for *all* people, that He is the light to lighten the Gentiles. Simeon is completely soaked in the universalist prophecy of Isaiah whose vocabulary he even employs:

'For the Lord has comforted his people, he has redeemed Jerusalem. The Lord has bared his holy arm before the eyes of all the nations; and all the ends of the earth shall see the salvation of our God' (Isa. 52: 9–10).

In the first two Servant songs, which pre-figure the Messiah for him, Isaiah says again:

'I have given you as a covenant to the people, as a light to the nations . . . ' (42: 6).

'It is too light a thing that you should be my servant, to raise up the tribes of Jacob and restore the preserved of Israel; I will give you as a light to the nations, that my salvation may reach to the end of the earth' (49: 6).

Simeon, however, goes further than Isaiah as he sees for the first time the universal mission of the Messiah, 'a light to lighten the Gentiles,' and only then his mission to the people of God: 'to be a glory to Israel.'

After the Annunciation and the Nativity, the Presentation brings to Mary a new and clearer revelation of the universal mission of the Son of God. He, whom she has borne, is the salvation for all peoples, a light to lighten the Gentiles at the same time as being the glory of Yahveh in Israel. What astonishment these words of Simeon, the man who only lives in the Holy Spirit, produce in Joseph and Mary! Their joy and wonder are at their fullest (Luke 2: 33). And it is in this spirit of joy and exultation and the act of grace that they are able at that moment to fulfil the liturgical act of Presentation and Sacrifice for this first-born who is not only a sign and memorial of the past deliverance of Israel and who is the salvation of all peoples, the Light of all the Gentiles, but at the same time is the glory of Israel and the deliverer of Jerusalem (Luke 2: 38).

Simeon, after he has sung of the unique glory of the Messiah whom he has held in his arms, pronounces a benediction over Joseph and Mary. He gives thanks for their submissiveness and he gives them the blessing of the Lord whose assistance they will need in order to understand and bring to pass the prophecy which he is going to address especially to Mary. Following the manner of the canticles of Isaiah about the servant of Yahveh, Simeon gives the Virgin to understand that her son is not only the Messiah King who is also universal and glorious but that He is also the Suffering Servant prophesied by Isaiah in the third and fourth songs of the Servant of Yahveh (Isa. 50: 4–9; 52: 13–53: 12):

'I hid not my face from shame and spitting. . . .
He had no form and comeliness that we should look at him, and no beauty that we should desire him. He was despised and rejected of men; a man of sorrows, and acquainted with grief . . . ' (50: 6; 53: 2–3).

The Messiah, as King and Suffering Servant, must fulfil His mission in gainsaying and grief. In the presence of Christ the thoughts of all hearts will be revealed; some will be closed to Him, and this will be their downfall, others will follow Him and find their revelation, and their spiritual resurrection. It will be a sign to be spoken against and He will thus be drawn to the love of some and the hate of others; and this hate will lead Him to suffering. Mary here realizes that her Son is not only the Messiah King but also the Suffering Servant foretold by Isaiah. She must therefore expect to see Him 'scorned and despised.' He will indeed have to bear the sufferings of men and He will be burdened with their sorrows. He will be pierced on account of their sins and crushed on account of their misdeeds. The chastisement which will bring their peace will be upon Him and it is thanks to His wounds that men will be healed (Isa. 53: 4–5). Of course Mary does not fully appreciate here the whole of this drama, but she is here prepared for it by the prophecy of Simeon who reveals to her the gainsaying which will concern her beloved Son since He is the Messiah and the Servant of Yahveh who is foretold by Isaiah.

And then the word that Simeon is speaking to her personally on the subject of her son is interrupted abruptly by an interpolation which refers to her own suffering. We must note here that Simeon's prophecy is addressed explicitly to Mary, as Mother of Jesus. The Evangelist has taken care to indicate this. It is she, personally, who having received the joyous promises of the Annunciation and the Nativity, must also bear the prophecies of opposition, concerning Jesus, and of the sword, concerning herself: ' . . . and a sword will pierce through thine own soul also.' The text thus underlines the person of Mary twice. It is as if the old man Simeon now specially fixed his gaze on Mary in order to make her understand clearly that the suffering of which he speaks concerns her personally. Because of the suffering of the Messiah, her Son, Mary will know suffering as well. And this suffering is spoken of as great suffering for the word 'romphaia' means a sword of great size, a redoubtable weapon. This suffering of the sword will touch Mary in the very depths of her being, and will pierce her soul through and through. The image is very definite and very forceful. It is not simply a matter of her feelings being hurt but truly a question of the most acute kind of suffering in the depths of her being. What suffering is this?

The sword or the great weapon which is here referred to is only found elsewhere in the Apocalypse, where it is mentioned six times and where in five of those occasions it symbolizes the Word of God which comes forth from the mouth of Christ glorified in final judgment (Rev. 1: 16; 2: 12, 16; 19: 15, 21; and in 6: 8 it is only a hand-to-hand sword which is referred to): 'In his right hand there were seven stars, and from his mouth there came forth a sharp two-edged sword . . .'

We must compare these texts with that of the Epistle to the Hebrews which speaks of the Word of God as a sword; '(here, "machaira," and not: "romphaia"), like the double-edged sword (distomos),' 'for the Word of God is living and active, sharper than any two-edged sword, piercing to the division of soul and spirit, of joints and marrow, and discerning the thoughts and intentions of the heart ' (Heb. 4: 12). The two-edged sword is here, as in the Revelation, the symbol of the Word of God which judges and reveals the depths of one's being. And there we are brought back to the prophecy of Simeon who speaks of this judgment and the revealing of the thoughts of all hearts by the Messiah, a sign to be spoken against which brings the destruction or the resurrection of men. Christ, the living and active Word, is going to become the revealer of active thoughts and thus bring about the judgment of men, who will fall or be raised up by His voice. The sword, which is here in question, in the interpolation concerning the Virgin Mary, is no other than this living and active Word which makes clear the depths of our being and judges all hearts. The sword which is going to pierce her soul is the Word of God, living and active in her Son, which will penetrate even to the dividing of soul and spirit, of joint and marrow, and which will judge the feelings and thoughts of all hearts (Heb. 4: 12).

The living Word of God for Mary is her Son, His whole life and His whole mission, all that as Messiah He is and represents, the Son of God and the Suffering Servant. Since she has accepted this divine motherhood she must accept all the consequences of it in her life. This sword of the Word of God which must pierce her soul is the total reality of the Incarnation and the Redemption which are going to be summed up in the Sacrifice of the Cross. The reality of the redemptive sacrifice will sear her heart like a sword of sorrow; and she will experience this reality of faith likewise in her motherly flesh.

Because she is also the blessed believer it will be necessary for her to accept in faith the sacrifice of her Son. She will also know the temptation of doubt. The reality of the suffering of her Son will penetrate her being as a test of faith in His messianic mission, and in His nature as Son of God. The sword of the Word of God will make plain the thoughts of her heart, will test her faithfulness and prove her faith, and it is through much suffering experienced in her flesh and in her soul that she will know the victory of faith and the spiritual resurrection of which Simeon speaks. In that, as Mother of the Suffering Servant who is the Son of God, Mary is the figure of the Church, of the community of believers who have been tested in their faith by suffering. Every Christian also sees in her the realities of faith, promises of hope and signs of the love of God jostling with the realities of life, the test of suffering and the signs of men's hate. All this is a test of faith which demands an heroic perseverance. A Christian experiences the struggle between Christ whom he loves by faith and the trials of the world which affect him in his flesh. Mary herself will undergo this struggle between the good Christian whom she loves in faith as believer, and in the flesh as mother, and the trials of the world which will bring her Son even to the death of the Cross. She will thus be, in this struggle, the very type of the Church; but she will suffer more than any other Christian, since the object of her faith, He who is exposed to the world's persecution, is at the same time the Son to whom she has given birth and whom she loves as a human mother. Mary's sword is the Christ planted in the heart of a mother to whom the most marvellous promises have been given. Like every other Christian, Mary will have to undergo this test of faith which will lay bare her heart, but she will experience it in all the reality of human motherhood. In this prophecy of Simeon Mary appears as the type of the people of Israel and of the Church in which the

test of faith, through the sword of the Word of God, is in operation, the sorting of the tares and the wheat to decide their fall or
their resurrection.

The Virgin Mary will not emerge from this grievous trial of the
sword victorious unless she totally accepts in faith that her Son can
be at the same time both Messiah King and Suffering Servant, the
Son of God and the Crucified. She will not carry off the victory of
faith unless she accepts the life of the Cross in her Son, Son of God
as He is, and in her own life as believer and mother. Mary, as the
first Christian woman and as the type of the Church, must accept
fully what St. Paul expressed in Col. 1: 24, viz., that she would find
her joy in suffering and thus complete in her flesh that which was
lacking in the suffering of Christ for His Body, which is the Church.

Even if Jesus has accomplished all for us in dying on the Cross,
and we are able to add nothing to His redemptive suffering, there is
a secret longing of God that this suffering shall be completed in a
similar fashion in our human flesh. It is necessary that Mary, the
type of the Church, and the Church which is the actual human form
on earth of Jesus glorified, *and* the Christian in whom Christ lives
by faith, in the Gospel, Baptism and Eucharist, should be like Him
in His dying. We should read our text therefore like this: 'I fill up
what is lacking "in my flesh" of the suffering of Christ.' There is
nothing lacking of the suffering of Jesus Christ in Himself: as
Redeemer He has fulfilled all things. But it is necessary that Mary
and every Christian should bear in themselves that same death of
His. There is something lacking in their flesh, indeed an infinite
amount, if they are to realize this conformity with Him in themselves. Throughout the whole of her life therefore Mary will have
to perfect in her heart and in her flesh the image of Jesus the
Crucified. As St. Thomas wrote: 'What is lacking in the Passion of
Christ, that is to say in the entire Church of which Christ is the
head, I complete and add to in my own way, in my flesh, by
suffering in myself, or again by passing through such suffering as
was lacking, in my flesh: what was lacking in Christ, in that he
suffered in his own Body, was suffered by Paul, one of his members, and similarly by all others.' One might say: '. . . it was lacking in Christ in order that Mary might suffer it.' And Calvin echoes
this idea in much the same way: 'As Christ endured once himself
so this continues all and every day in his members.'

108

It is therefore 'in his own flesh' that there is lacking something which Mary will complete, by her own suffering, of the whole Christ who is the Church. But why should there be that suffering? What use can be served by undergoing this suffering, these pains, these tribulations, these distresses and these lonely engagements of Mary and of each Christian, since only the suffering of Jesus Christ is redemptive and that alone can save us? Why should we bear the death of Jesus in *our* souls? Why should we thus conform to His Passion since we are the risen ones sharing in the marks of the Resurrection? It is because the Cross of Christ must be proclaimed in the world, not only by words but also by deeds. God wills that we should be a living proclamation of the Lord Crucified and Risen. If, like St. Paul, we do not wish to know anything but Jesus Christ and Him crucified, it is essential that we should live that out in our whole life. Not only in our hearts, by a deep and permanent meditation on the Passion of Jesus, but in our souls and in our bodies, by the distresses, persecutions, outrages and extreme suffering which we bear for Christ. It is necessary that we feel the hardness of life in the very fibre of our being and in our body by the weaknesses of our nature and the outrages which it can bear. Like St. Paul we have to bear in our bodies the marks of the Lord Jesus. And Mary, as the first Christian and type of the Church, bore in her heart in the most acute and exemplary manner the suffering of Christ, since she was in every sense His mother.

Jesus associates us with His Passion, and sets us on Calvary at the foot of the Cross with Mary His mother and John His beloved disciple. These sufferings encountered in the course of our Christian life, which is hard and full of Christian travail, gain for us a quite special intimacy with Christ. We are very close to the Crucified. We pierce the sad mystery of His self-offering and His death and thus become living and powerful witnesses of His Passion. We understand men then in their many different modes of suffering and we are able to be for them, not only in words, but in deeds, friends full of compassion, rich in consolation and overflowing with affection, sharing with them their suffering as Christ did ours in His.

But what can we do for all these men who suffer throughout the world and whom we do not know? If we can be witnesses for our neighbours, suffer with them and console them in Christ, what can we do for all the others? We here touch a second aspect of Christian suffering. What is needed is not only a lively preaching of the Cross but also intercession for all men in the whole world.

In order to understand this aspect of suffering by Christians for others, we need first to realize that we are members of the Body of Christ, the Church. St. Paul writes to the Colossians that he suffers for them. Now he did not himself preach the gospel to them; it was Epaphras, his dear companion in the ministry, who brought them to the knowledge of their love for Christ; he is now separated from them in space, and separated by captivity. No human bond can explain how the apostle could suffer for the Colossians. St. Paul does not here speak of any example of fidelity and endurance which he would give them by his patience and bearing of the evils of prison. That would indeed be presumptuous. If he says that he suffers for them, it is because he believes in a mystical relationship amongst all those who confess Jesus Christ and who are bound up with His Body, the Church.

The suffering which brings us into that very special intimacy with Jesus Christ enables us to undertake a more fervent and more effective intercession. We are then so close to Him that we are the better able to confide to Him the distress of our brother men. We are like St. John, the beloved disciple, who leant upon His breast on the evening of Maundy Thursday to hear from Him words of true consolation, and to put to Him the questions of his troubled brethren. And this intercession bears fruit for these brethren who suffer, even if they are far removed from us, for in the Communion of Saints we are all gathered up in Christ, in His Body the Church. Our sorrows, which finally bring about in us the image of Jesus Christ crucified, enable us to speak more effectively and better with Him. Our suffering then becomes a living intercession. We are able, by our sorrows which have become prayers, to act with power for our brethren in the whole world. Even then, of course, we are useless serfs, God could by-pass us but He wills to make us His collaborators.

What we have just said of the Church and of each Christian is fulfilled for Mary in the prophecy of the sword which will pierce her soul. She is going to live through all that pre-eminently as the first Christian and as the type of the Church, and yet more sorrowfully, since she is the Mother of the Suffering Servant and of the Crucified. She will bear in her heart the suffering and the death of her Son and her Saviour. She will each day complete in her flesh what is lacking still of the sorrows of Christ for His Body, the Church. By the spoliation and separation of her human mother-

hood, and by the acceptance of the sad mission of her Son, she will
have to inscribe on her heart, and every day the more, the imprint
of Christ's suffering and a day like that of His Cross. In this sharing
of His suffering and His passion, she will know the intimacy of the
Saviour, then of the Crucified, since she will live with Him His
sorrowful life. And she will not experience this only for herself in
order that her faith might indeed be faith in the Messiah who
suffers and in the Saviour in His Passion, but she will experience it
also for the sake of the Church, the Body of Christ. In this unique
intimacy with the Saviour whom she will know better in suffering,
she will be able to know the suffering of men and intercede for
them. In the mystery of the Communion of Saints, her suffering,
like ours, will become an intercession full of compassion for all
mankind, she will obtain from God their consolation and their
peace.

In this communion with the sufferings of Christ, the Virgin
Mary, as the first Christian and type of the Church, enables us to
reproduce in our hearts the image of the Crucified and not to flee
before the suffering which comes close to us through Christ and
with our brethren. Here the Virgin is with us in order to draw us
in the wake of the Suffering Servant; yet more than us she has
known the sorrows of Christ since her human motherhood has
united her to the Saviour by bonds which no one after her will ever
be able to know. Like us, and like the Church, of which she is the
type, she receives in her heart the suffering of Christ the Redeemer
and ours, but the Cross is marked on her more deeply and sadly
since she is the Mother of the Saviour and since she suffers in her
humanity as a mother what we suffer in our flesh. On account of
this unique place in communion with the sufferings of Christ, and
because of this peculiar sword which pierces her Christian and
motherly soul she becomes for us a unique example on the way of
the Cross which leads us with her to the resurrection.

With the example of the Mother of the Redeemer before us,
knowing that nothing is in vain in our suffering, and if it is truly
for Christ that we endure it, and are certain that by suffering we
reproduce the image of Jesus Christ crucified in our flesh, and that
our prayer for others becomes powerful, then we are truly able to
find our joy in the sorrows of Christ in us.[5]

How is this sword predicted by Simeon as likely to manifest itself

111

in the life of Mary? After the Presentation in the Temple, when the consecration of the first-born son and the sacrifice of the offering have taken the aspect indicated by Simeon, an exultant act of grace and personal spoliation, in order to enable the mission of the Suffering Servant to be accomplished, Mary and Joseph will not have long to wait to see written on their life the marks of suffering. The visit of the wise men, who reveal to them anew the universality of the messianic mission of Jesus, is followed by the flight into Egypt to escape the persecution of Herod. Until the death of the King they are to live as refugees in a foreign land, and there is the massacre of the innocents who pay with their martyrdom for the life of the infant Messiah. Mary must endure the sorrow of exile, and even more the suffering of all the mothers of Judæa who undergo in her place the cruel mourning of their little children. The night of the Passover is repeated: Jesus, the first-born, is spared whilst all the other children of His age are put to death; it is indeed the sign *par excellence* of the deliverance, but at the price of such suffering that Mary can only be deeply touched by this tragedy from which she escapes by becoming an exile, a refugee.

On their return they will go to Nazareth, in order to live there the hidden life in Galilee of the Gentiles, where Mary previously received the promise of the angel. We can imagine that this hidden life will not always by exempt from fear, for Joseph and Mary know that their Son, the Messiah, is only likely to evoke opposition from the powerful ones of this world if He is going to reveal His messianic kingliness.

When He is twelve years old they take Jesus to Jerusalem for the Feast of the Passover. Time has passed and things are calm again. We now have the fourth and final stage of the ascent of Jesus to the Temple. But on leaving Jerusalem Jesus is not with them: there is the agonizing search of three days amongst the members of the party, their friends and acquaintances in Jerusalem. We can conjure up a picture of the grief of Mary during this search. These three days of Jesus' absence spent in the House of the Father are perhaps a symbol of His absence at His future death; when they find Him again Mary and Joseph are seized with emotion, and this emotion Mary will know again on the day of the Resurrection. This sorrowful absence and then this recovery are to establish in Mary the mystery of the Passion. It is essential that she should become used to the independence of her Son in regard to her human motherhood. She will have to be detached and separated from all that there is of natural humanity in her relationship with Christ so as no longer to see in Him any one but the Son of God. She has admitted that on the day of the Presentation when, warned by Simeon of the real meaning of her act, she totally consecrated her Son in the House of the Father by making a sacrifice of herself. She cannot, however, stop herself speaking of her motherly disturbance: 'Child why have you done this? Behold thy father and I have sought you sorrowing' (Luke 2: 48). The human motherliness of Mary is here revealed in all its rich emotion. Jesus is going to call His parents back to the meaning of their earlier act when they consecrated Him in the Temple: 'Why have you searched for me? Do you not know that I must be about my Father's business?' (Luke 2: 49). Jesus here takes His place in the logical development of the Incarnation and the Presentation in the Temple. Since His birth and since His consecration to the Lord His parents have to learn that His natural place is in the Temple. For the fourth time, that is to say following the Visitation, His birth, and the Presentation, the Son of God has come to Jerusalem and to the Temple His natural seat; His parents had now to understand that He has come upon earth in order to busy Himself with the affairs of His Father whose seat is in the Temple. Mary has called forth before Jesus the concern of his father Joseph. Jesus, in His reply, reminds them that His Father is God and He must withdraw Himself somewhat from the relationship with His human parents, His legal father and His mother. They must live with Him according to their intention on the day of the Presentation, and according to the prophecy of Simeon; they must accept the sacrifice of their human love in order to permit their son to begin His messianic task in the service of His Father, in the house of and amongst the business of His Father in Heaven.

But Joseph and Mary, the Gospel tells us, did not understand the word which He had just spoken to them. They still experienced a certain darkness of faith and their sacrifice is all the greater because of that. Little by little, the consequences of the mission of the Suffering Servant will become clear for Mary. She faithfully keeps all these sayings and all these events in her heart. She sets them in relation the one to the other, and one day she will be able to experience the Passion of her Son, standing at the foot of the Cross, and will be able to rejoice in His Resurrection receiving at last the full light of the Holy Spirit at Pentecost. For the moment, however, Jesus returns with her to Nazareth; He is submissive to His human parents who continue His education. The sad parenthesis of the Passover and Jerusalem has renewed their spirit of sacrifice; they live in faith awaiting the public manifestation of the Messiah when His hour will come.

Some eighteen years later, at the end of a long and hidden life, spent with Joseph, who apparently dies during this time,[6] and with Mary, His mother, who has now become a widow, Jesus is called to His mission as Messiah by the baptism of John and gathers His disciples. It is at Cana in Galilee, at the wedding festivities, that we find Mary and Jesus who has been invited with His disciples, and there He will perform the first miraculous sign of His messianic mission, manifesting His glory and awakening the faith of His disciples (John 2: 11). We shall see later the meaning of this episode which involves Mary. We can only note at this stage the refusal of Jesus to Mary's invitation: 'They have no wine. What do you wish of me, woman? My hour has not yet come' (John 2: 3–4). Whatever interpretation we give to this text it suggests that Mary must move on from the stage of her human motherhood of the Messiah in order to take her place in the Church: 'Woman,' Jesus says to her. This title is at one and the same time a solemn title and the indication that Mary is no longer able to play in the presence of her son the rôle of a mother who has had control of Him. She will be made great because of this, but it is certain that this stage marks for her a new experience of humbling: the hour of the Messiah approaches and she must sacrifice her human motherhood, when her Son enters resolutely upon His grievous task.

It is the same detachment which is indicated in another episode of the Gospel. One day, His mother and brethren (the men of His kindred) come to Him, when He is preaching to the crowd; they seek to speak with Him; and when He is told that they are there he says: 'Who is my mother, and who are my brethren?' Then, pointing to His disciples with a gesture of the hand He adds: 'Behold my mother and my brethren; for whoever doeth the will of my Father who is in heaven, he is my brother and sister and mother' (Matt. 12: 46–50 and other places). The heavenly Fatherhood, the motherhood and the brotherhood of the Church surpass all human kindred. More than the human motherhood of Mary is that of the Church, the spiritual mother who now matters to Jesus. The human motherhood of Mary must diminish in the presence of the spiritual motherhood of the Church. Certainly Mary has her part with those who fulfil the will of the Father for she is in the Church; but it is precisely on this ground that she must now consider her kinship with her Son and no longer on that of being His human mother. We shall see later what this signifies. Here we will only note the sacrifice which this truth involves for Mary; she must be stripped of her status as the human mother of the Son of God, in order to discover in the Church a kinship more spiritual and profound which links those who believe in Him. Motherhood according to the flesh must be effaced before the spiritual motherhood of the Church, and in the face of the brotherhood of faith in the Church. Even if Mary accepts this new development, even if she understands the superior nature of this spiritual kinship within the Church as over the fleshly kinship of the family, she will still suffer human sadness at this stripping and necessary detachment from her earlier bond.

Finally, it is at the foot of the Cross that Mary will know the most acute pain of the 'sword' spoken of by Simeon, which has never ceased to pierce her heart and test her faith. This Son, to whom she gave birth, whom she has brought up and loved, and for whom she has desired the promise of messianic royalty, she now sees crucified as a malefactor at the culmination of His ministry. As a mother's heart is here pierced more than ever by the grief of the sword, her believing heart is faced with the surest act of faith: to believe against all the evidence that God will be faithful to His promise. The darkness which envelops the world in a material sense envelops also her motherly love and her Christian faith. She must pass with her Son through the agony of His abandonment in order to know with Him the joy of the Resurrection. At the foot of the Cross she is, more than anywhere else, the type of the Church and of every Christian who, persecuted or on the very edge of distress, believes and hopes against all hope. More than ever, this sad mother is also the placid believer because more than anything she holds only to a pure faith. A sign of the love and care of her son, however, comes to soften her suffering and maintain her faith: Jesus commits her to the beloved disciple who will take her to his home (John 19: 26–7). This word, as we shall see, has also another meaning; but that does not entirely exclude the quite human sense of a last act of compassion on the part of this Son, who has not been able to be a Son like other sons and yet who here shows the tenderest compassion.

115

The Pastor Charles Drelincourt expressed the supreme suffering of Mary in words full of meaning: 'There was no blood flowing from the wounds of our Lord which did not mingle with the tears of the Virgin; and with the dead body of Jesus there was buried the heart of Mary.'[7]

At the foot of the Cross Mary experienced in her flesh the sorrows of Christ more than any other Christian after her, since, being the human mother of the Son of God, her whole being could only shudder with agony and suffering in the presence of this Crucified One. Thus, the marks of the Cross, which she must bear in her heart as the first Christian woman and type of the Church, she has experienced again most cruelly because she was the human mother of her crucified Saviour. There she completed what was lacking in her flesh of the sorrows of Christ, for His Body and for the Church: she reveals to us the way of this likeness to Christ crucified which we must experience in our flesh in order to arrive one day at the glory of His Resurrection.

Chapter 9

Mary and the Church

In the Gospel according to St. John, the intention and theological structure of which are not in question, Mary only appears twice at important moments in the life of Christ: at the marriage in Cana and at the foot of the Cross (John 2: 1–12; 19: 25–7). In these two accounts Mary is called 'the Mother of Jesus' ('His mother') by the Evangelist (four times at Cana, and four times at the Cross), and 'woman' by Jesus Himself. On the other hand, at the marriage of Cana, Jesus speaks of His 'Hour' which, for St. John, means the moment when the Son shall pass from this world to the Father (13: 1), or of His glorification (12: 23–7; 17: 1), meaning the elevation on the Cross; after the words of the Crucified to Mary and St. John, when all had been accomplished, the hour is also mentioned (19: 27). It is certain that these two accounts are closely linked in both a literary and logical sense.[1] We shall see that these two events, at different stages, bring Mary to the same awareness of her new function in regard to the human motherhood she bears to the Son of God who has been her first vocation.

Mary, the Mother of God, the human mother of the Son of God, such as St. Luke has depicted her at the start of his gospel, is made aware at Cana and then at the Cross, in St. John's Gospel and in two other episodes related by the Synoptic Gospels (Matt. 12: 46–50 and elsewhere; St. Luke 11: 27–8), of a new dimension to her vocation.

THE MARRIAGE AT CANA

It is difficult to cut a path through the innumerable exegeses of the account of Cana which have appeared in the course of past traditions; if we are silent about any of those which we shall not discuss this does not mean that we exclude these interpretations; it is not our purpose here to give a history of the various explanations for this has often been done elsewhere. We only want to pursue this very rich and important text by choosing the suggestions which appear to us to be the least unreliable and the most likely, and which throw light on Mary's vocation.

The Meaning of Cana

'Then, on the third day, there was a marriage at Cana of Galilee; and the mother of Jesus was there. Jesus and his disciples also were invited to the wedding' (John 2: 1–2).

It is essential first of all to set this account in the whole context of St. John's Gospel. This gospel is built on a liturgical plan. It is around the occasions of the liturgical feasts of Israel that Jesus develops His mission, and it is on their symbolism that He builds His teaching. On the other hand the messianic task of Jesus consists in fulfilling certain signs which manifest the glory that has come amongst men so as to set up its Tabernacle among them.

'The Word became flesh,
And was tabernacled amongst us,
And we saw his glory, the glory as of the only begotten Son,
Coming from the Father,
Full of grace and truth' (John 1: 14).

The whole meaning of the Incarnation and the mission of the Son is summed up in the prologue of the Gospel: He became flesh, and was amongst us as the sacred tent of the Israelites in the desert, where the glory of Yahveh dwelt; this glory He manifested by miraculous signs so that the Apostles might see it; it is the glory of God, that is to say, His Holy Presence amongst men, because He is the only Son, and in Him is found the fullness of grace and truth. At the end of his Gospel John will sum up by writing, 'Jesus did many other such signs in the presence of his disciples which have not been described in this book, these signs (contained in the Gospel) have been described in order that you may believe that Jesus is the Christ, the Son of God, that in believing you might have life in his name' (John 20: 30–1). The Gospel of John has thus been a selection of the miraculous signs of Christ, accompanied by the words which throw light on them, in order to demonstrate that Jesus is the Messiah and the Son of God and to awaken the faith which gives life in Him.

The Gospel can therefore be divided according to the plan of the liturgical feasts at which Jesus was present, and on the occasion of which He performed His signs and gave His teaching:

Prologue: 'The Word became flesh . . . we saw his glory:' (1: 1–18).

The Opening week of seven days finishing with the first sign at Cana:
The water changed into wine (1: 19–2: 12).

The First Passover and return to Galilee through Judæa and Samaria,
finishing with the second sign at Cana:
The healing of the nobleman's son (2: 13–4: 54).

The Second Feast, perhaps Pentecost:
The sign of the healing of the sick woman of Bethesda.[5]

The other Passover: the signs of the multiplying of the bread and the walking on the lake.[6]

The Feast of Tabernacles; in the autumn:
The sign of the healing of the man born blind (7: 1–10: 21).

The Feast of the Dedication; in winter:
The sign of the resurrection of Lazarus (10: 22–11: 54).

The week of the Passion (11: 55–18: 27).

The Last Passover: the sign of the elevation on the Cross and the thrusting in of the spear which gives birth to the Church (18: 28–19: 42).

The final week of the appearances of the Resurrection:
From the Sunday of the Passover to the Sunday of Thomas:
The signs of the Resurrection finishing with the words about faith in signs without the sight of signs:
'Blessed are those who believe and have not seen' (20: 1–29).

Conclusion to the Gospel of the signs (20: 30–1).

Appendix on the life of the Church and the return of Christ (21: 1–23),
with a new ending alluding to signs (21: 24–5; cf. 21: 25 with 20: 30).

In the light of this arrangement we can see that the first sign at Cana is set at the end of the opening week of the ministry of Jesus and just before the first Passover, during which Jesus is going to cleanse the Temple and predict the resurrection of His Body, the new Temple (2: 13–25), after which He will give His teaching to Nicodemus on the new birth by water and the spirit (3: 1–21), then to the Samaritan woman on the new worship in spirit and in truth (4: 1–42); whilst between these two discourses John the Baptist will point Christ out as being the Bridegroom of the Bride, the messianic community, the Church (3: 22–36). Finally, having returned

119

to Galilee, Jesus will fulfil His second sign at Cana: the healing of the nobleman's son (4: 43–54). The week of the Passion, preceding the last Passover, will be completed by the final manifestation of the Messiah's glory, as Cana, at the end of the first week, had been the first revealing of this glory. The appearances of the Resurrection will be set in a final week which will end on the Sunday of Thomas. Thus the Gospel is constructed on a plan of six liturgical feasts, three Passovers, one Pentecost (probably), a feast of Tabernacles and a feast of Dedication, with three principal weeks: the opening week and the week of the Passion are both of them completed with the manifesting of the glory of Christ (the first: Cana; the last: the raising on the Cross followed by the Resurrection) and finally, the last week with the appearances after the Resurrection. The details in the indication of days, the literary parallelisms, the structure of the accounts, is all too striking for exegesis not to note these comparisons and relationships which the Evangelist himself suggests, and which are so fitting for his theological manner of considering and presenting the history of Jesus.

'The third day there was a marriage at Cana of Galilee.' The precise mention of the days, for the beginning of the ministry of Jesus, reveals a succession of seven whole days which constitute the opening week of the gospel. The impossibility of there being such movement in the country-side as is demanded by this rapid succession of time shows that we must not attach an exact chronological meaning to this 'week,' but rather a theological sense. The theological Gospel writer wished to give a mystical sense to this 'week' of seven 'days.' The three 'next days' (1: 29, 35, 43), and the precise mention of the 'third day' after the fourth (2: 1), indicate a succession of symbolic days recalling the seven 'days' of the Creation. The Prologue of the Gospel of John begins like Genesis: 'In the beginning . . . En archei . . . ' (Gen. 1: 1; John 1: 1); the beginning of the ministry of Christ unfolds like the Creation in a symbolic week. The Evangelist wishes to show that the messianic salvation is a new creation in Christ, the Word which was at the beginning, by which all was made (1: 1–3), and which has become flesh (1: 14). The priestly author of the first account of the Creation (Gen. 1: 1–2: 3) had constructed his plan on six symbolic days to show the divine origin of the seventh day as a day of rest for God (Gen. 2: 1– 3). St. John in the same way sets the act of the new creation in a week, of which the seventh day coincides with the marriage at Cana when Jesus fulfils a first sign of His messianic status: in a symbolic week, Christ lays the foundation of a new creation of the messianic community, the Church, by calling one by one those who will be the pillars of this new building, the Apostles; and then, the seventh day, the sign of final rest, He shares in the joy of the marriage at Cana which symbolizes and pre-figures the eschatological marriage of God with His people, the messianic banquet of the Kingdom, and He reveals His glory in the first sign of His divine Sonship. This symbolic week is thus divided as follows:

First Day: The first witness of John the Baptist:
'I am not the Christ . . . he is coming' (1: 19–28).

Second Day: The second witness of John the Baptist:
'Behold the lamb of God who taketh away the sin of the world. . . .
'I have seen the Spirit like a dove descending from the heavens and resting on him. He is the chosen of God' (1: 29–34).

Third Day: The calling of Andrew and another disciple of John the Baptist:
'Behold the lamb of God.'
'Come and see' (1: 35–9):
The calling of Simon Peter:
'Thou shalt be called Peter' (1: 40–2).

Fourth Day: The calling of Philip:
'Follow me!' (1: 43–4).
The calling of Nathanael:
'Rabbi, thou art the Son of God, the king of Israel' (1: 45–51).

The Seventh Day: The marriage at Cana, the seventh day after the calling of Philip and Nathanael.[2]

The progress then of this opening week is very clear: John the Baptist withdraws (first day), Jesus appears (second day), the disciples of John the Baptist leave him in order to follow Jesus (third day), two other disciples follow Jesus, of whom Nathanael, who represents the true Israel, is joined to Christ (fourth day). Finally, the marriage of Cana in which the new Israel, the messianic community, is established in the faith of the Son of God who fulfils the first sign of His glory. This opening week is dominated by the witness of John: 'Behold the Lamb of God, the chosen of God,' taken up by Nathanael: 'Thou art the Son of God, thou art the king of Israel.' This double witness, which gives four major titles to the Messiah, will find its justification and explanation in

121

the miracle at Cana, in which the Messiah will reveal Himself as the Son of God in His mystical marriage as the Chosen, the Son, the King, in the sign of His messianic status.

The theological Schemata of the opening week would have demanded that every 'day' should be named, as in the account of the Creation. Now there is a gap in the numbering, and it is necessary to see here the intention of the Evangelist as describing the seventh day as the third after the last which has been underlined, the calling of Nathanael and Philip.

The indication of the third day is frequent and significant in John's Gospel. It becomes part of Christian tradition in the earliest times to describe the day of Christ's resurrection: 'For I delivered to you as of first importance that which I also received,' wrote St. Paul to the Corinthians, that 'Christ died for our sins in accordance with the Scriptures' (1 Cor. 15: 3–4). There is here a tradition of a very primitive confession of faith.[3] We have seen that the account of the miracle of the marriage at Cana, and that of the healing of the nobleman's son at Cana (4: 46–54) must have been related, according to the very intention of St. John, who sets them both in relation to one another (4: 46); they are the first and second of the signs which are both accomplished at Cana. Now the second account is placed 'after two days,' in relation to the event which precedes it just as the first account was set on 'the third day.' Is John thinking of the prophecy of Hosea in regard to the restoration of Israel? It is possible:

'Come, let us return to the Lord, for he hath torn that he may heal us; he has stricken and he will bind us up. After two days he will revive us and on the third day he will raise us up, that we may live before him' (Hosea 6: 1–2).

In every sense the miracles of healing are signs revealing the almightiness of Christ over the body and prefiguring the Resurrection. The second sign at Cana was a sign of healing-resurrection which the Evangelist takes care to set 'after two days' in order to call to mind the Resurrection of Christ which is thus foreshadowed.

Before the resurrection of Lazarus (11: 1–44), which is the great sign of the glory of Christ who is powerful even over death, we notice a similar indication of days. Jesus has retired to the other side of Jordan, and when He learned of the sickness of Lazarus he 'remained there *two days* in the place where he was; and only then did he say to his disciples, Let us go into Judæa' (11: 6–7). Here again, in relation to the great sign of the resurrection of Lazarus, John notes that Jesus voluntarily waits two days and that He then comes a third day to Bethany in order to bring back His friend to life. Here again the mention of *two days* sets the tone for the event of the resurrection of Christ.

Thus the setting of the marriage of Cana at the end of the week, the new Creation, and the mention of the three days which bring to mind for John the Resurrection of Christ, set forth this first sign of the water changed into wine, and the whole context of the miracle, as a revelation first and foremost of the glory of Christ, a manifestation which will find its fulfilment and its fullness in the last sign to which all the others point: the Resurrection on Easter morning. Let us here still note that this opening week, finishing with the marriage at Cana, is almost immediately followed, in the Gospel, by the Feast of the Passover at Jerusalem, in which Christ will reveal His power as the Son of God over the Temple: for there again, the three days are mentioned as a direct allusion to the resurrection.

'Destroy this sanctuary and in three days I will raise it up. . . . He spoke of the sanctuary of his Body' (2: 19, 21). Just before this first Easter when the resurrection is proclaimed in what is still a mysterious sense, the marriage at Cana takes on an altogether Paschal significance. Let us finally recall that the week of the Passion will be completed by the last sign of the glory of Christ in the course of the last Passover: in the final week, with which the Gospel closes, the manifestation of the glory of the resurrection will be the only sign which we are given, bursting forth on Easter morning before the eyes of Peter, John, and Mary Magdalene, and then in the evening before the eyes of all the Apostles, except Thomas; this will be a special manifestation of the glory of Christ, eight days later, when even he will believe.

The whole Gospel of John must be read in this Paschal sense of the Resurrection which burst out in the last eight days; and the opening week of the messianic mission [4] and the crowning of this week in the marriage at Cana must be understood especially in a paschal sense of the glory of the Risen Lord.

123

The marriage at Cana set on the seventh day of the opening week symbolizes the new sabbath of God, the day of Christ's rest, after the day of the new creation, the founding of the messianic community by the calling of the disciples; this new day of rest prefigures the rest of the Church in the Kingdom of God: the marriage at Cana has an eschatological significance. Furthermore the marriage of Cana, set on 'a third day,' and just before Passover, symbolizes the day of Christ's resurrection in glory; it is in this Paschal light of the Resurrection that we have to interpret this account, following the Evangelist's intention. The marriage at Cana has, in view of its chronological setting, a paschal and eschatological significance.

On the other hand, it is in the course of the marriage festivities, that Christ fulfils His first messianic sign. We know very well how the theme of the marriage of Yahveh with His people plays an important part in the Old Testament, to indicate the final deliverance (*vide* Hosea). In the New Testament, marriage has a symbolic meaning of union between the Son of God and His Church in the end of time: 'The kingdom of heaven is likened unto a king who made a marriage feast for his son . . . ' (Matt. 22: 2). In the Revelation, the coming of the final kingdom is spoken of as the marriage of the Lamb: 'Let us rejoice and exult and give him the glory, for the marriage of the Lamb has come and his bride has made herself ready . . . blessed are those who are invited to the marriage of the Lamb . . . ' (Rev. 19: 7, 9). Twice, in the opening week, Christ is called by John the Baptist the 'Lamb of God,' an important title used by the Evangelist to indicate the Suffering Servant, and later John the Baptist points Christ out as the 'bridegroom' of the community of the Messiah. John the Baptist describes Christ as 'the Lamb,' and 'the Bridegroom,' which are eschatological titles designating the Messiah who, by His sacrifice as Suffering Servant, will bring about the indissoluble union of the people of God with their Lord in a mystical marriage. St. Paul will unite these ideas: 'Husbands love your wives as Christ loved the Church and gave himself for it . . . this is a great mystery; I mean that it concerns Christ and the Church' (Ephes. 5: 25, 32).

The theme of the *meal* is also a messianic and eschatological theme. The Messiah eats with His own a messianic banquet and the kingdom will be often compared to a feast. 'Many will come from the east and from the west to take their place at the feast with

Abraham and Jacob in the kingdom of heaven' (Matt. 8: 11). The
Evangelist insists very much on the place of wine in the proceed-
ings of the marriage at Cana. Six times the word recurs and the
quantity of wine provided by the miracle of Christ was enormous:
six pots, containing each of them two or three measures of 45 litres,
that is about 600 litres in all. In the Old Testament, wine and its
abundance had assumed a messianic and symbolic significance:
the blessing of the Lord accompanying the deliverance had to be
expressed in the symbol of an abundance of wine, corn and also
oil, sometimes joined by the theme of marriage:

> 'For as a young man marries a virgin, so shall your son marry
> you and as the bridegroom rejoices over the bride, so shall
> your God rejoice over you . . . and those who garner the
> harvest shall eat it and praise the Lord, and those who gather
> it shall drink it in the courts of my sanctuary' (Isa. 62: 5, 9).
> 'They shall come and sing aloud on the height of Zion and
> they shall be radiant over the goodness of the Lord, over the
> grain, over the wine and the oil . . . ' (Jer. 31: 12; Hosea 2:
> 7–11 and 14: 8; Amos 9: 14).

The Apochryphal writers develop this theme of the abundance of
corn and wine which takes on enormous proportions. The messianic blessing of Judah by Jacob similarly mentioned the symbol
of wine:

> 'The sceptre shall not pass away from Judah, nor the ruler's
> staff from between his feet, until he comes to whom it belongs,
> and to whom it shall be the obedience of the peoples. Binding
> his foal to the vine and his ass's colt to the choice vine, he
> washes his garments and his vesture in the blood of grapes; his
> eyes shall be red with wine and his teeth white with milk'
> (Gen. 49: 10–12).

The blessing of Isaac upon Jacob had also called forth this symbol of the wine: 'May God give unto thee the dew of heaven and
the fatness of the earth and plenty of grain and wine' (Gen. 27:
28, 37).

Wine is the sign of God's blessing and it symbolizes the restoration of Israel by the Messiah, who will establish for ever the People
of God in the Promised Land which is overflowing with wine, corn
and oil. The wine at Cana symbolizes this messianic restoration
which is fulfilled by Christ. Indeed its abundance is too great for

it to be needed just for a human marriage—it was too plentiful for that. By this sign of considerable superabundance the miracle at Cana sets before us a marriage in which Christ and His disciples take part in the symbolic setting of the restoration of Israel within the superabundant blessing of its Lord.

The wine at Cana is a sign of the kingdom which is coming according to the Word of Christ, according to the first Lord's supper over the Cup at the Paschal meal: 'Verily I tell you I shall not drink henceforth of the fruit of the vine until the kingdom of God comes' (Luke 22: 18). The new wine at Cana is a good wine which follows a less good wine, as is remarked by the master of the feast: 'Every man serves the good wine first and when men have drunk freely then the poor wine; but you have kept the good wine until now' (John 2: 10). The wine at Cana is the sign of the new world which Christ had just created during this first week of the new creation. The good wine of the new creation succeeds the less good of the old world; the new Covenant succeeds the old which has perished; the Kingdom of God will succeed the time of the Church according to the words of the last Supper: 'Truly I tell you I will not drink of the fruit of the vine until the day that I shall drink the new wine in the kingdom of God' (Mark 14: 25; see also 2: 22). This theme of the newness of the world which Christ is coming to inaugurate is repeated elsewhere in the following passage of the gospel. After the miracle of the good wine of Cana, the sign of the 'new creation,' Christ will go forth to fulfil the purification of the Temple at Jerusalem, where He will speak of His Body as the 'New Temple' (John 2: 19); to Nicodemus He will explain the mystery of the 'New Birth' by water and the spirit (3: 5); to the Samaritan He will announce the 'New Worship' of spirit and in truth (4: 23); and finally the miracle of the healing and resurrection of Lazarus will indicate the 'New Life' in Christ (4: 50 etc. . . .).

The wine of the marriage feast is, in its abundance, not only the symbol of the messianic restoration, or, by its quality, of the new covenant, but is also the symbol of the Word of Christ, His Wisdom and the Word of God, and of the Eucharist of the Body and Blood of Christ, the two tables of the liturgical feast of the Church.

The liturgical meaning of the wine at the marriage of Cana is indicated by the fact that it is substituted for the ritual water of purification for the Jews, which was contained in the six stone water pots.[5] This water was prepared in order to permit those taking part in the feast to make their 'legal' purification, and to wash their hands before sitting at table. Christ will cause the water pots to be filled once more, and this water will be changed into wine. The water of 'legal' purification is to become miraculously the wine of Christian 'spiritual' purification by truth and by the blood of Christ, by the Word and by the Eucharist. Origen of Alexandria and others of the Fathers will see in the wine at Cana, the new doctrine of Christ; Ephrem will see in the wine that is less good the law of Moses and in that which is better Grace and Truth.[6] Irenaeus of Lyons is to see in the wine at Cana a sacramental symbol of the Eucharistic Blood.

Two texts from the Old Testament which refer to Wisdom speak of wine as the symbol of truth which it is fitting to hear:

'Wisdom has built her house, she has set up her seven pillars, she has slaughtered her beasts, she has mixed her wine, she has also set her tables . . . come eat of my bread and drink of the wine I have mixed! Leave simpleness and live, and walk in the way of insight' (Proverbs 9: 1–5).

'Ho, everyone who thirsts, come to the waters; and he who has no money, come, buy and eat! Come, buy wine and milk without money and without price. . . . Hearken diligently to me, and eat what is good, and delight yourselves in fatness. Incline your ear to me; hear, that your soul may live . . . ' (Isa. 55: 1–3).

Christ is Wisdom who leads His disciples to the feast that is prepared in order to give them the wine of the new teaching and to communicate life to them. The purification of the law and its rites has perished (the Water), the law and the prophets are no longer sufficient (the wine that was less good), and now it is necessary that those who are thirsty shall have their need met by drawing new wine that is excellent, from the Word of Christ, from the true Wisdom, the perfect Truth which Christ gives and which is Himself, which purifies, not only symbolically as the ritual water of the Jews, but truly. Christ will later underline this idea of purification by the Word of Truth: 'You are already made clean by the Word that I have spoken to you' (John 15: 3). In the High Priestly prayer, Christ says again: 'Sanctify them in the Truth, thy Word is Truth. . . . I sanctify myself before them, in order that they also might be sanctified in the Truth' (John 17: 17, 19).

The good wine of Cana, replacing the ritual water of the purifying of the Jews, which is better than the first wine given at the
feast, therefore is a sign of the Word of Christ, the Wisdom of God,
the sign of the Truth, which sanctifies, purifies and consecrates
those who hear a new teaching of the Messiah. But nothing prevents
this symbol from being even more rich. There are certain signs
which direct us equally to a sacramental explanation of the wine at
Cana. We have already been shown the undertones of the Johannine theology and the intention of the Evangelist to illustrate the
sacramental life of the Church by the account of historical events
in the life of Christ.[8] Baptism and the Eucharist are called forth by
the different scenes in the life of Jesus.

The miracle at Cana and the multiplying of the bread are both
of them set in relation to the Feast of the Passover. Immediately
after the account of the marriage and just before the miracle of the
loaves, the Evangelist notes precisely 'and the Passover, the feast
of the Jews was nigh' (2: 13; 6: 4). That is His way of underlining
the major incidents in the life of Christ and these liturgical occasions; a third time that one finds this phrase is before the week of
the Passion and the last Passover: 'And the Passover of the Jews
was nigh' (11: 55); before the week of the Feast of Tabernacles,
the Evangelist also draws the attention of the reader by the same
phrase: 'And a feast of the Jews was nigh, the feast of tabernacles'
(7: 2). Hence, the three feasts of Passover referred to by St. John
are introduced with this somewhat solemn phrase which catches the
attention. The marriage of Cana and the multiplying of the loaves
are thus set in relation to the Passover. Mention of the Passover
follows the miracle of Cana, whilst it precedes the multiplying of
the bread; however, between the marriage of Cana and the mention
of Passover, the Evangelist takes care to emphasize that Jesus, His
mother and His disciples did not dwell at Capernaum save for a
few days. There is a quite clear determination to link the account
at Cana with the ascent of Jesus to Jerusalem for the Passover.

The marriage at Cana and the multiplying of the loaves have a
certain connection with the Paschal meal and the Eucharist. Christ
is the perfect Paschal Lamb which takes away the sin of the world;
He died at the moment of the slaughtering of the Paschal Lamb,
at the last feast of Passover. As the bread at the feeding of the five
thousand prefigures the Eucharistic bread, so the wine at Cana pre-
figures the Eucharistic wine. The multiplying of the bread is followed

by the discourse on the Bread of Life at the synagogue at Capernaum (6: 32–59). This liturgical sermon expounds the symbolic significance of the increase of the loaves. The material bread was the sign of spiritual feeding: 'Labour not for the bread which perishes, but for the food which remains till eternal life which the Son of man will give you, for it is he that the Father, yea even God, has sealed' (6: 27). If the Son had been marked at His baptism by the seal of the Mighty One, and by the Holy Spirit, it is not only to do miracles in the natural order, but signs which symbolize a more profound divine reality which will last until eternity. Hence the miracle of the bread is a sign which directs faith towards a spiritual reality: the food which lasts even to life eternal, the Bread of Life. Jesus is the Bread of Life 'who comes down from heaven and gives life to the world' (6: 32–40): the Bread of Life is also His Word: 'the teaching which comes from the Father,' which one feeds on and which one takes by faith (6: 44–50); the Bread of Life is yet again the Eucharist, 'the flesh of the Son of Man,' which we must eat, and with that 'His Blood' which we must drink in order that we might have life eternal and rise again at the last day (6: 51–8). Hence the miracle of the multiplying of the loaves is a sign which directs faith towards Christ who is the Bread of Life and who gives the Bread of Life in His Word and in His Eucharist. The discourse on the Bread of Life is a discourse on the person of Christ, on His teaching and on His Eucharistic Body. It is at one and the same time a case here of Christ who is Wisdom, who gives His Word, and who gives His Body and His Blood.

Just as the sign of the increase of the loaves directs faith above all towards the theme of bread, the bread of the Word and the bread of the Eucharist, the sign at the marriage at Cana directs faith above all towards the theme of wine, the wine of Wisdom and the wine of the Eucharist. The festivities of the marriage at Cana, with its paschal and eschatological character, is a type of the Eucharist. The wine is not only a symbol of the new doctrine of Christ who is Wisdom but is also the prefiguring of the Eucharistic wine which Christ will distribute to His disciples at the Last Supper on Maundy Thursday, as a sign of His Blood poured forth, the prefiguring of that wine which Christ may no longer drink until the Kingdom of God has come (Luke 22: 18), of that new wine which He will drink in the Kingdom of God (Mark 14: 25). One might well be astonished that only the wine should be a sufficient and clear allusion to the Eucharist, when the last part of the discourse

I

on the Bread of Life introduces the indication of blood, side by side with the flesh, to call forth the Last Supper with its two species. But if one sees a connection with the episode of the thrusting-in of the spear at the end of the Gospel (19: 31-7; 1 John 5: 6-8), the sacrament of the Eucharist is only called out in regard to the Blood which pours forth from the pierced side of the Crucified, whilst the water is a type of Baptism.[9]

The wine at Cana, which takes the place of the ritual water used for purifying, bears a very rich symbolism: it is the sign of the messianic restoration, on account of its abundance, of a new and better covenant, on account of its quality, of the Word of Christ, and of His Eucharistic Blood, for it is given in the course of this marriage feast which calls up the image of the banquet of the Wisdom and that of the Kingdom.

We are now able to estimate the total theological importance of this marriage at Cana for the gospel writer and for the Church. For the first time, at the end of the opening week of His ministry, Christ manifests in a type His glory as Messiah and Son of God, which He will manifest in the fullness of His resurrection. In the sign of the wine He proclaims the messianic restoration and the new covenant, symbolizes His Word and His Truth and His Blood which is His real Presence in the Church. Of course the disciples are not yet aware of all that this mystery means as they will understand it later. After the Word of Christ about 'the temple of his body' (2: 19-21), the Evangelist notes that 'when Jesus rose from the dead his disciples remembered that he had said this; and they believed the scripture and the Word that Jesus had spoken' (2: 22). It is in the light of His Resurrection, with the help of His spirit and in the life of His Church, that the disciples will understand the mystery contained in the signs which have been fulfilled by Christ. It is necessary to distinguish in this account of Cana, as in the whole Gospel of John, the historical plan, perceptible to the understanding of the disciples, and the theological and mystical plan, of which the gospel writer alone is aware and which determines the structure of his account, his insistence on certain themes and his literary style.

One can understand, given the theological richness of this event of the marriage at Cana, why John has underlined its importance, in making of this first miracle 'the beginning of the signs' which reveal the glory of the Messiah, and the origin of the explicit faith of the disciples in the divinity of their Master. The miracle of the marriage at Cana is a 'primordial sign which, in some manner, contains within its symbolism the meaning of all other signs.' [10] It is not only the first sign, but as the text says, 'the beginning of signs, *archē tôn sēmeiôn.*'

And as in no other part of the Gospel of John, except in the Prologue ('We have seen his glory') the actual glory of the Son of God in His earthly life is explicitly affirmed as an Epiphany: 'He manifested his glory.' It is as if the conclusion of the account abruptly threw us beyond the life and death of Jesus into the glory of His Resurrection. He appears here in His glory as the Son of God and He awakens the explicit faith of the disciples in His messianic status. This overwhelming ending to the story is really its point. The whole event of the marriage at Cana has no significance save as a manifestation of divine glory. It is impossible to read it simply as the next event in a novel which carries forward a sort of psychological plot. From the very outset of the account John has in view the point which we meet in the conclusion: 'He manifested his glory.' From the outset it is the Son of God, Christ, who is Wisdom, who acts in full knowledge of what He is doing, of what He is saying, and of the end to which He is moving. From the outset of the account of the marriage at Cana Christ has the intention of performing His first miracle, of beginning the signs of His messianic task, and accomplishing this primordial and decisive sign of changing water into wine, one which contains the paschal significance of the other signs, but which is truly the beginning, the archetype of all the signs of the Messiah.[11]

It is not only a case of a miracle of power, but of a sign which manifests the glory of the Son of God, that is to say which reveals the presence in Him of God Himself with all the gifts which result from that for the faith of the disciples. There is there the sense of the sign, of 'sēmeion,' in the Gospel of John. Christ *is* in person what He *gives* in the miracle.[12] Christ is the glory and He gives the fruits of the presence of the glory which is in Him; these fruits are the historic miracles of Jesus and the sacraments of the Church prefigured in these miracles. For John the historical miracle and the ecclesiastical sacrament are united by the concept of this sign; the miracle, as a sign of God's gift, is the prefiguring of sacrament in the history of Jesus; sacrament, as a sign of the glory of God,

131

is the continuing of miracle in the life of the Church. Jesus is the Light of the world (9: 5) and He gives light to the man born blind (9: 7); He is the resurrection (11: 25) and He gives resurrection to Lazarus (11: 43); He is the Bread of Life (6: 35) and He gives His flesh, the Living Bread for the life of the world (6: 51); He is Truth and the Glory of God (1: 14) and He gives the Wine of Wisdom, the vine of His sacramental presence, in the marriage at Cana.

Jesus has come to this wedding to manifest His glory, to reveal that He is the Glory of God and to give the disciples faith in Him through this sign.

The Presence of Mary at Cana

'The mother of Jesus was there; and Jesus and his disciples were also invited to the wedding.'

We have already seen the significance and importance of the sign of the marriage at Cana in the Gospel of John; the presence of 'the Mother of Jesus' on this occasion is certainly not without meaning and importance. We know that, in this Gospel, she will only appear at one other crucial moment: at the foot of the Cross, when the decisive Hour of the death of the Messiah will have arrived. Both here, and in the other place, the gospel writer gives her the title of 'Mother of Jesus' (or 'Mother,' four times at Cana, four times at the Cross); he thus underlines her close relationship with Christ as being the human Mother of the Son of God. However, Mary is not in the group of the disciples; she is not just one of them; she is separate. She has her own part in the setting of this event; she is already there. It seems that the gospel writer is wanting to record a change in Mary's relationship to Christ in the course of this marriage feast at Cana. At the outset she seems to have come on her own, in her own right, and to be entering into the scene at Cana as a person of some importance. The disciples have been chosen and are now united with Christ, and so are invited to the wedding with Him: they arrive there as a messianic community which has already been formed. Mary, for her part, has no place in this community, and she has not been called by Christ. She has played her part as Mother of God, which is completed with the entering of Christ upon His own ministry and now she is alone, humanly speaking, and it is alone that she comes, of her own right, to be present at the first revealing of the glory of Christ. She represents the time of Jesus' own humanity in which there was no miraculous sign to make known in public the glory that was His as the Son of God; the miracle of Cana was the first sign of that glory. Until now Jesus has not been able to appear outwardly except in His human nature; but the first week of His mission has already shown Him as the Master, as the Wisdom of God, who gathers His disciples, and as the Messiah, who is laying the foundations of His messianic community; at Cana, the beginning of these signs is going to reveal Him to the faith of His disciples, as the Son of God, indwelt by Glory.

We shall see that the reply of Jesus to Mary: 'What have I to do with thee, woman,' marks the distinction between Mother and Son. This separation has already been indicated by the setting of the marriage at Cana: Mary is there, having come on her own, and Jesus and the disciples are also invited, and they arrive on their own. There is going to be a dialogue between Mary and Jesus which will cause us to appreciate even more the difference between the levels on which these persons stand. For, in the course of the dialogue, Mary seems to be awakened by a new sense of reality, as though she understands her new situation, and she enters into the messianic community. At the end of the scene, the persons who had come separately from two different directions go out together as one: 'After which,' said John, 'he went down to Capernaum with his mother, his brethren, and his disciples, and they remained there a few days' (2: 12). Jesus, His Mother, His brethren, and His disciples form a united group in which particular members will no longer be distinguished.

It is now necessary to follow the unfolding of the scene, in order to grasp this development which involves Mary. As we have already said, it is necessary to understand each part of the scene in relation to the whole point of the account: viz., a miraculous sign which manifests the glory of the Messiah and awakens the faith of the disciples. John is not writing a psychological novel, but about a theological event, a miraculous sign, and, from the outset each person is there in relation to this miraculous sign. When the sickness of Lazarus is announced, Jesus knows from the outset that 'This sickness is not unto death, but is to the glory of God, that it may serve to glorify the Son of God, according to his own word' (11: 4). This is very much in the style of the accounts of the miracles. For John, the words of Mary and Jesus are all related to the miracle which is going to be accomplished at Cana, they prepare for it, they

133

wait for it. For the writer of the Gospel the shortage of wine is both providential and intentional in order that the miracle can take place; the first words of Mary are the affirmation of a hope for such a miracle: 'They have no more wine.' As a person at the scene, Mary knows that Jesus is able to accomplish a miracle, and she asks it of Him. It is not simply a case of a comment of purely human concern, according to which Mary requests her Son to concern Himself with a matter which is really the affair of the host, asking Him, for example, to send His disciples to buy wine in the village. Such a psychological approach to the tale has no justification whatever in such an account of a miraculous sign, or in the theological perspective of John. Mary's remark prepares for the miracle; it reveals a hope of miracle, and is even a prayer that one might be performed.

One can here measure the development of Mary's awareness since the Gospel of the infancy. She now knows that her Son, who is the Messiah and the Son of God, possesses the power to do miracles. Judaism was waiting indeed for a Messiah, a new Moses who would renew the miracles of the Exodus. If Jesus was this Messiah, the prophet *par excellence*, the new Moses, He was going to accomplish the miraculous signs which had been expected (2: 18). Faith in the possible miracle accompanies, in Mary, faith in Jesus as Messiah and Son of God. This faith is therefore well established in her. She thus represents, at the outset of the scene, the messianic faith which will be stirred up in the disciples after the miracle.

However, if Jesus, as the Messiah, consents to do miracles it seems that it may be with some reticence for He fears that men would be more attached to the marvellous and prodigious nature of these miracles than to their character as signs of the glory of the Son of God, which would awaken faith. The Jews demand wonderful signs which will reveal the messianic status of Jesus: 'What sign have you to show us for doing this?' (2: 18). But Jesus defies this appeal to miracle: 'Now when he was in Jerusalem at the Passover feast, many believed in his name when they saw the signs that he did, but Jesus did not trust himself to them, because he knew all men and needed no one to bear witness of man; for he himself knew what was in man' (2: 23-5). Even after the multiplying of the bread and the discourse on the Bread of Life: 'Several of the disciples withdrew and walked with him no more' (6: 66). 'For

Jesus knew from the first who those were who did not believe, and who it was that should betray him' (6: 64). Miracle is inadequate for drawing men to Christ. It is necessary that it should be 'granted him by the Father' (6: 65). One should not be drawn by the marvels of miracle, but by the Word which they signify, as Peter will be: 'Lord to whom shall we go? You have the word of eternal life, we believe and know that thou art the holy one of God' (6: 68–9). What counts is the significance of the miracle and the faith which that draws out, not its wonder-working character. That is why Jesus always added to the miracles which manifest His glory a word to feed faith. 'See, you are well, he says to the sick man of Bethesda, sin no more that nothing worse befall you' (5: 14). After the increase of the bread He utters the discourse on the Bread of Life (Chap. 6). Meeting the blind man who has been healed, He puts to him the question of faith in the Son of man (9: 35) and the man on whom a miracle has been worked prostrates himself before Him, saying: 'Lord, I believe' (9: 38). Before the resurrection of Lazarus, Jesus puts to Martha the question of faith in the resurrection, and she replies: 'Yes, Lord, I believe that thou art the Christ, the Son of God, who must come into the world' (11: 27).

In the account of the second sign, the healing of the nobleman's son, Jesus begins by indicating His reticence even before the miracle: 'If you do not see signs and miracles you will not believe?' (4: 48). This is not a refusal to do a miracle but a warning against the attraction of the marvellous and an insistence on the power of faith, the only fruit worthy of a sign. The nobleman will believe in the Word of Jesus since it will support the miracle; and the account finishes: 'He believed, he and his whole house' (4: 53).

Mary at Cana believes in the Messiah and His power to perform miracles, and this is why she asks Him to perform one: 'They have no more wine.' However, her faith rests perhaps a little too much on the miraculous power of the Messiah and His efficaciousness on the human side. The hosts are in a difficulty; the Messiah is there; He has the power to perform a miracle; this miracle can save a human situation. The nobleman has exactly the same spiritual attitude; his son is sick; Jesus is coming; He has the power to heal; this miracle can save his son from death. We saw the parallelism of these two accounts in the structure of the gospel. The one throws light upon the other. Mary, like the nobleman, is too bound up with the relation between miracle and the difficult situation which has to be dealt with. She is plainly human in her attitude to faith in the all powerful Messiah; she also represents the situation of the faith of Judaism at this time; the Messiah, like Moses, is expected to produce signs like those of the Exodus.

In her act of faith and in her prayer, Mary appears as one who represents humanity in difficulty and Judaism in its messianic hope; she is the type of humanity and of Israel which are awaiting their deliverance, a mysterious deliverance for humanity, a messianic but still very human deliverance for Israel. Faced with the plea of the nobleman, Jesus will warn those around Him about signs and mighty works, in order to awaken a purer faith which does not demand miracles. The reply of Jesus to His Mother must first be interpreted as a warning and an appeal to a more surrendered faith: 'What have I to do with thee, woman?' It is, let me repeat, not a refusal to work a miracle, but an invitation to faith which has no need of miracle. At the end of the Resurrection appearances, Thomas will hear these words spoken by Christ to him: 'Because you have seen me Thomas you have believed; blessed are those who having not seen believe' (20: 29). It is towards this point that the Gospel of these signs is moving: Jesus does not refuse a miracle, but it is essential that faith should be deeply linked with the meaning of a sign which is worked, that is to say, with the very person of Christ Himself, in order to reach a faith without signs, which is perfect faith, and blessed are those indeed who have that faith without having seen.

In this first part of the account, Mary symbolizes an anxious humanity which is awaiting deliverance, and also that Jewish faith in the Messiah which expects Him to be revealed by signs. Fully human in her expectations, she is the type of all humanity; being still Jewish in her faith she is the type of Israel; but Christ by the reply that He addresses to her, though it is not a refusal, but an appeal to take a wider look, is going to draw her out of this human situation and this Jewish faith in order to raise her up with Christian faith to a place of being the type of the believing Church.

The writer of the Gospel gives Mary the title of 'Mother of Jesus' (or 'His mother') in this account, but Christ Himself gives His mother the title of 'Woman' when He speaks to her. It will be just the same at the foot of the Cross. This parallel is too striking not

136

to be significant. Normally a Jew spoke of his mother as 'Imma,' in Aramaic, 'Mother' or 'my mother.' It is very strange for a son to speak of his mother as 'Woman' (Aramaic: Itta). Jesus did use this address in speaking to various women, to the Samaritan woman (John 4: 21), to the Canaanite woman (Matt. 15: 28), to the woman taken in adultery (John 8: 10), to the woman who was bent (Luke 13: 12), and to Mary Magdalene (John 20: 13); but here, in addressing His mother, this title sounds very odd. On one side it replaces the normal title of 'mother' and on the other side, by the fact of this very replacement, it takes on a solemn, emphatic note. There will be exactly the same sort of situation when, from the Cross, Jesus says to His mother with regard to the disciple whom He loved: 'Woman, behold thy son' (John 19: 26).

Before accomplishing this primordial sign which will reveal His glory as Messiah, Jesus will have to indicate that the time of human family relationship has had to come to an end. He is no longer able to be considered as the human son of Mary, and the Virgin has finished her rôle as the human mother of God. In her divine motherhood, as 'theotokos,' Mary was a sign of the true humanity of the Son of God, the reality of the Incarnation: 'The Word became flesh' (John 1: 14). Now, this sign is no longer necessary; Christ the man reveals His divine glory in His own humanity; the bond of human parenthood would simply endanger or veil His nature as the Son of God. The time of the 'theotokos' is over; and now comes that of 'Bride of the Church,' which will be the true and final parenthood of the son of God. Mary must pass from her function as 'Mother of Jesus' to that of 'Woman' in the Church, but this title of 'Woman' which Jesus gives her, in place of that of 'Mother,' is of a more solemn character. There is a relation between the two titles. As Mother, Mary passes from the function of Mother of God to that of the type of the Church, from the human and spiritual rôle of the Mother of the Messiah, to the purely spiritual rôle of the believing woman in the Church. The Mother of God becomes the Believing Woman.

'What to me and to thee?' This very Semitic idiom expresses the relationship of these two human beings, in union or in opposition.[13] In this particular case, and having been given the context, the expression should be translated thus: 'What is our relation, between me and thee, Woman?' There is no need to see this as a harsh word on Christ's part, nor as a refusal of the request made

137

by Mary for a miracle; this would contradict the fact that Jesus certainly had the intention of fulfilling His first sign, and He was going to do so directly. One cannot imagine, in the style of the account of the miracle, above all in John's Gospel, Christ not knowing at the outset what He is going to do, that Mary may ask a miracle of Him; and though Jesus will first refuse it, in the end He will accomplish it as the result of a curious insistence by Mary. The phrase used by Jesus is a question which must lead His mother to reflect on the relationship with Him, on her own rôle, and on the significance of the miracle for which she is asking. One might quite legitimately paraphrase the reply of Jesus thus: 'What are the relationship between me and thee? Reflect Woman, I am the Son of God, you are my human mother, but now our relationship cannot be that of a son with his mother. I have entered upon my messianic mission, and you have no more maternal authority over me but you are to have your part in the messianic community, as a woman in the Church of which I am the head. You ask for a miracle and I am going to do it, but do you realize what this miracle signifies for the Son of God, whom I am? It is not a mighty work destined to meet some human difficulty only; it is the sign of my glory which must evoke faith in My Word.' The second part of this paraphrase is based on the parallelism of the two miracles of Cana. To the nobleman who asked the miracle of healing, Jesus replies in spite of His intention to do it: 'If you do not *see* signs and miracles you will not *believe?*' (4: 48). By this question, Jesus is wanting to get those around to pass beyond the conception simply of 'wonder' and the too 'visual nature' of miracle, to a more inward conception of 'the sign' which addresses itself to spiritual faith, which should tend to pass beyond the miracle, because such will be, after the appearances of the Resurrection, the normal situation in the faith of the Church.

Jesus' reply therefore marks, in one sense, a new stage for Mary: He does not any longer call her 'Mother' but 'Woman': the Mother of God becomes a member of the Church community; on the other hand, the human and Judaic character of this cry for miracle by Mary, as a miraculous solution to a human difficulty, is raised by Christ's question to a more interior perception of the sign of the Messiah's glory which will awaken faith. This latter aspect will reappear at the end of the story, in particular at the second intervention by Mary.

But the reply of Jesus continues: 'What is the relationship between thee and me, Woman? It is not yet my hour.' The Hour of which Jesus speaks is, according to St. John, the decisive hour of His being raised upon the Cross, of His glorification, and of His return to the Father. During the Feast of Tabernacles, they twice wish to arrest Jesus, but no one can raise a hand against Him, because, said St. John, 'His hour had not yet come' (7: 30; 8: 20). When the day of His death is to appear, Jesus will announce it as His glorification: 'The hour is come in which the Son of man must be glorified . . . now my soul is troubled, and what shall I say: Father save me from this hour? but it is for that that I have come even to this hour: Father, glorify thy name! ' (12: 23, 27). And before the washing of the feet, the initiation of the disciples into the mystery of the perfect love which will be accomplished on the Cross, the Evangelist introduces the account: 'Before the feast of Passover, Jesus, knowing that his hour was come in which he must pass from this world to the Father, and having loved his own loved them to the utmost of his love' (13: 1). In the High Priestly prayer Jesus will say yet again: 'Father the hour is come: glorify thy Son, that thy Son may glorify thee . . . ' (17: 1). This Hour is the final moment of the Cross which elevates the Son, and glorifies Him in order that He may pass from this world to the Father. After the words of the Crucified to His mother and to His beloved disciple the Evangelist will write: 'From this very hour the disciple took her unto his own home' (19: 27).

Jesus, in His reply to Mary, directs His mother to the decisive Hour, and sets her in the way of the final dénouement of the Cross, His elevation and glorification. This direction does not imply a refusal to work a miracle in the present hour; that would mean that Jesus has not the intention of performing a miracle before the coming of the dénouement of His mission. Why then should He change His point of view so quickly? It is so unlikely and impossible.[14] Jesus' reply is not the kind of refusal to do a miracle which means that she is to wait for an hour far distant, for one could not then understand the insistence of Mary which would amount to insolence in regard to the Master. Jesus' reply is not concerned with the accomplishing of a miracle for that is already decided, as the beginning of His messianic signs, but with the attitude of Mary in relation to the miracle in order that she might understand it in faith as a sign. This reply also concerns Mary's function. This is no longer the motherly function in regard to the Messiah, but a new function which she will later grasp in the Hour of the Cross; however, she is able to begin it from this moment on by being set in the context of the messianic community and in the position of a believing woman in the Church.

Jesus' reply therefore concerns essentially the development of Mary's faith and her new function, which follows on her human motherhood of the Son of God. One might even paraphrase the reply of Jesus once more as: 'You and I, we are not seeing things in the same way; you want a miracle, and I am going to perform a sign which is going to awaken faith; as mother, you are still too human; you are to grow up to a pure faith which will see, through these signs, or even without them, the glory of the Son of God and those that put their trust in his word. Woman, you are called to a greater function still than that of historic motherhood of the Messiah; my hour is still not come and you are still not able to understand; but at that hour (at the Cross) this situation and new function will be revealed to you in their fullness.' Mary is called to a superior, spiritual purpose and is directed to that decisive hour even though she evidently does not know what this final dénouement may be. She is only able to sense that the glory of the Messiah will not come without suffering, according to the prophecy of Simeon in the Temple.

We must now return to the Synoptic gospels in order to understand, in the light of an event which concerns Mary, what this passage about the function of the Mother of the Son of God signifies for her in the situation of a believer in the messianic community, the Church, a situation which will take on its full significance at the Hour of the Crucifixion.

One day when Jesus is speaking to the crowd, His mother and some members of His kindred come to speak with Him but they are not able to reach Him because of the crowd (Matt. 12: 46–50; Mark 3: 31–5; Luke 8: 19–21). They tell Jesus of the request of His mother and His brethren and He replies to those who tell Him: 'Who is my mother, and who are my brethren?' Then, pointing with a gesture to His disciples, He adds: 'Behold my mother and my brethren, for whosoever does the will of my Father which is in heaven, he is my brother, and my sister, and my mother' (Matt. 12: 49–50; Mark 3: 35). St. Luke records these words thus: 'My mother and my brethren are those who hear and perform the Word of God' (Luke 8: 21).

This account clarifies the words of Jesus to Mary at the marriage at Cana: 'What is the relationship between me and thee, Woman?' The response is found in part in this later episode in the history of Jesus, and it was given in full at the last Hour by the Crucified as He addressed His mother and the beloved disciple. Yet another episode, reported by Luke, carries the same meaning. One day, to a woman who proclaimed the human motherhood of Mary as blessed, Jesus replied: 'Yea, blessed rather are those who hear the Word of God and keep it' (Luke 11: 28).

The explanation of these words is simple. Jesus, having entered upon His ministry, and surrounded by the messianic community, does not wish the bonds of earthly and human parenthood to play any part in His life since they might conceal His divine origin and impede His mission. Mary has completed her rôle as the human mother of the Messiah, and the mother of God. The mother, who now enters upon her task, is the messianic community that is the Church; the true parents of Jesus and His brethren are the disciples who surround Him. A definitive and spiritual parenthood succeeds His temporary and earthly parenthood. The temporary and maternal function of Mary in regard to the historic Christ makes way for the final, motherly function of the Church, in regard to the mystical Christ, the Body of Christ and its members, to its disciples and faithful, to the sons of the Father in Heaven who are born by the Word of God. Jesus here underlines the Fatherhood of God and the motherhood of the ecclesiastical community which gives birth to the faithful, thanks to the Word of God, the fraternity of the disciples and of the members of the Body of Christ. The Church, the Mother of the faithful, is more happy than Mary, the Mother of God, for the motherhood of the Church is perpetual, whereas that of Mary was only temporary. Certainly Mary also has her part in the Church; she also has been engendered by faith in the Word of God which she hears, keeps and fulfils; she has also the Church as her Mother, and the disciples and all the faithful as her brothers and sisters. Her place now is to be there in the Church and to rejoice in the spiritual motherhood of the Church community, in the spiritual fraternity of the members of the Body of Christ, greater than all human motherliness and fraternity, or all earthly parenthood. At the Hour of the Cross she will understand even more; she will know then that a particular relationship is established between her human motherhood of the Son of God and the spiritual motherhood of the Church. But, for the moment, she must take her place amongst those who, engendered by the Word of the Father, are brothers and sisters in the words of the messianic community, their spiritual mother. Christ is amongst them, as the eldest son who leads them to the love of the Father and in obedience to His will.

Mary has understood the word of Jesus on the matter of the miracle she has requested. The account of Cana, concise as it is, immediately leads to a new intervention by Mary which indicates a change in her. John has presented in this very brief dialogue a complete spiritual pilgrimage in response to the monition of Jesus. She continues to believe in the miracle and to ask for it, for Jesus has not refused it. She knows that the Hour will come in which she will the better understand her place in regard to her Son. Already she is prepared to understand, in the faith longed-for by Christ, the sign which the Messiah is going to give in order to show forth His glory.[15]

'His mother said to the servants: whatsoever he tells you, do it' (2: 5).

Mary has understood Christ's intention of accomplishing a sign of His glory, in reply to her first demand, but she has also understood that she must put herself on another level than that of her human motherhood, in order that her relationship with her Son might be conformed to the new situation, that of a believing woman in the messianic community; this setting will be explained at the decisive Hour of Jesus' mission. After having first demanded a miracle in order to save a human situation for which she was concerned and after having hoped for this miracle of power from her Son, Mary commits herself totally to Him and to His Word, thus revealing that she has understood that what matters is not the miracle but the person of the Messiah who will thus be glorified, and hence calls for total abandonment to His will, in pure faith and obedience to His orders whatever they may be. Mary has so well understood the will of Christ in regard to Him and in regard to the miracle that she no more importunes her Son with an insistence that would be unfitting but turns to the servants to invite them to believe, and obey, whatever the word and the will of Jesus may be. She communicates to them in some kind of way her faith and her obedience to the Word of the all-powerful Messiah. She is truly of those who hear and fulfil the Word of God, and in that she finds her true and real place in the messianic community, as a spiritual mother and sister of Him of whom she has been until now the human mother: 'My mother and my brethren are those who hear and fulfil the Word of God' (Luke 8: 21). By inviting the servants to hear the Word of Christ, and to do the orders of the Messiah whatever they may be, and to abandon themselves to Him in faith and obedience, she ceases to be the human mother of Christ who had power over her Son and becomes the spiritual mother in the community of the Messiah, and gives birth, by faith and obedience, to the servants of the Master. Her faith and her obedience precede the faith and obedience of both the servants and the disciples; Mary here shares in the spiritual motherhood of the Church which, by the Word of Christ, gives birth to the sons of the Father in heaven by causing them to be born by faith and obedience. We shall find with St. Paul this idea of engendering or bearing of the faithful of the Church in faith. Before speaking to the Galatians of the Jerusalem which is on high, the Church, as a Mother, he says to them: 'My little children, with whom I am again in travail until Christ be performed in you!' (Gal. 4: 19, 26). Here the Apostle sees his ministry as a motherly child-bearing which has its part in the spiritual motherhood of the Church. Besides, he considers himself as a father: 'It is I who, by the Gospel, have borne you in Christ Jesus' (1 Cor. 4: 15; see also 1 Thess. 2: 11; Philemon 10). In all these cases the conversion to Christ by faith is seen as a giving birth by the ministry of the Word of God, a giving birth by Mother Church, in whose motherhood the Apostle takes his part.

Mary, here, also participates in the spiritual motherhood of the Church which gives birth to the disciples of Christ in the light of faith. Mary's faith, which is total abandon to the will and word of Christ ('Whatsoever he says'), communicates itself to the servants ('. . . do it'), and precedes and prepares for the glory of the Messiah which will awaken the faith of the disciples ('. . . and the disciples believed in him'). Mary here fulfils the ministry of communicating the faith, she gives birth to the faith of others, and shares in the motherhood of the Church.

Now, the account of the miracle has been completely introduced, the occasion can pursue its way and enable us to assist in this sign which will show forth the glory of the Messiah and draw out the explicit faith of the disciples, following the faith of Mary.

'After which, he went down to Capernaum as did his mother, brethren and disciples and there they rested a few days' (John 2: 12). At the end of the account Mary and the disciples formed the messianic community, united with faith to the Son of God who has just manifested his glory; there is the kernel of the Church around its Lord, hearing His Word and fulfilling the will of the Father. Mary is present in this ecclesiastical community and one can imagine Christ looking round on the group around Him saying: 'Behold my mother and my brethren; whoever does the will of my Father which is in heaven he is my brother and my sister and my mother.' In Mother Church Mary is no longer only the human mother of the Son of God but is the believing woman, the spiritual mother sharing in the motherhood of the Church which gives birth by faith. Certainly we do not see her following Jesus in His movements from place to place with the other women mentioned in the Gospel, Mary Magdalene, Mary the mother of James and Joses, Salome the mother of the sons of Zebedee, Joanna wife of Chuza, Susanna and many others (Matt. 27: 55–6; Mark 15: 40–1; Luke 8: 2–3; 24: 10; John 19: 25); but that does not imply that Mary was outside the messianic community. She plays her part by faith within it, if not by a life spent at the side of Jesus all the time.

All these women will be found at the foot of the Cross and then Mary will be there, mentioned by St. John, and amongst them all she will be chosen to receive the last words of the Crucified.

THE HOUR OF THE CROSS

The crucifying of Jesus is for St. John the decisive Hour in the messianic mission. It is the Hour to which Jesus has directed His mother at the marriage at Cana, it is the Hour in which the Jewish Paschal Lamb is sacrificed for the feast and in which Christ, the true and final Lamb, who takes away the sin of the world, is Himself offered on the Cross; it is the Hour in which the love of the Saviour is manifested to the end; it is the Hour of the passing of the Son of God from this world to the Father (13: 1); it is the Hour of the glorification of the Son by the Father (12: 23, 27–8; 17: 1); it is the Hour of raising-up from the earth which united in one single act both the raising of the Cross for death and the raising to Heaven in the Resurrection. 'And I, if I be lifted up, will draw all men unto me' (12: 32). By this Jesus signified what death He would die (12: 33) and that His being raised up on the Cross would be at the same time His glorification and His passing from this world to the Father: 'No one ascends into heaven, he said to Nicodemus, but he that descended from heaven, even the Son of man who is in heaven. As Moses lifted up the serpent in the desert, even so must the Son of man be lifted up in order that all men may believe that in Him they may have eternal life' (3: 13–15).

Mary is present at this decisive Hour of the Cross, in order to share with the messianic community, represented by the beloved disciple and the women, in the last mystery of Christ's mission and at this last sign of the raising-up which will be completed by the mysterious thrust of the spear into the side of the Crucified.

The words of Christ to Mary and to the disciple constitute the supreme moment in the Crucifixion. Very shortly afterwards there is mention made of the Hour and the final fulfilment: 'From this very hour the disciple took her into his own home after which, knowing that from this moment all was accomplished, Jesus said, in order that the Scripture might be fulfilled, I thirst' (19: 27–8). Then He takes the vinegar and He says: 'It is finished: and, bowing his head, he gave up the ghost' (19: 30). The words of the Crucified to His mother and His disciple whom He loved are thus placed at the summit and accomplishment of the redemption by Christ according to the Scripture.

The Significance of the Words of the Crucified

'Standing by the cross of Jesus were his mother, his mother's sister, Mary the wife of Cleophas and Mary Magdalene. When Jesus saw his mother and the disciple whom he loved standing near he said to his mother: "Woman, behold your son! " Then he said to the disciple, "Behold your mother! ", and from that hour the disciple took her unto his own home. After this Jesus knowing that all was now finished . . . ' (19: 25–8).

There have been many and varied interpretations of this text in the course of tradition.[16] It is possible to divide them into five general groups each of which have fewer or more exponents.

Firstly, we encounter the idea that this text describes John as the beloved disciple, 'the perfect disciple,' who, by reason of his perfection, is in so intimate a relation with Christ that He gives him the task of replacing him near to His own mother; he thus becomes the type of perfect Christian who knows Christ intimately. 'Every man

145

K

who becomes perfect no longer lives to himself, but Christ lives in him, and since Christ lives in him, Mary is told concerning him: "Behold thy son, the Christ! " ' [17] This line of interpretation of the text which might be called Johannine and not Marian, and which sets the prerogatives of John more to the fore than those of Mary, is supported by Tertullian,[18] Origen, St. John Chrysostom,[19] and Theodore of Mopsuestia.[20]

Secondly, we meet the idea that this text is evidence for the 'perpetual virginity' of Mary. This interpretation is particularly favoured by the Fathers of the fourth century who had to defend the doctrine of Mary's perpetual virginity: St. Athanasius of Alexandria, St. Epiphanius of Cyprus, St. Hilary of Poitier, St. Jerome, and St. Ambrose.[21] 'If Mary had had children, and if her husband was still alive, why was Mary committed to the care of John . . .' [22]

Thirdly, we encounter the idea that this text emphasizes the 'filial love' of Christ in regard to His mother, which is an example for all Christians; this interpretation is one of the most widespread, because, in the West, it was held by great Doctors like St. Ambrose and St. Augustine; this idea will also be taken over by St. Thomas Aquinas; in the east St. John Chrysostom and St. Cyril of Alexandria also share it. 'The master of the saints, wrote St. Augustine in the year 415, has thus been given as an example for this so salutary precept, when he saw before him another son in his place, in the presence of the mother from whom as a man he had come forth and whom he now was leaving . . .' [23]

Fourthly, an interpretation which is more rare, but is certainly more theological and certainly more according to the style of St. John, sees in Mary a 'symbol of the Church.' St. Ephraem (died A.D. 373) in his commentary on the Diatessaron ('the compound Gospel,' attributed to Tatian), explains our text in relation to the discourse on the Bread of Life (St. John 6). Jesus is the new Moses who gives us the true bread from heaven, He is the fulfilment of the prophecy of Moses: 'The Lord God will raise up a prophet like me from among you, from your brethren whom you shall heed . . .' (Deut. 18: 15). St. Ephraem writes: 'Jesus walked across the sea; he appeared in the cloud; his Church will be redeemed from circumcision; he established John who was chaste in place of Joshua, the son of Nun (God's leader), and he gave him Mary, his Church, as Moses had given Joshua the people, in order to act even as Moses had said: "in my stead." ' [24] In the very moment when Jesus, the new Moses, is going to die He commits Mary to John, that is to say he commits the Church to the faithful Apostle, as Moses had committed the people to Joshua in order that he might lead them into the Promised Land.

To this Syrian testimony may be added a western interpretation, that of St. Ambrose of Milan. The exegesis of this great bishop evolved in the course of his ministry following the pastoral requirements which he encountered. He is the one patristic author who makes the most use of this text of John 19: 25-7. In the first stage of his interpretation he uses the text to demonstrate the perpetual virginity of Mary against her detractors. He still imagines Joseph to be alive when Jesus is crucified, which is very debatable, and writes: 'If there had been a union between them, and if she had never left her husband, then this just man would never have consented that she should be separated from him.' [25] Ambrose also sees in this text the proof of the reality of the Incarnation: 'Christ does not deny having a mother—according to the traps which are spread out by certain heretics (in regard to Luke 8: 21)—since on the very Cross he will recognize her . . . ' [26] At the second stage, and this is the most important, St. Ambrose is to see in the Word of Christ an act of filial piety, a 'testamentum domesticum' [27]: 'We have therefore a master of piety; the text teaches us what our model should be for maternal love and how filial respect should be expressed. Mothers should be willing to share in the dangers that their sons undergo, and they in their turn must be full of concern for the care of their mothers rather than for the suffering of their own death.' [28] But this interpretation is linked still with the argument of Mary's virginity. Her Son gives her a protector: 'To the mother is committed the defence of her virginity, the witness of her integrity, and to the disciple, the care of this mother, the grace of piety.' [29]

In a third stage, St. Ambrose moves away from the literal sense (the proof of perpetual virginity) and from the moral sense (the sign of filial piety) to a mystical sense of the text, which is more like St. Ephraem and which is more in keeping with the Gospel writer: Mary, at the foot of the Cross, is a type of the Church. 'There is a mystery in the fact that Mary is committed to John, the youngest of the Apostles; and we do not need to accept this with a

strange ear . . . for this has to do with the mystery of the Church:
formerly united with her ancient people in type, but not effectively,
and after having given birth to the Word, and having sown him in
the bodies and souls of men by faith in the Cross and by burial in
the Body of the Lord, she has, by God's command, chosen the
society of the youngest people.' [30] Mary here appears as a type of
the Church which is being detached from Israel in order to adopt
the Gentiles, the younger people who are represented by the beloved
disciple like John, the young Apostle. Furthermore St. Ambrose
underlines this theme of Mary, the type of the Church, in regard
to John, who is the type of the Christian disciple; addressing himself to Christians the bishop exhorts them to follow the steps of
Peter, James and John, the two 'sons of thunder.' He writes: 'You
will be a son of thunder if you are a son of the Church; since from
the gibbet of the Cross Christ may say to you also: "Behold thy
mother"; and also He may say to the Church: "Behold thy son";
it is then that you will begin to be a son of the Church, when you
shall see Christ victorious on his Cross . . . ; the son of the Church
is he who sees in the sign of the Cross a triumph and who recognizes the voice of Christ triumphant.' [31]

If we have spoken at length about this fourth interpretation it is
because it seems to us the most interesting and also the one which
is nearest to the Johannine spirit.[32]

Fifthly, however, and somewhat later in history, we find the idea
that the words of the Crucified to Mary and to John establish the
'spiritual maternity' of the virgin over all men. It is in the east in
the ninth century, with the Bishop George Nicomedia (died after
A.D. 880), that this Marian interpretation of the text begins to
appear. In a sermon of *Parasceva*, he paraphrases the words of
Christ to Mary: 'I bequeath to you also, through him (the beloved
disciple), the rest of my disciples. And as long as my will is that you
should live with them and remain with them, you shall let them
share your corporeal presence in my place. Be for them all that a
mother naturally should be for her children, or rather all that I
would be were I present; and they will be for thee all that sons and
subjects should be. They will render you the respect that is your
due as the mother of the Lord, and as I have been present to them
in thee, they will similarly possess thee as an easy mediator for
obtaining things towards me.' [33] Then, paraphrasing the words of
Jesus Christ to His beloved disciple, he continues: 'Henceforth, I

constitute her (Mary) a guide for the disciples, as a mother not only for thee, but for all the other disciples, and I will that she should be honoured with the full rights of her maternal dignity. If therefore I have warned you not to call any one on earth "father," yet I will that you should call her "mother" and that you should honour her as such . . . ' [34] One can here assess the development in the interpretation of our text.

In the West, the idea of Mary's spiritual maternity is developed from the eighth century; Ambrose Autpert (died 784), Odo of Cluny (died 942), Fulbert of Chartres (died A.D. 1029) are witnesses to this interpretation; Mary is called: 'Mother of the believers, Mother of all, Mother of mercy.' [35] But the first interpretation of the text, John 19: 25-7, in the sense of a spiritual motherhood of Mary, we owe to Bishop Anselm of Lucca (died 1086) who became the spiritual director of the Countess Matilda of Tuscany; he wrote in regard to 'behold thy son' that this word signifies 'that the glorious mother intercedes for all true believers in so great and pious an affection that she keeps by a special protection those whom she has adopted for her children, the captives who have been redeemed.' [36] St. Anselm of Canterbury, thus consulted by Matilda of Tuscany, will pursue this same vision of the spiritual motherhood of Mary, which he will transmit to his disciples: 'Mary is our mother, Jesus is our brother.' [37] Eadmer, one of his disciples (died 1124), will sum up this conclusion of the medieval interpretation of John 19: 25-7: 'O sovereign lady, if thy Son has become for thee our brother, art thou not thyself our mother? For when he was on the point of dying on the Cross for us, he said to John who represented no other than ourselves in this condition: "Behold thy mother . . ." ' [38] The Abbé Rupert Deutz (died A.D. 1130) finished up with the idea of a birth of the faithful in salvation, by Mary, thanks to her communion in the sufferings of Christ: 'Hence, suffering here truly the pains of birth (Psalm 48) in the fashion of her only Son, the Blessed Virgin has brought to the world our universal salvation; that is why she is the mother of us all.' [39]

It is a long way from the interpretation of St. Ambrose ('perpetual virginity, filial piety, and a type of the Church'), which very well sums up the Patristic interpretation, to that of the twelfth century ('Mary, the mother of believers who gives birth to them in her compassion').

The interpretation which sees in these words of the Crucified an act of filial piety is far and away the most widespread. Is it the only possible interpretation? Does it go deep enough theologically? Does it really fit, alone and by itself, an account by a mystical theologian such as the writer of the Fourth Gospel? If we do not see in the words of Jesus anything but the intention of providing for the future of His mother, we shall then run into a great many difficulties.

If the words of Christ have only a charitable import, one must ask why Christ waits until the moment before His death before providing for His mother's future. From the outset of His ministry, at Cana, we have seen Mary alone, and certainly a widow. She does not follow Jesus from place to place; Jesus has therefore abandoned the company of His mother, and throughout the time of His earthly mission her needs have had to be met until this very moment. Besides we see Mary in the company of the members of His kindred (the 'brethren' of Jesus, Matt. 12: 46 and similar passages). At the foot of the Cross, she is with her sister, or relative, Salome, mother of the Sons of Zebedee, or Mary, the wife of Cleophas (Matt. 27: 56; Mark 15: 40; John 19: 25). She is therefore surrounded by her kindred, she is not isolated, and it is not necessary for any one to be specially preoccupied with provision for her future purely from the material point of view.

On the other hand Jesus addresses His mother in order to commit the disciple to her and only secondly speaks to him in order to commit His mother to his care. If this were only a case of an act of filial love, the first word should surely be addressed to the disciple in order to commit Mary to him, and this word would then be sufficient. If Jesus begins with Mary, in order to designate the disciple as her son, it is because this word has more than a purely private interpretation; it has another import. Further, the solemn character of the situation and of these words of Jesus fit a simply moral explanation with great difficulty. Five episodes compose the account of the Crucifixion (19: 16–37) and each of them conveys a significant act, either in itself or by reason of the fulfilment of a prophecy:
1. The Placing on the Cross, with the superscription 'The King of the Jews';
2. The parting of the vestments, with the quoting of Ps. 22: 18;
3. Mary and the disciple, with the words of Jesus;

4. The death of Jesus, with the allusion to Ps. 69: 22;
5. The thrusting-in of the spear, with the allusion to Exod. 12: 46 and the quotations of Ps. 34: 21 and from Zech. 12: 10.

On the three occasions when there is a reference to the Old Testament the act is linked with the quotation by the phrase: 'in order that the scripture might be fulfilled' (the second, fourth and fifth episodes: 19: 24, 28 and 36–7). The first episode thus speaks of the 'scripture' which cannot be revoked: 'What I have written I have written' (19: 22). The third episode, with Mary and the disciple, is completed by the solemn words, which, without making any allusion to scripture, set the words of Christ in the plan of the redeeming act: 'After that, seeing that from that moment, all was accomplished (tētēlestai), in order that the scripture might be fulfilled (tēleiōthei), Jesus said: "I thirst" ' (19: 28). These five episodes are thus united by the same intention of the Evangelist by setting them in relation to a prophecy, with a 'piece of scripture,' and in relation to the redemptive act accomplished on the Cross. How, in such an important and solemn context, can the episode of the disciple and Mary alone be accepted as having simply a domestic and private interpretation? And finally, it must be added, that if the Evangelist is simply pointing out Mary as the Mother of Jesus, then Jesus, in speaking to her, addresses her, not with the title of 'Mother,' but with that of 'Woman.' If the episode were simply concerned with a filial consideration by Jesus, why would He not address her by calling her quite naturally 'Mother,' which would then be more fitting to the moral sense of the text and to Jewish custom. But on the contrary, Jesus gives His mother a title which, as at Cana, expresses a separation between them, and puts to one side a too human consideration of the motherhood of Mary and the sonship of Christ by setting Mary on a more objective level: 'Woman, behold thy son.'

It is not a question of putting aside the exegesis which sees in this episode a filial act by Christ towards His mother. The conclusive phrase: ' . . . the disciple took her to his own home,' whatever might be the fashion in which one understands it, implies a welcome to Mary by the disciple to his own home. Jesus has indeed committed His mother materially to His beloved disciple; but, as we have just seen, the context prevents us from resting with this interpretation alone. One cannot exclude it, but no more is one able to exclude the historic sense of other episodes of the Cruci-

151

fixion; the superscription by Pilate, the predicted tearing of the robe, the thirst of Jesus, and the piercing of the side of Christ. But, like these other episodes, that of Mary and of the disciple demands a deepening sense of mystery, according to the style of the Johannine Gospel. It is, therefore, necessary to admit first the immediately historic sense of the episode, as has been done by the majority of the commentators. One can add further, as an additional comment, the consideration that Mary must be a widow, and without other children, or else it is indeed very strange that she should go and dwell with the disciple. Therefore we discover here two interpretations of the patristic tradition: it is an act of 'filial piety' by Christ and there is no sense in this remark unless Mary is 'alone.'

But, to this immediately historic sense, the context obliges us to join the intentionally mystical sense of both Christ and the Evangelist.

The Meaning of the Events of the Crucifixion

If we once more take up the context, we are led to note several important points which set our episode against the whole plan of the redemptive act and not only that of a domestic record. The general use of the five Johannine episodes of the Crucifixion may be summed up in the theme of the fulfilment of redemption and of scripture. The raising-up of Christ upon the Cross is only one with His glorification, and therefore constitutes the Hour of the fulfilment of the messianic mission of the Lamb which taketh away the sin of the world.

The Crucifixion took place on the day of the preparation of the Passover, the day on which one prepared the Paschal meal which had to take place after the setting of the sun. After midday anything that was leavened had to be removed in order to make place for the 'azymes,' for the unleavened bread of the Passover. The Evangelist underlines this hour of midday (19: 14) in order to set the Crucifixion and the death of Christ clearly in relation with the Passover. Jesus is going to be sacrificed on the Cross at the very moment the Paschal Lamb is sacrificed for the liturgical feast of the Passover. Christ is the true and final 'Passover Lamb' who takes away the sins of the world, according to the double prophecy of the Baptist at the outset of the Johannine Gospel (1: 29, 36). For the Gospel writer the Messiah is the Suffering Servant of the prophecy of Isaiah (ch. 53), and the Passover Lamb of the Passover of the Exodus (ch. 12) a sign of the deliverance of Israel. Jesus dies on the Cross at the moment of the liturgical sacrifice of the Passover Lamb: 'There shall not be one bone of him broken' (John 19: 36), as with the Passover Lamb (Exod. 12: 46). As St. Paul is to say: 'Christ our Passover has been slain, let us therefore celebrate the feast, not with the old leaven, nor with the leaven of malice and wickedness but with the unleavened bread of purity and truth' (1 Cor. 5: 7–8). This theme of the Lamb is to be central for the Apostolic preaching (Acts 8: 32–5; 1 Peter 1: 18–20; Rev. 5: 6, 12, etc.). It is quite clearly set before us in the Johannine chronology of the events of the Passion story.

1. In the first episode of the account of the Crucifixion in John's Gospel, Pilate plays a providential rôle in order to set down in evidence the royal title of the Messiah: Jesus is the 'King of the Jews.' The soldiers have already mocked Christ by crowning Him with thorns and clothing Him with purple; they have saluted Him with the title of 'King of the Jews'; here are once more united the glory and humiliation of the Messiah, the King and Suffering Servant; wishing to humiliate Him the soldiers show forth His glory as King, Pilate, after having presented Him to the crowd in His humanity, 'Behold the man' (19: 5), is going to present Him once again in His royal status, 'Behold your king' (19: 14). Pilate here appears as an unwitting instrument of the Word of God: he expresses the truth about Christ, and even goes so far as to write in three languages on the superscription that will be fixed to the Cross: 'Jesus of Nazareth, the King of the Jews' (19: 19, 21). By doing that he expresses the humanity and the glory of the Messiah without realizing it: Jesus is Man, or the Nazarene, and He is the King of the Jews. When the High Priest wants to change the text, however, Pilate maintains his 'scripture' with authority: 'What I have written I have written' (19: 22). His authority on Jesus Christ he holds on high as Jesus declares it to him: 'You would have no authority over me had it not been given to you from above . . .' (19: 11). Pilate therefore appears as an instrument of God to lead the Messiah to the fulfilment of His redemptive work by saying and writing the Word of God: Jesus is Man and He is King. Hence, the first of the five episodes of the Crucifixion have a revelatory function concerning the person of Jesus; the Nazarene is the King of the Jews; what is written has been indeed well written (19: 16–22).

2. The second episode, the parting of His clothes, stands in con-

trast with the third. On the one hand the soldiers divide amongst themselves the robes of Christ, they draw lots for the robe without seam. On the other hand, the women, Mary and John gather in a little group of piety and unity at the foot of the Cross of Jesus. On the one hand the gesture of stripping and dividing; and on the other an attitude of piety uniting men. In addition to this the allusion to the seamless robe of Christ clearly reminds us of the robe of the High Priest which had to be seamless. The Gospel writer's care in describing clothes thus tends to show Christ as the true and final 'High Priest' of the people of God. This third episode makes allusion to the supreme priesthood of the Messiah on the Cross, who offers the perfect sacrifice of which He is Himself the Victim and who taketh away the sin of the world (19: 23–4).

These three themes of the Lamb, of the King and of the High Priest provide the evidence for the passing from the Old to the New Testament which takes place on the Cross and in the Messiah. Christ takes His place in the new people of God as their final sacrifice, their true King and the perfect High Priest. In Him, Israel fulfils her journey and her renewal in the Church.

3. We shall return later to the third episode, that of Mary and John, in order to interpret it in the light of its context. Let us here only note that it is completed by the theme of 'fulfilment' of the redemptive act and of scripture: 'After that, knowing that from this moment all was accomplished, in order that the scripture might be fulfilled, Jesus said: I thirst' (19: 28). This episode marks a decisive moment in the Crucifixion. From this moment 'all' has been accomplished. Jesus has reached the height of His messianic mission, He has just accomplished the decisive act which will be followed by His death.

4. The fourth episode, that of the death of Jesus, underlines the final fulfilment of His messianic work and of scripture. The text of the Gospel still indicates a fulfilment of scripture in the thirst of the Crucified which is quenched by the sponge filled with vinegar (cf. Ps. 69: 22), and then the Christ Himself announces completion of His redemptive work, 'It is finished.' Then He bows His head, and, according to the Evangelist, 'he gives up the ghost' (19: 30). The other Evangelists record the death of Jesus in rather more dramatic terms ('He gave a great cry,' Matt. 27: 50; Mark 15: 37; Luke 23: 46), or in terms more customary for describing death

(Matt. 27: 50, 'He gave up the spirit'; Mark 15: 37, 39; Luke 23: 46, 'He died'). John alone mentions the bowing of the head of Jesus, and the term which He uses for expressing the death is expressively intentional: 'Gave up the spirit, parēdōken to pneuma.'

The Gospel writer certainly plays upon the repeated expression 'to give up the spirit' to indicate that at the death of Jesus a 'transmission' of the spirit took place; the Crucified bowed His head towards the nucleus of the Church which Mary and John represent at the foot of the Cross, and He transmits to them His Spirit, the Holy Spirit. The verb 'to transmit,' 'paradidonai,' often indicates, in the New Testament, an act of handing over or transmission of wisdom or of divine truths (Matt. 11: 27; 25: 14; Luke 1: 2; 10: 22; Acts 6: 14; 16: 4; 1 Cor. 11: 2, 23; 15: 3; 2 Peter 2: 21; Jude 3). It is in this sense that we have to interpret the 'transmission of the spirit' by Jesus at His death. This wisdom that was called forth by the wine at Cana, at the start of His ministry, is transmitted by the Crucified to His own as He dies. It is all that there is in Himself that He transmits to them. The Spirit of truth, the other Comforter promised in His final discourse, Jesus now begins to transmit to His Church. We have here the first act of the Johannine Pentecost; the Pentecost of the Crucified who bows His head to transmit the Spirit to His Church, represented by Mary and the disciple. Later we have the account of the second act of the Johannine Pentecost; the Pentecost of the Risen Lord who breathes upon His disciples, sending them out and saying to them: 'Receive the Holy Spirit; those whose sins you remit the same will be remitted to them; and those whose sins you retain, the same will be retained' (20: 22–3). On the one hand the Spirit is transmitted to the Church symbolized in her motherliness and her unity by Mary and the beloved disciple. On the other hand it is transmitted to the Church by reason of her apostolic mission; the remission of sins by the disciples sent into the world.

We understand in what sense all is fulfilled of the work of God when Jesus entrusts the disciple to His mother, and her to the disciple, and when He bows towards them His head in order to transmit the Spirit. It is the work of creation and redemption which is fulfilled and accomplished by the new creation of the Church according to the Spirit, symbolized in her motherliness by Mary and in her unity by the spiritual and material solidarity of the beloved disciple with Mary. We see here the bond between the different episodes of the Crucifixion: the Messiah, Lamb, King and Priest, establishes in His death and in the Holy Spirit the Church, a new creation, symbolized by Mary and the beloved disciple.

5. The fifth episode, that of the piercing with the spear, is going to complete the ecclesiastical symbolism of the events of the Crucifixion. The Gospel writer attaches great importance to it. 'He who has seen these things bears witness, and his witness is true, and he knows that he speaks the truth . . . ' There follow two references to scripture which this event fulfils and which in turn throw light on the meaning of the event. The soldiers had broken the legs of the two thieves who were crucified with Jesus in order to hasten their death. 'But when they came to Jesus and found him already dead, they did not break his limbs, but one of the soldiers, with his spear, pierced his side and immediately there flowed out blood and water' (19: 33-4). The immediate and literal sense of this event is the reality of the death of Christ. There has been no mere *appearance* of death, but veritable death. The first text of scripture which is referred to, 'They shall not break a bone of his body,' gives to the event a primarily spiritual sense: Christ is indeed the Paschal Lamb of which no bone must be broken according to Jewish ritual (Exod. 12: 46). Jesus has been indeed sacrificed as the Lamb which taketh away the sin of the world. The blood which emerges from His side attests the reality of this true and final Paschal Lamb. The second text of scripture which is quoted, 'They shall look upon him whom they have pierced,' gives the event a second spiritual sense. This is a little verse from Zachariah which it is essential to replace in its context. It concerns an eschatological prophecy: that the time of salvation will depend upon suffering which recalls that of the Suffering Servant (Isa. 53): 'And I will pour out on the house of David and the inhabitants of Jerusalem a spirit of compassion and supplication, so that when they look on him whom they have pierced they shall mourn for him as one mourns for an only child . . . on that day there shall be a fountain opened for the house of David and the inhabitants of Jerusalem to cleanse them from sin and uncleanness' (Zech. 12: 10; 13: 1). The themes of the fountain and the living water which flow from it characterize, in the Old Testament, the time of the Messiah; this symbol of living water coming from a fountain or spring is linked with the gift of the Spirit (breath) of the Lord which must regenerate the people of God. We must quote Ezekiel here: 'I will sprinkle clean water on you, and

you shall be clean from all your uncleannesses, and from all your idols I will cleanse you. A new heart I will give you and a new spirit I will put within you; and I will take out of your flesh the heart of stone and give you a heart of flesh, and I will put my spirit (ruach, pneuma) within you . . . ' (Ezek. 36: 25-7), and 'then he brought me back to the door of the Temple, and behold water was issuing from below the threshold of the Temple from the east (for the Temple faced east); and the water was flowing down from below the south end of the threshold of the Temple, south of the altar . . . this water flows towards the eastern region . . . and wherever the river goes every living creature which swarms will live . . . for this water goes there, that the waters of the sea may become fresh; so everything will live where the river goes . . . and on the banks, on both sides of the river, there will grow all kinds of trees. Their leaves will not wither nor their fruits fail, but they will bear fresh fruit every month because the water for them flows from the sanctuary. Their fruit will be for food and their leaves for healing' (Ezek. 36: 25-7; 47: 1-12). Zechariah is also aware of this theme of living water of the messianic salvation: 'On that day living water shall flow out from Jerusalem . . . ' (Zech. 14: 8). The book of Revelation takes up this theme: 'Then the angel showed me the river of the water of life, bright as a crystal flowing from the throne of God and of the Lamb' (Rev. 22: 1).

The Gospel of John, recounting this episode of the thrusting-in of the spear, alludes to this prophetic vision of the Messiah who is pierced, the only Son, the first-born, as connected with the vision of the open spring, a sign of the spirit of grace and of prayer which is poured out over the house of David and the dwellers in Jerusalem in order to purify them from sin and impurity (Zech. 12: 10; 13: 1). The pierced side of the Crucified is the open spring of Zechariah's vision, from which the life-giving water of His redemptive death springs, a symbol of the Spirit which He has handed on as He dies; it is the sign of the temple, the vision of Ezekiel, from which the water springs which cleanses and develops life wherever it flows.

After the Feast of Tabernacles, Christ spoke of the river of living water as the sign of the Spirit spread abroad. In the liturgical setting of the Feast of Tabernacles there was prayer for rain (showing the agrarian origin of the feast) in which was recalled the miracle of the water that poured forth from the rock in the wilderness (Exod. 17: 1–7; the historic sense of the feast, which was grafted on to the earlier and agrarian one), and prophecies about the regenerative spring were read (Zech. 14: 8; Ezek. 47: 1ff.). It is in this setting that 'on the last day of the feast, the great day, Jesus stood up and proclaimed, "If anyone thirst let him come to me and drink. He who believes in me, as the scripture has said, out of his heart shall flow rivers of living waters." He spoke about the spirit which those who believed in him were to receive; for as yet the spirit had not been given, for Jesus was not yet glorified' (John 7: 37–9). Here the water symbolizes the gift of the Spirit without any doubt. If one compares 'He who believes in me' with what precedes it, the quotation from scripture can be related to Jesus; it probably has to do with the prophecy of Ezekiel concerning the water which flowed from the heart of the Temple; this text of John can be related to the episode of the thrusting-in of the spear. Jesus on the Cross is lifted up and glorified: from His side flows the living water which symbolizes the Spirit spread abroad.[40] Those who will have to receive the Spirit, flowing from His side like the living waters, are the believers, and in the first place, those who, at the foot of the Cross, symbolize the Church; Mary and the disciple.

In this episode of the thrusting-in of the spear, the blood signifies the true sacrifice of the Lamb which takes away the sin of the world, and the water signifies the spirit of life which He has 'handed on,' to the Church, Mary and the disciple, as He bends His head and dies. Many of the Fathers of the Church saw in the blood and the water an indication of the two sacraments of the Eucharist and Baptism. In the liturgical and sacramental perspective of John's Gospel, that is very likely. Numerous exegetes to-day uphold this sacramental interpretation.[41]

This episode of the thrusting-in of the spear therefore bears, as the Evangelist is insistent on telling us (19: 35), a very important meaning in the plan of the Messiah's redemptive work. Christ, the Paschal Lamb, lifted up, glorified and sacrificed for the salvation of the world (the blood), hands on to the messianic community, the Church, and pours out upon her, His spirit (the water); this Pentecost of the Cross will be completed by a Pentecost of the Resurrection in which Christ will breathe the spirit upon His disciples by giving them the power of the remission of sins (20: 21–3). Thus, at the Cross, the Church receives from the Crucified the Holy Spirit in order to be constituted the mother of the faithful, under the symbol of Mary, the mother of the beloved disciple; and, on the evening of the Resurrection, she receives the Holy Spirit from the Risen Lord in order that she may be constituted a ministry of pardon by means of the Apostles' mission. At the Cross, the water and the blood which flows from the side of Him who is pierced symbolize the two fundamental sacraments of Baptism and the Eucharist, the signs and instruments of motherhood and the ministry of the Church: by Baptism she gives birth to, and by the Eucharist she nourishes, believers in the Holy Spirit.

Mary, the Type of Mother Church

In His last discourses with His disciples, Jesus had compared His death to a grievous birth: 'You will be sorrowful but your sorrow will be turned into joy. When a woman is in travail she has sorrow because her hour has come; but when she is delivered of the child she no longer remembers the anguish for joy that a man is born into the world. So you have sorrow now, but I will see you again and your hearts will rejoice, and no one will take your joy from you' (John 16: 20-2). In this Johannine discourse, one is again faced with the image of the birth of the messianic deliverance by the Daughter of Zion, personifying the people of promise. The textual similarities with Isaiah are too striking not to be intentional. In his apocalyptic poem, the prophet saw Jerusalem giving birth to a new people:

'Chapter 66, v. 7: Before she was in labour she gave birth; before her pain came upon her she was delivered of a son.

v. 8: Who has heard such a thing? Who has seen such a thing? Shall a land be born in one day? Shall a nation be brought forth in one moment? For as soon as Zion was in labour she brought forth a son! . . .

v. 10: Rejoice with Jerusalem, and be glad for her, all you who love her! Rejoice with her in joy, all you mourn over her; . . .

v. 12: For thus says the Lord: behold I will extend peace to her like a river, and the wealth of the nations like an over-flowing stream, and you shall suck, and you shall be carried upon her hip, and dandled upon her knees.

v. 13: As one whom her mother comforts, so will I comfort you. You shall be comforted in Jerusalem.

v. 14: You shall see, and your hearts shall rejoice; your bones shall flourish like the grass . . . '

The promises of the Johannine discourses (chs. 13–16) are very close to those of the Book of Consolation, i.e. Isa. 40–66. Christ promises to His disciples, called 'little children' (John 13: 33), not to leave them orphans (14: 18), to return to them and to see them again (16: 22), and to send them the Spirit, the Comforter.[42] In these farewell discourses Jesus reveals the maternal tenderness of God, of the Holy Spirit and of the Church which will continue His work. The relation of these discourses to the Spirit of the Book of Consolation of Isaiah (40–66) is quite clear. When Christ speaks of His death and its effect on the hearts of the disciples, He quite naturally draws upon the prophetic image of the Woman, the Daughter of Zion, sad and grief-stricken in her child-bearing, but joyous that a man is come into the world. 'Like a son whom his mother consoles, I also will console you; at this sight your hearts will rejoice,' proclaimed the Lord to Isaiah (in 66: 14) and Christ echoes that as He speaks to the disciples, having spoken of the woman in joy: 'I will see you again and your hearts will rejoice' (John 16: 22).

The text of the last discourse by Jesus (John 16: 20–2) alludes to the woman, to motherhood, to the hour ('because her hour is come'), and hence announces the moment of the Crucifixion, 'the coming Hour,' in which Mary is called strangely, 'Woman,' and 'Mother' of the beloved disciple. In the proclamation of the sad child-bearing of the Hour of His death, Jesus has conjured up the prophetic image of the Daughter of Zion, who, when her hour is come, gives birth in grief, and then, like a mother, consoles the sons of Israel. In the Hour of the Cross, a woman, the Mother of Jesus, will be this daughter of Zion in a symbolic way, personifying Mother Church who is the consoler of orphans, which, without the Holy Spirit having come from the Father, the disciples, the brethren of Jesus, gathered in person around the beloved disciple would be. Mary, called 'Woman' by the Crucified, and then given as 'Mother' to the 'disciple,' is, at the foot of the Cross, the figure of the Church, the consoling Mother of the faithful. The Holy Spirit, the Comforter, is transmitted to her, as to the disciples, in order that the joy of the Church might be realized, which, having given birth, forgets the pains of her child-bearing by reason of the new people of God at the foot of the Cross and in the power of the Spirit.

The sorrows of the woman who gives birth (16: 20–1) announce the suffering of the disciples at the death of Christ: 'Truly, truly, I say to you, you will weep and lament but the world will rejoice; you will be sorrowful but your sorrow will turn into joy. When a woman is in travail she has sorrow because her hour is come; . . .' The disciples will know a suffering comparable to that of child-bearing; the messianic community at the death of its Saviour, will be like a woman who gives birth, in sadness and grief, but this sadness and grief will be turned into joy on the day of Christ's resurrection. There is a sharing of the messianic community in the suffering of Christ, which is comparable to the giving birth of the new people by the Daughter of Zion (Isa. 66: 7–9). At the death of Christ, the community of the apostles is going to know the griefs of the childbearing of the Church, in faith against all evidence, in hope against all hope. And, at the foot of the Cross, the messianic community is represented by no more than a small group of women from which the Mother of Jesus is detached, and by the beloved disciple who symbolizes faithfulness even unto death.

It is this little remnant of the apostolic community which is going to learn at the foot of the Cross the sorrows of the Daughter of Zion, in communion with the Suffering Servant. Mary, particularly, as the one who gave birth to the Son of God, suffers in soul and body, together with her Saviour, who is also her beloved Son. She knows the human sorrow of a woman who sees her only Son die; she knows also the spiritual grief of a believer who sees hope die, and she gives birth to faith in the resurrection, in the sadness of seeing what seems altogether apparently lost. It is here in her extremity that the prophecy of Simeon is fulfilled: 'A sword shall pierce thy soul.'

As a type of the Church, Mary intimately shares in the suffering of the Crucified; and this suffering of the Daughter of Zion, who gives birth to her hope in the resurrection, and in the birth of the new people, the Church, is also experienced by her in her human and motherly flesh. The Church can only be given birth at the foot of the Cross, by the power of the spirit transmitted by the Crucified, if the faithful remnant of the messianic community believe in the face of all the evidence, and hope against all hope: 'From his side there will flow rivers of living water. He spoke of the spirit which they must receive who believe in him' (John 7: 38–9).

161

Mary is there, at the foot of the Cross, giving birth in her grief to faith in the promises of Christ: 'The Son of man must be delivered into the hands of men, and they will kill him, and on the third day he will rise again' (Matt. 17: 22–3). By faith she is completely the Daughter of Zion who gives birth to hope even in grief, the Church believing and faithful even to the end. By faith in the Crucified who will rise again, in her grief as a mother and as a believer, she is truly the type of the Mother Church of the faithful. It is as such that Jesus regards her and speaks to her: 'Woman, behold thy son.' The beloved and faithful disciple is the true son of the Church of which Mary is the type in the sharing of the suffering of the Crucified, in her faith and in her hope in the Resurrection.

The text of this episode, in its literal translation, lays this symbolic interpretation on the persons of Mary and of the beloved disciple:

'Jesus therefore, seeing his mother and the disciple whom he loved close to her, said to his mother: Woman, behold thy son; then he said to the disciple: behold thy mother; and from that hour, the disciple took her to his own home' (John 19: 26–7).

As at Cana, Mary is not called by her name, but presented as 'the mother of Jesus' (19: 25). It is the title of her vocation which matters to the Gospel writer. Then, the Gospel text finishes by no longer describing her except by the single title of 'the mother' (19: 26, twice), in the same way that he who is first described as 'the disciple whom Jesus loved,' is not called except by the single title of 'the disciple' (19: 27, twice). It seems that the Gospel writer wishes to emphasize thus the symbolic character of Mary, mother of Jesus, who is finally called 'the mother,' as if this title was her own new name.[43] It is just the same for 'the disciple.' At the foot of the Cross, when the Hour has come, to which Jesus had directed His mother's attention after the marriage at Cana, 'the mother of Jesus' becomes 'the Mother,' the type of Mother Church, and 'the disciple whom Jesus loved' becomes 'the disciple,' the type of the faithful in the Church. In the Gospel of St. John, neither 'the mother' nor 'the disciple' bear their proper names of Mary and John; they are described by their vocations, they are persons who have been set by their calling in the history of salvation on a symbolic and mystical level: they are 'types,' 'icons' of Mother Church and of the faithful brethren of Jesus. The Gospel writer is not interested in their individual history, but in their personal calling, and their theological setting in the Gospel, or in their symbolic function *vis-à-vis* the Church and their mystical relationship with Christ and His messianic work.

When He speaks to His mother: 'Woman, behold thy son,' He is speaking to Mother Church, symbolized by Mary, who shares in His suffering, who believes, hopes, loves and who is entrusted by Jesus with the beloved and faithful disciple, who symbolizes all the faithful, the beloved brethren of Christ, indeed all His brethren.[44]

The context of all the words of the Crucified to His mother and to the beloved disciple make clear to us that the symbolic sense which they bear is much more than their literal sense: it is not simply a matter of a simple act of filial piety but much rather an act which has an important significance in the plan of the work of redemption.

The disciple spoken of as 'him who Jesus loved' is without question the personification of the perfect disciple, the true and faithful Christian and the believer who has received the Spirit. It is not simply a question here of a special affection shown by Jesus to one of His apostles, but the symbolic personification of all faithfulness to the Lord. Christ wished that one of His disciples should represent all faithfulness even unto the end, even when the others have abandoned Him at the decisive moment. The beloved disciple therefore embodies the faithfulness of all believers, the brethren of Jesus, even unto death. If there can be no doubt that the disciple at the foot of the Cross stands for more than his own individuality, the same is certainly true for Mary. The title of 'Woman' which her crucified son gives her, as at Cana, contrary to all the customs of Jewish family life, reveals that He sets His mother on another level than that simply of a relationship between a son and his mother. He sees in her the 'Woman' who symbolizes the people of God in her maternal rôle, the Daughter of Zion representing the childbearing of the new Israel, the messianic deliverance in sorrow followed finally by eschatological joy, the Church which will be the consoling Mother of those who have received the Holy Spirit the Comforter, which will give birth to the children of the Father and the brethren of Christ until the end of time, by the Word and Baptism, and which will nourish them with that same Word and the Eucharist.

163

It is because Mary is the type of the Church that Jesus commits her to the beloved disciple and him to her. The period of Mary's human motherhood in regard to the Son of God incarnate, the fulfilment of which Christ had already declared at Cana, here finds its completion: she, the Mother of God, becomes the type of Mother Church. Henceforth it will not be possible to speak of the Church, of her humility, motherliness, her faith or her joy . . . without conceiving of Mary, the Mother of the Lord, as her pure expression, her archetype, and as her first realization. 'Maria-Ecclesia: Ecclesia-Maria.' These two names will be interchanged constantly in the writings and thought of the Fathers of the Church.[45]

On Calvary, as we have seen, scripture is fulfilled and all the types of the Old Testament: the Paschal Lamb, the King, the High Priest, all have Christ as their fulfilment. In Mary is fulfilled the transition from the old to the new Israel, since Jesus as He dies 'gives up the Ghost' to her and to him who represent the Church, in both her motherhood and her faithfulness. St. Ambrose noted this transition from the Daughter of Zion to the new Israel when he wrote, 'We deal here with the mystery of the Church: already (Mary), linked not very effectively with her ancient people, as a type, after having given birth to the Word and having sown him in the bodies and souls of men, by faith in the Cross and the burial of the body of the Lord, has, at God's command, chosen the society of the youngest people (John).' [46]

The double phrase used by the Crucified: 'Woman, behold thy son; behold thy mother' recalls the covenant formulæ of the Old Testament: 'I will be to him a Father and he will be to me a son' (2 Sam. 7: 14); 'I thought how I would set you among my sons, and give you a pleasant land, a heritage most beauteous of all nations! and I thought you would call me, my Father, and would not turn from following me . . . ' (Jer. 3: 19). ' . . . and I will sow him for myself in the land. And I will have pity on Not-Loved, and I will say to Not-my-people, "You are my people," and he shall say, "Thou art my God" ' (Hosea 2: 23; see also Jer. 24: 7; 31: 33; Ezek. 36: 28). In the book of Revelation this double formula of the covenant will reappear in the vision of the New Jerusalem, the young bride adorned for her husband: 'Behold, the dwelling of God is with men. He will dwell with them, and they shall be his people, and God himself will be with them and be their God' (Rev. 21: 3).

The New Covenant was established between the Father and the beloved disciples, Christ's brethren, by the motherhood of the Church, the 'Jerusalem from on high which is free, our mother' (Gal. 4: 26). The Church, symbolized by Mary, receives at the foot of the Cross this maternal mission in the presence of Christ's brethren, the children of the Father; thus the New Covenant is expressed in family terms: the people of God becomes the family of the Father, with the Church in the Holy Spirit as mother and the Son as the first-born brother of the beloved and faithful disciples. It is striking to note in the Gospel of John that it is after the Resurrection that Jesus for the first time gives His disciples the title of 'brethren'; the Risen Lord says to Mary Magdalene: 'Go to my brethren and tell them: I ascend to my Father and your Father, to my God and your God' (John 20: 17).

By the death of Christ and in the sorrows of this childbearing of the Daughter of Zion, in which the messianic community, represented at the foot of the Cross by Jesus' mother and His beloved disciple, has shared, the people of the New Covenant is born; the Crucified has transmitted to them the Spirit and, from the side of the Pierced One, there have appeared the sacramental signs of water and blood, of Baptism and Eucharist; this new people is consecrated as the family of the Father; the Church in the Spirit is from then onwards the Mother of the faithful, and the disciples are the brethren of Jesus. The Risen Lord will explain this fact by calling the disciples 'His brethren' and God 'His Father and their Father.' This fact of the family of God, Mother Church and the Church of the brethren, appeared in a type at the foot of the Cross in Mary, the mother of the beloved disciple, her son.

This motherhood of the Church, under the type of Mary, the mother of the disciple, is the fount of unity amongst the disciples, brethren and faithful of Christ. Jesus, in His high-priestly prayer (John 17), had prayed for their unity: 'The glory which thou hast given me I have given to them, that they may be one even as we are one, I in them and thou in me, that they may become perfectly one, so that the world may know that thou hast sent me and hast loved them even as thou hast loved me' (John 17: 22–3). The unity of Father and Son is the ground and example of unity among the brethren; it is possible thanks to the dwelling of Christ in His Body, the Church, by means of the Holy Spirit. The Church, as the Mother of the faithful, awakens and promotes the unity of the brethren of Christ. Like a mother, the Church has a constant concern for the unity of her children, the children of the Father and the brethren of Christ.

Mary, the type of Mother Church, receives the faithful disciple as her son, and he receives her into his home; together they symbolize the unity of the Church. This scene at the foot of the Cross contrasts with that which immediately precedes it. The soldiers part the robes of the Crucified, they draw lots for His seamless robe. For them, who have no faith, Christ is the object of division and separation; they fulfil the prophecy of men's division: 'They divided my clothes amongst them, and for my vesture they drew lots' (Ps. 22: 18). Over against this, the group of faithful women at the foot of the Cross, and above all the words of the Crucified to His mother and disciple, indicate the unity of the believers in the one Church. Alas! Christians to-day too much resemble the soldiers who parted the garments stripped from Christ, rather than Mary and the disciple who were united by the Crucified in one and the same physical and spiritual community!

United with Mother Church, we are true, beloved and faithful disciples and true brethren of Jesus, like the beloved disciple who became the son of Mary. Like him who received Mary his mother into his own home we have to receive the Church our mother into our lives, like true sons of the Father and true brethren of Jesus.

The Hour announced by Christ to Mary, at the marriage at Cana, has now arrived. If Jesus, at Cana, pointed Mary to the Hour of the Cross, it was in order that at this decisive moment she might understand His new vocation, matured in the course of the life of her son on earth: after the title and rôle of 'Mother of God,' she now receives the title and rôle of 'the type of Mother Church.' We understand the motherhood of the Church as we meditate on the motherhood of Mary, the mother of the Lord and the mother of the blessed disciple.

Mary, Mother in the Church

Jesus had made this solemn promise to His disciples 'Truly, I say to you, there is no one who has left house, or brothers, or sisters, or mother, or father, or children, or lands, for my sake and the gospel's, who will not receive a hundredfold, now in this time, houses, and brothers, and sisters, and mothers, and children, and lands, with persecutions, and in the age to come eternal life' (Mark 10: 29–30; Matt. 19: 29; Luke 18: 29–30). He who, because of Christ and the Good News of the Kingdom, has renounced the good things of this world, in order to consecrate himself to the love and service of Christ, receives the promise of a hundredfold hereafter. If he has left home and family, he is going to discover in the present time homes, brethren, sisters and mothers. . . . Such is the domestic picture of the Church which is here laid out before us.

For the disciple who has left everything the Church is a home with innumerable dwelling-places in which he is called to serve. In this house of the Church he will find the great community of Christ's brethren and sisters; all the faithful Christians with whom he can share the fraternal life, the work of the ministry, the joy of worship and the eucharistic feast. Whereas the phrase about sacrifice spoke of the 'father' whom one leaves behind (Mark 10: 29), that which speaks of our reward omits all mention of 'fathers' whom one would discover. Do we not see in this a concern to underline the fact that for the Christian there is only one Father, God Himself? It is certainly possible; for that would agree with other statements by Christ: 'But you are not to be called Rabbi; for you have one teacher, and you are all brethren. And call no man your father on earth, for you have one Father, who is in heaven' (Matt. 23: 8–9).

This text mentions the reward of the disciple who, having left his mother, receives other mothers a hundredfold. The image of the Church as a spiritual family is here made more precise. The Church is the new home of the sons of the Father and brethren of Jesus; they there re-discover fraternal dwellings to receive them and innumerable brothers and sisters and mothers too.[47] The greetings at the close of the Epistles of St. Paul bear witness to this Church life thought of as a supernatural family life. Those who had been called to poverty for Christ's sake, to a life of renunciation and detachment, had all things in common (Acts 2: 44) and their Church life was that of one great family in which they again discover houses, brethren, sisters, mothers, children and possessions in a perfect common life. St. Paul underlines, at the end of his letters, this supernatural family sense of the Church; he speaks constantly of it as being that of 'brethren' and of 'sisters': 'I commend to you Phoebe, our sister. . . . As for our brother Apollos I strongly urged him to visit you with the other brethren . . . ' (Rom.

167

16: 1; 1 Cor. 16: 12 . . .). He alludes to 'houses' where the Church meets, those of Priscilla and Aquila, Aristobulus and Narcissus . . . (Rom. 16: 3, 10, 11 . . .). He also speaks of his spiritual children: Timothy is 'as a son with his father,' he is the 'true son' of Paul in the faith; Onesimus is his 'child whom he has borne in chains' (Phil. 2: 22; 1 Tim. 1: 2; 2 Tim. 2: 1; Philemon 10). Mark is the 'son' of Peter (1 Peter 5: 13). The 'fields,' the possessions, are held in common, as if by one and the same family: 'And they sold their possessions and goods and distributed them to all as any had need . . .' (Acts 2: 44–5; 4: 32, 34–5). Truly, the multitude of the believers were of one heart and of one mind, like one great supernatural family.

The second Epistle of John completes this image of the Christian family community, which finds its principle of unity in the fraternal love and maternal care of the Church. 'The Elder (the head of the Church), to the elect lady (the Church) and her children, whom I love in the truth. . . . I rejoice greatly to find some of your children following the truth, just as we have been commanded by the Father. And now, lady, . . . I beg of you that we love one another . . . the children of your elect Sister greet you' (2 John: 1, 4–5, 13). A head of a church writes to another church. He calls this church 'the elect lady' and he thinks of her as the mother of her faithful ones some of whom he actually knows. He invites her to share in mutual charity between their neighbouring churches, charity which flows from truth, the possession of the Father and of the Son. Finally he sends her the greeting of the Church over which he is head and in which he dwells; he speaks of this church as 'the elect sister' of which the faithful are his children. Here, the personification of the local church, by the title of 'elect lady' (Eklektē Kyria) derived from the title of Christ, 'elect, Lord' (Eklektos, Kyrios), and her motherhood, emphasized by the title of 'children' (Tekna) given to her faithful ones, are clearly indicated. God is the Father of the believers who confess 'Jesus Christ come in the flesh,' his Son, the Elect, the Lord; the local churches, the Elect Ladies, are sisters one with another and each are mothers of their faithful members.

But, to return to St. Mark's text, who are these 'mothers' discovered in the Church, with the houses of the brotherly community, the brethren and the sisters and these fields which are shared? Here again St. Paul is able to throw light upon the matter. 'Salute

168

Rufus,' he writes to the Romans (16: 13), 'the elect in the Lord, also his mother and mine.' And in his pastoral injunctions to Timothy, he writes: 'Do not rebuke an older man but exhort him as you would a father; treat younger men like brothers, older women like mothers and younger women like sisters in all purity' (1 Tim. 5: 1–2). Then there follow the recommendations with regard to widows and in particular those who are 'left all alone, having set their hope on God and continuing in supplication and prayers night and day' (1 Tim. 5: 5).

The various ages of life preserve a significance in the Church and those whom one regards as 'brothers,' when they are young, must be considered as 'fathers' when they attain riper years. It is the same with Christian women, who, though thought of at some time as 'sisters' become 'mothers' according to the Spirit. St. Paul would regard the mother of Rufus as his own mother. In the ordering of faith and piety older women, on account of their experience in the Christian life, can play this rôle of spiritual maternity which is an essential function of the Church. The 'order' of widows in the primitive Church (1 Tim. 5: 3–16) was probably born out of this conviction that a Christian woman, freed from family cares and rich in spiritual experience, can play an important rôle in the service of the Church community. St. Paul sees these widows as principally dedicated to prayer and supplication. But they are not only women wholly dedicated to Christ's service but also Christian mothers who can assume this rôle of spiritual maternity in the Church, thus revealing one aspect of the Church's own motherhood. Hence, in the Church, the whole natural family life finds itself transformed; and those who have left all to follow Christ discover a hundred-fold, in the present time, in the heart of the Church, the family of the Father, dwellings, brethren, sisters, children and mothers, in a fullness of family community spiritualized in Christ.

St. Paul would consider the mother of Rufus, his brother in Christ, as his own spiritual mother. The disciple whom Jesus loved at the Cross received Mary as his mother and he took her to his own home. Of course, as we have seen, the event has a mystical sense concerning the motherhood of the Church; however, the words of the Crucified had also this consequence that the disciple received the mother of Jesus into his house. Thereafter, by Christ's command, he will live with Mary, the type of Mother Church, regarding her as his own mother according to the Spirit. We can

169

guess, from all the evidence, that Mary will teach him a great deal about the person and the life of her son, and that she will be for him, and for all the other disciples, a source of gospel knowledge. Mary is going to play, in the life of the beloved disciple as of all the disciples, a pre-eminent part in the tradition of the truths of the faith; she will have a real task as the spiritual mother in the primitive Church. Since Jesus Himself has described her as 'the mother' symbolizing Mother Church, how could she not be pre-eminently of the number of those mothers whom the disciples will discover a hundredfold, in the present time, in the heart of the family community of the Church? Indeed, according to the words of the Crucified, she will be, even for the disciple, and all the disciples whom He represents, the first of those mothers rediscovered in the Church. In her love for the risen and glorified Lord, her own son, in her faith, hope and piety, she will be an example to them, a spiritual mother who watches, prays and serves. She will be like those widows of the primitive Church 'who set their hopes on God and continued in supplication and prayer night and day' (1 Tim. 5: 5).

The disciple whom Jesus loved can say of Mary that she is the Mother of Jesus and also his own mother; he realizes then the intimacy which unites him with Christ, his Lord and his brother. Mary, the Mother of Jesus and his mother, is the person who is able to draw him closer to Christ, his Lord and his God. With him, she has been a witness of the last moments of the Crucifixion, she has heard the last words of Jesus, and has received the Spirit which He has transmitted to the Church. Mary is therefore for him, and, through him, for all the disciples, and for the Church which gathers about them, a very close sign of the presence of the Lord, a spiritual mother in the Christian community, the most venerated of all spiritual mothers found in the Church, the spiritual mother *par excellence* of the beloved and faithful disciple, of the brother of Jesus, which every Christian is called to be.

Immediately after the Ascension, we see, in the Acts of the Apostles (1: 12–14), the group of the Eleven, returning to Jerusalem and going into the Upper Room where they had habitually met with Christ. There they are to await the outpouring of the Spirit at Pentecost. 'All these with one accord devoted themselves to prayer, together with the women, Mary, the mother of Jesus, and with his brothers' (Acts 1: 14). Mary, the Mother of Jesus, is here integrated with the whole group of the disciples: the apostles, the women and the relatives of the Lord. With them, and in the midst of them, being of one heart and mind with them, she is assiduous in prayer, awaiting the great outpouring of the Holy Spirit which will open the missionary era of the Church. A type of Mother Church, she has no place of a ministerial or hierarchical kind, as have Peter, John, James and the other Apostles who are first named. She is mentioned among the women and relatives of Jesus. She is in the midst of the primitive Church, as a humble and praying example, as a handmaid of the Lord and of the Church. It is thus that she will receive the Spirit at Pentecost, in order that she may be fulfilled with the fullness of her vocation, in the very heart of the Church.

She appears indeed as the widow of the ancient Church 'who sets her hope on God and continues in supplication and prayer night and day' (1 Tim. 5: 5). However, she is not alone; she has a son in the disciple whom Jesus loved; she is the spiritual mother *par excellence* in the midst of the faithful women who have followed Christ and who are always there. She is for the disciple, and for all the disciples, the type of Mother Church and the spiritual mother rediscovered in the Church. In the power of the Spirit, she will be able to transmit to the disciples and to the primitive Church all that she knew of Jesus, her beloved Son, and what she has so preciously guarded and pondered in her heart (Luke 2: 19, 51). She will be a humble bearer of the Gospel of her Son, not in the same fashion as the missionary apostles, but in the manner of a discreet and loving mother, a human mother, the mother of the Son of God whom she has known better than any one in the intimacy of His company, a spiritual mother of the disciples, to recall all that Christ said and did, and of whom she has been able to be a faithful and attentive hearer. By her faith, her hope, her charity, and her prayers she will be a spiritual mother of Mother Church, of whom she is the living and humble representative.

Luther made very clear the rôle of Mary as the type of Mother Church, and her rôle also as spiritual mother in the Church. In regard to the prophecy of the sword which would pierce her, made by Simeon, Luther freely comments:

'What does the fact that Simeon only and personally addresses his remarks to Mary, his mother, and not to Joseph signify? Surely

171

it signifies that the Christian Church on earth remains the spiritual Virgin Mary, and that it will not be destroyed, however much her preachers, her faith and her gospel, which is the spiritual Christ, may be persecuted. Although Joseph will die first and Christ will be martyred, although Mary will be made a widow and will be parted from her Son, yet she will remain and all this great sorrow will pierce her heart. Hence, the Christian Church will always remain as it were a widow, and her heart is pierced though Joseph and the Holy Fathers die and though the Gospel is persecuted; she must bear the sword and yet remain always even unto the end.' [48]

Luther applies an ecclesiological typology to the persons of Mary, Elizabeth and Anna under the title of a spiritual meditation:

'Now any one who wishes can meditate even further on the spiritual significance of all this. Mary represents Christianity after the synagogue, Elizabeth represents the people under the synagogue; although it may be a pious people it is wrapped up much more in external precepts. But Mary, who transcends the mountains and yet does so with modesty, represents the Christian people who walk here free below under heaven . . . and who, however, in her freedom, is full of humility, not like a flapping flag of propaganda such as some false Christians are.' [49] In another version of the same sermon he says more precisely: 'Mary signifies the Church after the synagogue, Elizabeth the synagogue. Elizabeth is in her house, Mary is free. That symbolizes the people who are under the law, locked up under the law. When Christ comes in the flesh, Mary was made free, that is to say that the Church is made free and raised above the mountains. Elizabeth and Mary are at one accord amongst themselves which means that the Old and the New Testaments are above all in harmony on the matter of the Only Christ.' [50]

In his 'Table Talk,' Luther calls Mary 'the new Church'; the old woman Anna represents the synagogue which perceives the prophetic sign; she is old at the time of the birth of Christ, whereas Mary is young; here, in very truth, a 'new Church' has begun. [51]

Mary is the type of the young, free and suffering Church; she is also the type of Mother Church:

'According to physical birth we are all different, but in Baptism we are all the first-born of the Virgin, that is to say, of the Church, which is the pure Virgin in the Spirit. She possesses the pure Word of God, she is pregnant with it [52]; hence we are truly the first fruits, in order to belong to our Lord God . . .'[53]

But, for Luther, Mary, the type of Mother Church, young, free and suffering, is also a mother in the Church: 'Oh, it is a great joy of which the angel speaks! It is God's consolation and overflowing goodness that man should be honoured with such treasure: Mary as his very mother, Christ as his brother and God as his father.'[54]

At Christmas 1523, Luther said: 'I believe that there is no one amongst us who would not leave his own mother to become a son of Mary. And that you can do; all the more because that has been offered as a choice to you and it is an even greater joy than if you embraced your mother with real embraces.'[55] And the next day but one he said again: 'Thus this child was given to us as a gift, and we are the children of Mary; we are able to hear the song of the Angels.'[56]

Five years later, in 1528, he still holds the same view: 'In very truth Mary is our mother. But if we wanted to erect a structure with her at its heart ("auf sie bauen"), and to take from Christ His honour and His task and give them to His mother, that would mean a denial of Christ's suffering.'[57]

Finally, at Christmas 1529, he declares: 'Thus, Mary is the mother of Jesus, and the mother of us all. If Christ is ours, we must be where he is; and where he is we must be also, and all that he has must be ours, and his mother therefore also is ours.'[58]

Luther thinks of Mary in her function as a representative of the Church, and he considers her also a spiritual mother within the Church, by reason of her intimate communion with Jesus, the Son of Mary. Of course these assertions, often very poetic, must not be detached from the context of the preaching in which they occur. Always the very coherence of Luther's thought on this point shows that he gave a real place to Mary in his faith and piety, and that he had this family conception of the Church which we noted in the New Testament. He discovered in Mary a spiritual mother in the Church: 'Mary is his true mother, Christ is his brother and God is his Father.'[59]

173

Mary therefore appears clearly as the type of the Church, our Mother. She helps us to think of this Motherhood of the Church in her ministry. When we think of the ministry of the Church, we must think of Mary as the type if we would understand her spiritual motherhood. The Church is the Bride of Christ: 'He loved her and gave himself up for her, that he might sanctify her, having cleansed her by the washing of water with the Word, that he might present the Church to himself with splendour, without spot or wrinkle or any such thing, that she might be holy and without blemish . . . ; he nourishes and cherishes her' (Ephes. 5: 25–32). And St. Paul added to this conjugal description of the Church: 'This is a great mystery, and I take it to mean Christ and the Church.' If, for St. Paul, the conjugal union of the Christian and his wife is a symbolic sign, a mystery, which directs our spirit towards the reality of the love of Christ for the Church, his Bride, then, for St. John, the motherhood of Mary in regard to Jesus and to the Beloved Disciple, a brother of Jesus, is a symbolic sign, a mystery, which directs our minds to the reality of the love for us of the Church our mother. The mystery of Mary is also of great import; it is applied to the Church, the mother of the faithful who are the brethren of Christ.

The Church bears, feeds, consoles and takes care of the children of the Father, the brethren of Christ in the power of the Holy Spirit. By the Word of God and Baptism, she brings into the world the new believers by faith, hope and charity; by the Eucharist, she nourishes them with the life-giving Body and Blood of the Lord; by absolution, she consoles them with the mercy of the Father; by unction, with the laying-on of hands, she brings them the healing of body and soul . . . [60] The whole ministry which she exercises is marked by this characteristic of spiritual motherhood. St. Paul wrote, for himself and for all the pastors who are ordained into the ministry of the Church in order to edify the royal priesthood of all the faithful: 'Our mouth is open to you, Corinthians; our heart is wide. You are not restricted by us . . . I speak to you as to my children—widen your hearts also . . . for I said before that you are in our hearts, to die together and to live together. I have great confidence in you; I have great pride in you; I am filled with comfort. With all our afflictions I am overjoyed. . . . And apart from other things, there is the daily pressure upon me of my anxiety for all the Churches. Who is weak and I am not weak? Who is made to fall, and I am not indignant? . . . ' (2 Cor. 6: 11–13; 7: 3–4; 11: 28–9).

Would you not say that this is a letter of a mother to her children? In his Epistles St. Paul sometimes appeared like a father, and sometimes like a mother; he realized in his ministry the motherly function of the Church. St. John also shows this tenderness and motherly concern in his pastoral ministry: 'And now, remain in him, little children. . . . Little children keep yourself from idols' (1 John 2: 1, 12, 28; 3: 7, 18; 4: 4; 5: 21; 'teknia, little children' appears seven times in the Epistle).

The authority of the minister must be united with his gentleness. The necessary authority of the Church must be expressed according to the motherly love of the Church, and Mary, the type of the motherly Church, is able to teach the ministers of the Church, the authority in the Church, and all the faithful, that only he who has a strong motherly concern for spiritual direction, without fancifulness, can truly express the love of the Father which gives rise to faith, nourishes, consoles and heals by His Word and by the signs of His presence.[61]

Chapter 10

A Great Sign in Heaven

1. 'And a great portent appeared in heaven,
   a woman clothed with the sun,
   and the moon under her feet
   And on her head a crown of twelve stars;
2. She was with child
   and she cried out in her pangs of birth, in anguish for delivery;

3. And another portent appeared in heaven;
   behold a great red dragon,
   with seven heads, and ten horns
   and seven diadems.
4. His tail swept down a third of the stars of heaven
   and cast them to the earth,

   And the dragon stood before the woman
   who was about to bear the child
   that he might devour the child
   when she brought it forth;

5. She brought forth a male child,
   one who is going to rule all the nations with a rod of iron,
   and her child was caught up to God
   and to his throne,

6. And the woman fled into the wilderness
   where she has a place prepared by God,
   where she is to be nourished
   for one thousand, two hundred and sixty days.

13. And when the dragon saw that he had been thrown down to
    the earth
    he pursued the woman who had borne the male child.

14. But the woman was given the two wings of the great eagle
that she might fly
from the serpent into the wilderness to the place
where she is to be nourished for a time, and times, and half
a time.

15. The serpent poured forth water like a river out of his mouth,
after the woman, to sweep her away with the flood,
16. But the earth came to the help of the woman, and the earth
opened its mouth.

and swallowed the river which the dragon had poured from
its mouth.

17. Then the dragon was angry with the woman
and went off to make war with the rest of her offspring,
those who keep the commandments
and bear testimony to Jesus.'
(Rev. 12: 1–6, 13–17).

The Victory of the Church

This 'great sign' (sēmeion mega) of John's revelation is in a style
similar to the 'signs' (Sēmeia, John 20: 30–1), recounted in the
Fourth Gospel. It bears, like them, some historical elements, some
theological and mystical meanings and some allusions to scripture
which thus find themselves fulfilled. Before we analyse the historical elements and the ecclesiological and mariological meanings,
we must, of course, first take notice of the definite biblical
allusions.[1]

There can be no doubt that this vision of the Woman in conflict
with the Dragon reminds us of the account at the opening of the
Book of Genesis in which that text is found which one calls the
'Protevangel' (Gen. 3: 15).[2] The common elements in these two
texts are quite clear: viz., the Woman, her offspring, the serpent,
and the struggle in which they engage, the sad victory of the
Woman, her bearing of a child and her mothering of all life.

After the Fall God addresses Himself to the serpent to condemn
him, and then He says to him:
'I will put enmity between you and the woman, and between
her seed and your seed; he shall bruise your head and you
shall bruise his heel.

177

M

'To the woman he said, I will greatly multiply your pain in
child-bearing; in pain you shall bring forth children . . .

'The man called his wife's name, Eve ("Havva" or, in Greek:
Life) because she was the mother of all living ("haya"—to
live) . . .

'Now the man knew Eve, his wife, and she conceived and
bore Cain saying, I have gotten (caniti) a man with the help of
God' (Gen. 3: 15, 16, 20; 4: 1).

The Fall of humanity, rebelling against God, has, as its consequence, the dreadful conflict between the serpent and the woman,
between the seed of the serpent, the powers of evil, and the offspring of the woman, all mankind. The Woman will thus know
pain and suffering. However, there is already hope. The offspring
of the Woman will one day bruise the serpent's head; it will deliver
him a fatal blow, but she will bear a grievous counter-blow and
will be wounded in her heel.

The hope is made even more definite in the name which the
Man gives to Woman: Eve, which means Life, for she is the mother
of the living. Finally, after her first childbearing, Eve considers her
son as a gift of God, a sign of His mercy: 'I have gotten a man by
the help of God.' But, if the mercy occurs but a little after the
punishment of first humanity, man's final deliverance is part of the
messianic expectation: it is the Messiah, the offspring of the
Woman, who will be victorious over Evil, and it is He who will
'bruise the serpent's head.'

The suffering of childbearing will be a sign of punishment and of
the pain which must precede the messianic deliverance; and as we
have already seen, Israel is often represented under the marks
of the Woman who knows the suffering of childbearing, the
Daughter of Zion who is laid low with child. This is a frequent
theme with the Prophets.[3] In the setting of the 'Protevangel' (Gen.
3: 15ff.), the people of God will often be symbolized by the
Woman: 'Being with child she cried out in her pangs of birth in
anguish for delivery' (Rev. 12: 2); and the final deliverance of the
people, their messianic salvation, their redemption to be achieved
by the Messiah of God, will be symbolized by the pain of child-
bearing followed by joy: 'A woman, when she is about to bear a
child, is sad, because her hour is come,' said Christ, announcing
His redemptive passion, 'But when she has given birth she forgets

straightway her sorrow, with joy that a man has come into the world' (John 16: 21). For Jesus also the work of Redemption by His death and resurrection is symbolized by this same prophetic image of the Woman who gives birth, through sorrow, to the joy of deliverance.[4]

This Woman of the Revelation, a great sign in heaven, therefore appears as the realization of the messianic hope already foreseen in Genesis; it is the fulfilment of the promise of Victory made to Eve, Woman, the mother of the living, whose offspring 'will bruise the serpent's head.' This Woman symbolizes Israel, the people of God, from whom the Messiah will be born. She symbolizes also the Church which one day will be totally victorious over the powers of evil and the serpent who has already been mortally wounded by Christ.

The people of God, Israel and the Church, victorious over the satanic powers, appear first of all as the image of the Temple of God in Heaven, and then under this symbol of the Woman clothed with the sun (Rev. 11: 19–12: 1):

'Then God's Temple in heaven was opened, and the Ark of his Covenant was seen within his Temple; and there were flashes of lightning, loud noises, peals of thunder, earthquakes and heavy hail. And a great portent appeared in heaven, a woman clothed with the sun. . . .'

This double symbolism of the Temple and of the Woman remind us of the Daughter of Zion, the personification of the people of God, of Israel, and then of the Church. The Woman-People is with child, like the Daughter of Zion, in order to give birth to the messianic salvation through suffering. It is the image of Israel waiting for the Messiah in the midst of the sad events of her history: the power of Evil is there, often incarnate in the kingdoms which persecute her, which torture the people of God, which sweep away her prophets and consume her hope. And then, all of a sudden, the Woman-Israel takes on a sharper appearance. The Woman bears a son, a man, the Messiah predicted by Psalm 2: He who will break the nations with a rod of iron; and this Son will be elevated to the throne of God.

The Woman-Israel has taken on the appearance of the Virgin Mary, the Daughter of Zion. Israel, symbolized by the Woman, ready to bear a child, becomes Mary, the Mother of the Messiah. It is as if, on to a vast canvas, still somewhat out of focus, there is of a sudden projected a sharp outline: upon the greater image of the Woman-Israel there is suddenly made clear the smaller figure of the Virgin, mother of the Messiah. The vision grows, and after having called forth the history of the Daughter of Zion, and of the history of the People of God who await their deliverance in sorrow, she makes her appearance as the Virgin Mary, 'the incarnation' of Israel, at the moment of the coming of the Messiah and His ascending to the presence of God.

Then the vision evolves still more and is altered. The Woman-Israel, who for a time has become the Virgin Mary, becomes the Woman-Church, who undergoes persecution, but who, protected by the Lord, is already assured of victory.

The same vision of the Woman, sad and yet victorious, therefore describes Mary, Israel and the Church. The Virgin Mary, who is outlined at the moment of the childbearing and rearing of the Messiah, serves, in this vision, as the link between Israel and the Church. In her, the Woman-Israel becomes the Woman-Church. This transition from Israel to Mary and from Mary to the Church, we have already noticed in the Gospels. At the Annunciation, the Daughter of Zion-Israel has become Mary; the Virgin has 'incarnated' all the sad waiting of the people of God with their messianic hope, has received the Saviour as her own son, in the name of all Israel. Then, at the Cross, the Daughter of Zion-Mary has been replaced by Mother Church; the messianic motherhood of Mary becomes the spiritual motherhood of the Church, of which Mary remains the type; the Church continues to bear the members of the *mystical* Body of Christ, of which the Virgin has borne the *physical*.

Mary, Daughter of Zion and Mother of the Messiah, is the sign of the transition of Israel, Daughter of Zion, the People of God, to the Church, Mother of the faithful, the Body of Christ. And it is this same apocalyptic symbol of the Woman which designates Israel, Mary and the Church.

The Woman-Israel is clothed with the sun of the presence and wisdom of God, assured of ruling over Creation by the power of the Lord ('the moon under her feet') crowned by His twelve tribes which shine like the stars; she awaits the Messiah in the sorrows of her past, in the remembrance of her past deliverance and in the hope of her final salvation. She wages war against the power of evil which is used by the nations to destroy her.

One day, a poor Virgin, full of grace, chosen to be the dwelling-place of God, becomes the Daughter of Zion and receives the fruit of the promises to the world. She gives birth to the Messiah, the Saviour and Lord, who is raised to the throne of God. The historic childbearing of the Woman certainly concerns the Incarnation, but influences much more its fulfilment in the Passion of Christ. Indeed, in a surprising manner the vision unites the childbearing and the rearing of the Messiah. On the other hand the allusion to Psalm 2 ('He who shall break all the nations with a rod of iron') calls forth all the more the Resurrection as well as the birth of Christ. The author of the Acts of the Apostles illustrates the Resurrection by one quotation from this psalm: 'God has raised Jesus, as it is written in the Second Psalm: Thou art my Son, this day have I begotten thee' (Acts 13: 33).

According to the fashion of this vision Christ is born for the resurrection life after passing through the Passion, in order then to be raised through the Ascension to the throne of God. The childbearing of the Messiah which is here our concern is the child-bearing of the Cross, which through the sorrows of the Passion leads Christ to the Resurrection and Ascension. The Woman-Church, in Mary, assists and shares in this sad childbearing of the Risen One, at the foot of the Cross; she is like the woman of whom St. John speaks and who calls forth the Daughter of Zion (John 16: 21). Here, the woman of Revelation reminds us of Mary, the type of the Church, suffering at the foot of the Cross, in her compassion for the Crucified One who is going to be born in the Resurrection through much suffering, in order that He might pass from this world to the Father, so as to be raised even to the Throne of God.[5]

Then there appears the Woman-Church of which the marks are like those of Mary who had in the vision risen to the occasion of the historic childbearing of the Messiah, crucified, risen and ascended.

The Woman-Church is going to undergo persecution like the Woman-Israel, but whilst the latter only had the hope of a future deliverance, the Church is assured of a salvation already won: the powers of Evil are still able to be unleashed against her but they will not have the victory. A symbolic period of three years and a half is indicated: it signifies a persecution which will not last for ever, and which will have at its close the victory of God, fully revealed. During this period the Church can find a retreat in the wilderness, in solitude with God, in contemplation of His love: there she will escape the torments of the world, like Israel, liberated from Egypt; there she is nourished by new manna, the Eucharist, which gives her the power to resist the persecution and run the gauntlet of her victorious entry into the Kingdom of God.

Indeed the Woman who has given birth to salvation is pursued by the conquered Dragon, thrown down upon the earth; but the all-powerful Lord gives her wings to fly to the place of His protection, the life in God by prayer, the Word and the Sacraments, with the fraternal communion of the Saints.

At the outset of her existence the Church is seen as menaced by the power of the Roman Empire: the Serpent has launched against the Woman the Roman flood in order to wash her away; but the earth, whose history is under the Lordship of God, comes also to the aid of the Church and by the play of the raising and abasing of the powers of this world the Church escapes from time to time the danger of annihilation. 'The earth came to the help of the woman and the earth opened its mouth and swallowed the river which the dragon had poured forth from his mouth.'

Because of the indefectibility of the Church, assisted in her victory by the history of the world itself, the powers of evil then attack individual Christians and it is the test of faith, the temptation to compromise and martyrdom which have to be faced: the dragon, in rage against the Woman, makes war on her offspring the faithful witnesses of Jesus. But there still martyrdom raises a bulwark against Satan and, by their union with the Body of Christ, the members of the Church, in their persecution, their suffering or their death, become a seed in the field which God cultivates in order to raise His final harvest; the blood of the martyrs is the seed of the Church.

At the Cross, Mary symbolized the Church, Mother of the Faithful; suffering in compassion with her crucified son, hoping against all hope, she symbolized the eschatological hope of the Church which, through the sufferings of the war with the powers of evil, awaits the final resurrection and glorious manifestation of the Kingdom of God. Mary, at the Cross, bends her very being towards Mother Church, which suffers persecution and awaits the Resurrection. In the vision of the book of Revelation the Woman, clothed with the sun, who is Mother Church, the inheritor of Israel, militant but already sure of final victory, recalls for us her historic image, Mary, mother of the Suffering Servant, and of the Messiah King, at the foot of the Cross in her suffering and in her hopefulness.

Thus Mary and the Church are closely united in the event of the Cross and in this event recorded in Revelation. These two moments of revelation present the Virgin Mary, mother of the Lord, as the symbol of the Church militant and triumphant: Mary, in the Church and with the Church, with all the members of Christ, shares in His humanity, in the suffering of the Crucified and the hope of the Resurrection.

The Woman of the Book of Revelation, the Church, mother of the faithful, militant and triumphant, and Mary, symbol of the maternal and spiritual ministry of the Church in suffering and hope, thus appear united in the ancestry of Israel, the Daughter of Zion, as the eschatological sign of the final victory of Christ over all the powers of evil. The great sign in Heaven is Mother Church marching towards the glorious Kingdom of the Risen One through the tribulations of this world, symbolized in history, and in particular at the foot of the Cross, by Mary, mother of the Crucified and Risen Lord.

Mary in the Church

Mary is truly 'proclaimed blessed by all generations' according to the Gospel (Luke 1: 48), in the liturgy, preaching and piety of the Church. Because Mary is present in the Church, as the first Christian, and because she is the type of the Church, she has her place in the proclamation of the Word of God by the Church and in the spiritual life of the faithful. Certainly this attention to Mary in the Church has known and still knows excesses which can compromise the adoration specially due to the Holy Trinity. But the fear of excess must not give way to a silence and avoidance of Mary in the Christian conscience which would be equally unfaithful to the Gospel of Christ.

In the course of this study we have emphasized, on the basis of scripture, all that Christian piety can learn of what is true and life-giving in meditation on the calling of Mary, mother of the Lord and type of the Church. There remains here for us only the task of defining how the proclamation of what God did in Mary can find a legitimate place in the liturgy and preaching of the Church, so that the Mother of the Lord might be 'proclaimed blessed by all generations,' according to Holy Writ.

The Virgin Mary has her place in the Liturgy, in which there can be proclaimed, as in preaching, the grace which He has bestowed upon her. Is not the whole of scripture an account of the marvellous acts of God performed for His people and for each of its members? Mary, in so far as she is an eminent member of the Church, as a type of the people of God, faithful and filled with His grace, is surely one who must provide in the Liturgy a special occasion for praise to the Lord. Luther, who kept many feasts of Mary in the Liturgy, expressed himself thus on March 25, 1539, the day of the Annunciation: 'This is one of the most important festivals which we celebrate as Christians, for we have been called, as St. Peter has said, to be a people who proclaim the marvellous acts of God.' It is surely in such a sense that we worship on the occasion of these festivals which recall the vocation of Mary in the plan of salvation, though we give thanks for the glory of God alone. The presence of Mary in the Liturgy, according to several feasts amongst the most ancient, gives an occasion for Christians to proclaim, with regard to Mary, mother of the Lord and type of the Church, the praises of Him who has called both her and us from darkness into His wonderful light.

The mention of Apostles, martyrs and confessors of the Church and the Virgin Mary in the Liturgy is necessary in order to make us realize that we are not alone in adoration and intercession for men, but that Christ unites in one single body with us the whole cloud of witnesses who surround us. The Communion of Saints unites all Christians in one and the same prayer, in one and the same life, in Christ; it unites the Church to-day with that of all the ages, the Church militant on earth with the Church triumphant in Heaven. In her struggle the Church needs to look upon the eschatological sign of Revelation; the Woman clothed with the sun, the cosmos beneath her feet, crowned with a dozen stars; this Woman is herself the Church, which, in spite of the hard struggle with this

world, has the promise of glory. The Lord offers her the wings of
His protection, the refuge of contemplation in the wilderness and
the manna of the Eucharist which enables her to stand firm in the
face of the powers of evil and of persecution. In order to hold on
in this world the Church needs to hold on to her eschatological
victory, and to see herself as the Woman lit up by the sun of Christ,
transfigured and glorified, reigning over the universe, crowned with
the twelve stars, the Twelve Apostles, who founded the new people
of God; the Church needs to feel herself encompassed by 'the great
cloud of witnesses' in order to run with patience the race that is set
before her (Heb. 11–12: 1). The Church marches towards the
Kingdom in a great festival procession: 'You have come to Mount
Zion and to the city of the living God, the heavenly Jerusalem, with
thousands of angels, in festal gathering, and to the assembly of the
firstborn who are enrolled in heaven, to a Judge who is God of all,
and to the spirits of just men made perfect, and to Jesus, the
mediator of a New Covenant, and to the sprinkled blood that speaks
more graciously than the blood of Abel' (Heb. 12: 22–4). This
Communion of Saints which accompanies the Church in her struggle and on her march towards the Kingdom, strengthens her in the
Faith, encourages her in Hope and spreads abroad in her its Love.[7]
This cloud of witnesses recalls for the Church that she is without
number and already triumphant in a struggle which sometimes must
seem as if it will overpower her. And Mary, the Mother of the
Lord and type of the Church, has her place in this immense community of the Saints, a place of pre-eminence as the first Christian
woman, filled with grace. She is all the more for the Church a symbol of her sorrowful motherhood which gives birth to the faithful
by the risen life. She is an example of faith, obedience, constancy
and saintliness: The Church militant, considering the Church
triumphant, sees there Mary, a symbol of her certain victory.

It is in the liturgical commemoration of the major events in the
life of Mary, and in the course of the simple Gospel festivals, that
the Mother of the Lord is able to be 'proclaimed blessed' by the
Church, in the praise of God alone, and to be set forward as an
example of faith, obedience, constancy and sainthood before all the
faithful in Christ.

Luther kept the principal feasts of Mary, on the occasion of
which he preached on the Gospel connected with them. Always, if
we consider his preaching on the occasion of the Conception,

Nativity or even Assumption of Mary, the last on December 8, 1520 (her conception), September 8, 1522 (her nativity) and August 15, 1523 (her assumption), we must notice that his interest in these feasts will decline as time passes, whilst it will continue unabated in observing the Annunciation, the Visitation and the Purification; his last sermons on the occasion of these festivals are dated respectively March 25, 1540, July 2, 1544, and February 2, 1546. The reason for this is that he found for these last three festivals an explicit basis in the Gospel account.

At Zurich, in the time of Zwingli, the feasts of the Apostles had been kept, as well as these three festivals of Mary: The Purification (February 2), the Annunciation (March 25) and the Assumption (August 15).[8] The radicalism of Calvin in regard to the festivals of the liturgical year, clearly led to the suppression of all the feasts of Mary, the Apostles and the Saints. In the face of the abuses of the time a particular attention to Mary, marked by a Feast Day, would have seemed to him to limit the peculiar glory due to God to whom alone we should render our worship. However, his preaching and his commentaries on the opening of the Gospel according to St. Luke insist on the praise which we must render to God in regard to the grace shown forth in Mary, His humble handmaid: 'To-day we cannot give praise for the blessing which Christ has given to us without remembering at the same time the glorious privilege which God bestowed on Mary by choosing her to be the mother of his only Son. . . . Now she is called Blessed because, receiving by faith the blessing which is offered to her, she opened the way for God to accomplish his work . . .'[9]

These quotations from Calvin indicate very well the sense in which we should regard the Virgin Mary, as magnifying the unique glory of God, because of the grace with which he endowed her for our salvation and joy in Christ. In the festivals which recall this grace of God in Mary, for the spiritual edification of the Church, the Liturgy will not want to express anything but an act of thanksgiving to the Lord for His marvellous acts of salvation, and intercession before Him in communion with the great cloud of witnesses in which Mary would have her place pre-eminently as an example of faith, obedience, constancy and saintliness which she radiates as mother and handmaid of the Lord.

There are FOUR amongst the most ancient feasts of Mary which ought to receive our attention:

The Annunciation to Mary by the Angel;
The Visitation by Mary to Elizabeth;
The Purification of Mary (or Presentation of Jesus in the
  Temple);
The Entry of Mary into God's rest.

The Annunciation, Visitation and the Presentation are tradition-
ally celebrated on March 25, July 2 and February 2 respectively.
Despite the respectable ancestry of these dates it is clear that they
do not fit easily into the year's liturgical cycle. The Annunciation
on March 25, for example, falls during Lent, and often during Holy
Week; in this latter case it is arranged that the feast shall be transferred to a date after the Octave of Easter. On the other hand, it is
very important that any memorial of Mary in the Liturgy should
be in close relation to the whole history of salvation and the mys-
teries of Christ. The most normal period for the feasts of the
Annunciation and Visitation, if we are to relate them to the
expectation of the Saviour, is the period of Advent. Why not in
fact transfer these ancient festivals to the third week of Advent
with the Annunciation on the Wednesday and the Visitation on the
Friday? The Feast of the Purification, or Presentation of Christ in
the Temple, would come better immediately after Christmas, rather
than forty days after (according to the exact requirements concerning the time in the Law). As it happens this latter feast, on
February 2, also often falls within the Easter cycle, after Septua-
gesima. The liturgical year follows a symbolic pattern which does
not have to stick too rigidly to the number of days between each
of the events that occur, except in the periods before and after
Easter, the Ascension and Pentecost. The traditional Western
Calendar for Christmas is complicated enough and does not make
easy a liturgy which seeks also to be pastoral.

In the Offices at Taizé, the Gospel of the Presentation in the
Temple is read on December 30.[11] Why do we not make January 1,
the Octave of Christmas, once more a really important liturgical
feast-day of Christ and His mother by celebrating, under the title
of the Presentation in the Temple, all the events recorded by
St. Luke in chapter 2, verses 21–40 (i.e. the circumcision, presentation, and the prophecies of Simeon and Anna)?

These three festivals of Mary (Annunciation, Visitation and the
Presentation), or rather of Christ and His mother, based on the

Gospel accounts, do not present any problems, especially if they are linked up with the seasons of Advent and Christmas. The very ancient feast of August 15 is a rather more delicate matter on account of the differing views that are held concerning the manner of Mary's 'falling asleep': our Catholic and Orthodox brethren believe in the corporeal assumption of the Blessed Virgin; Protestants believe that she died, entered into Heaven and awaits the Resurrection like any other Christian. None the less, it does appear that in a spirit of ecumenical understanding and without any doctrinal confusion, we could all keep the same day of Mary's 'falling asleep,' whatever may be the doctrine of this mystery which in faith we hold. Protestants could keep August 15 in the spirit of these lines from Charles Drelincourt, the Reformed French pastor of the seventeenth century, whom we have quoted several times already: 'As she received here below the most precious grace and the rarest favours with which any human being could be honoured, so also she now enjoys in highest heaven the glory most sublime which any human soul could receive. . . . If Joseph received his father with tears of joy when the latter came to Egypt to see his face once more and to share in the privileges of his high office, how much more the Son of God, the Saviour and Redeemer of the world, must have welcomed with delight this blessed and happy Mother . . . who is ascended into the heavens to contemplate the glory of his Paradise! ' [12]

In these four festivals it is not so much a matter of rendering thanks and glory to God for all that He has done in the life of His human mother, so much as asking for grace to follow the example of the Virgin Mary, by copying her faith, her obedience, her constancy and saintliness . . . as well as rejoicing in the Communion of Saints, awaiting the Resurrection and the Kingdom of God in which, with Mary and all the Saints, we shall enjoy life eternal and perfect joy.

An Example of Prayers (a Litany)

O Lord God, who hast responded to the messianic expectation of Israel, Thy chosen people, and to the uncertain hopes of all mankind, Thy beloved creatures, by sending Thine Angel to Mary, the Daughter of Zion; grant that we may ever attend Thy coming and await with joy Thy Kingdom of glory, through Christ, our Lord.

Come, Creator Spirit

Father of Mercies, who hast predestined and filled with grace the Virgin Mary, that she might become the mother of Thine only Son; enrich us with Thy blessing in the Well-beloved, Thou who hast chosen us in Him, that we may be holy and spotless in Thy presence and in Charity, through Christ, our Lord.

Come, Creator Spirit

Almighty God, who hast willed Thy son to be born of a poor virgin, that in her frailty and poverty Thy power and riches might be made plain; strengthen us in our poverty for we do not wish to possess anything but the gifts of Thy hand, through Christ, our Lord.

Come, Creator Spirit

O Holy God, who camest to dwell in Mary, to make in her Thy resting-place, and hast made of Christ's body a new and final Temple for those who worship Thee; come and dwell in us by Thy Holy Spirit, so that our bodies may more and more become temples dedicated to Thy presence, through Christ, our Lord.

Come, Creator Spirit

O God our Master, who hast granted to Mary the grace of pure faith, so that she could receive Thy word with the trust of an obedient and consecrated handmaid; make us to be Thy faithful servants, full of faith in Thy sure promises, through Christ, our Lord.

Come, Creator Spirit

O God of love, who didst cause the Virgin Mary to become Thy human mother, blessed amongst women and called blessed by all generations; renew in us faith in Thy Son, true God and true Man, and an act of thanksgiving for all the wonders of the Incarnation, through Christ, our Lord.

Come, Creator Spirit

189

O glorious God, who didst make Mary Thy humble handmaid to rejoice at the coming of the Messiah and didst inspire her to sing a song of Joy and Victory; destroy our pride, overthrow our power so that in humility and poverty we might find true might and true riches, through Christ, our Lord.

Come, Creator Spirit

God of Compassion, who didst draw Mary into the sufferings of her son, so as to fashion her heart by the passion of the Crucified; grant that we may find joy in suffering for the Gospel and complete in our own flesh what was lacking of the suffering of Jesus for His Body, the Church, through Christ, our Lord.

Come, Creator Spirit

O God our Father, who didst cause Mary to be the type of the Church, our Mother, and who gave her as a spiritual mother to the faithful disciple; grant us the grace to receive the Church in our hearts as a mother, and make us to rejoice in the spiritual family which you have given us, through Christ, our Lord.

Come, Creator Spirit

O God of Victory, who revealedst to Thy disciple John, in a vision, the final triumph of Thy Church; help us to perceive in the heavens the cloud of victorious witnesses so that we may have courage and might to wage war in this world; hear our prayer, we beseech Thee, and receive the prayers of Mary linked with ours in the communion of Saints. Make us follow the example of faith, of devotion, constancy and holiness given to us by her who was Thine earthly mother and who now remains the type of Thy Holy Church, through Christ, our Lord.

Come, Creator Spirit

Annunciation

Pour out, we beseech Thee, O Lord, Thy grace in our hearts; by the message of the Angel we have known the Incarnation of Jesus Christ, Thy Son; by His passion and His Cross, lead us to the glory of the Resurrection, because He lives and reigns with Thee, in the unity of the Holy Spirit, One God, world without end, AMEN

Visitation

O Lord God, who didst lead the blessed Virgin Mary to Elizabeth, and who didst permit them to meet to share their amazing joy; as Mary rejoiced to be called the Mother of the Lord, grant us also to find our joy in the Incarnation of Jesus Christ, Thy Son, our Lord, who liveth and reigneth with Thee, in the unity of the Holy Spirit, One God, world without end, AMEN

Presentation

Almighty and everlasting God, on this day on which Thy only Son, in a body like unto ours, was presented in the Temple, grant us the grace also to be presented to Thee, with hearts made pure by Jesus Christ, Thy Son, our Lord, who liveth and reigneth with Thee, in the unity of the Holy Spirit, One God, world without end, AMEN

Memorial

Almighty God, who hast filled with Thy especial grace the Blessed Virgin Mary, Mother of our Lord, sanctify, we beseech Thee, our hearts and bodies, and grant us like her to live in purity, humility and love, through Jesus Christ, Thy Son, our Lord, who liveth and reigneth with Thee, in the unity of the Holy Spirit, One God, world without end, AMEN.

NOTES ON THE INTRODUCTION

[1] We give here the principal works on Mariology, which we have found to be of invaluable help. Many of these authors have become our friends and we thank them for their assistance.

PROTESTANT

H. ASMUSSEN, *Maria, die Mutter Gottes,* Evangelisches Verlagswerk, Stuttgart 1951.

J. BOSC, P. BOURGUET, P. MAURY, H. ROUX, *Le protestantisme et la Vierge Marie,* Je Sers, Paris 1950.

P. BOURGUET, *La Vierge Marie,* Berger-Levrault, Paris 1955.

C. BRUTSCH, *La Vierge Marie,* Delachaux et Niestlé, Neuchâtel 1943.

J. CADIER, 'La Vierge Marie dans la dogmatique réformée au xvie et au xviie siècles,' in *La Revue Réformée,* 1958/4, pp. 46–58.

H. LAMPARTER, *Die Magd des Herrn,* Brunnquell-Verlag, Metzingen 1949.

G. MIEGGE, *La Vergine Maria,* Claudiana, Torre Pellice 1950; Eng. trans. 'The Virgin Mary,' Lutterworth Press, 1961.

R. SCHIMMELPFENNIG, *Die Geschichte der Marienverehrung im deutschen Protestantismus,* Verlag Ferdinand Schöningh, Paderborn 1952.

W. TAPPOLET, *Das Marienlob der Reformatoren,* Katzmann-Verlag, Tübingen 1962.

B.-D. DUPUY (catholic), 'La mariologie de Calvin,' in *Istina,* 1958/4, pp. 479–90.

S. CWIERTNIAK (catholic), *La Vierge Marie dans la tradition anglicane,* Fleurus, Paris 1958.

ORTHODOX

S. BOULGAKOF, *Du Verbe incarné,* Aubier, Paris 1943.

P. EVDOKIMOV, *L'orthodoxie,* Delachaux et Niestlé, Neuchâtel 1959.

P. EVDOKIMOV, *La femme et le salut du monde,* Casterman, Tournai 1958.

A. KNIAZEFF, 'Mariologie biblique et liturgie byzantine,' in *Irenikon,* 1955/3, pp. 268–89.

V. LOSSKY, *Essai sur la théologie mystique de l'Eglise d'Orient,* Aubier, Paris 1944.

METROPOLITE SERAPHIM, L'Eglise orthodoxe, Payot, Paris 1952.

L. S. THORNTON, V. LOSSKY, E. L. MASCALL, G. FLOROVSKY, T. M. PARKER, L. GILLET (Anglican and Orthodox), *The Mother of God,* Dacre Press, London 1949.

CATHOLIC

GENERAL MARIOLOGY

Maria, études sur la sainte Vierge. General editor: M. du Manoir, vols. I to VI, Beauchesne, Paris, 1949–61.

Etudes mariales, Bulletin de la Société Française d'études mariales, Lethielleux, Paris 1947 to 1961, 14 vols. especially on *Mary and the Church, The New Eve, The spiritual maternity of Mary.*

L. BOUYER, *Le trône de la sagesse,* Le Cerf, Paris 1957,

C. BOYER, *Synopsis praelectionum de beata Maria virgine,* Université Grégorienne, Rome 1952.

Y. M.-J. CONGAR, *Le Christ, Marie et l'Eglise,* Desclée de Brouwer, Paris 1952.

C. DILLENSCHNEIDER, *Le principe premier d'une théologie mariale organique*
— *Marie dans l'économie de la création rénovée*
— *Le mystère de Notre Dame*
Alsatia, Paris 1956-57–62.

C. Feckes, *Maria im Heilsplan Gottes,* Johannes-Verlag, Leutesdorf 1954.

R. Guardini, *Die Mutter des Herrn,* Werkbund-Verlag, Würzburg 1955, French translation, *Le Cerf,* Paris 1961.

J. Guitton, *La Vierge Marie,* Aubier, Paris 1949.

C. Journet, *Esquisse du développement du dogme marial,* Alsatia, Paris 1954.

R. Laurentin, *Court traité de théologie mariale,* Lethielleux, Paris 1953, and 1959 4th edition.

By the same author, excellent bibliographical notices in *La vie spirituelle* and *Revue des sciences philosophiques et théologiques,* 1962/2, pp. 324–75.

Lumière et Vie: Sainte Marie, Mère de Dieu, 16, 1954.

K. Rahner, *Marie mère du Seigneur,* Orante, Paris 1960.

H. Rahner, *Marie et l'Eglise,* Le Cerf, Paris 1955.

M. Riquet, *L'Eglise et la Vierge,* Spes, Paris 1954.

L. J. Suenens, Cardinal-Archbishop of Malines, *Quelle est Celle-ci?,* Arthème Fayard, Paris 1957.

MARY IN THE BIBLE

F. M. Braun, *La mère des fidèles,* Casterman, Tournai 1954.

J. Colson (C. Wiener et), *Un roi fit des noces à son fils,* Desclé de Brouwer, Paris 1962.

L. Deiss, *Marie, Fille de Sion,* Desclée de Brouwer, Paris 1959.

J. Galot, *Marie dans l'Evangile,* Desclée de Brouwer, Paris 1958.

R. Laurentin, *Structure et théologie de Luc I–II,* Gabalda, Paris 1957.

J.-J. Weber, Bishop of Strasbourg, *La Vierge Marie dans le Nouveau Testament,* Alsatia, Paris 1951.

MARY AND THE CHURCH

H. Coathalem, *Le parallélisme entre la sainte Vierge et l'Eglise dans la tradition latine jusqu'à la fin du* XIIᵉ *siècle,* Université grégorienne, Rome, 1954.

A. Kassing, *Die Kirche und Maria, Ihr Verhältnis im 12. Kapitel der Apokalypse,* Patmos-Verlag, Köln 1958.

H. de Lubac, *Méditation sur l'Eglise,* Aubier, Paris 1953, pp. 241–85.

A. Mueller, *Ecclesia—Maria, die Einheit Marias und der Kirche,* Universitätsverlag, Fribourg 1955.

Y. M.-J. Congar, 'Marie et l'Eglise dans la pensée patristique,' in *Revue des sciences philosophiques et théologiques,* 1954/1, pp. 3–38 (analysis of the preceding work).

J. Galot, 'Marie et l'Eglise,' in *Nouvelle revue théologique,* 1959/2, pp. 113–31.

Etudes mariales, Marie et l'Eglise, I, II et III, Lethielleux, Paris 1951, 1952, 1953.

THE RECENT POPES

Marian documents of Pius IX, Leo XIII, Pius X, Benedict XV, Pius XI and Pius XII, in *Laval théologique et philosophique,* Presses universitaires Laval, Quebec 1953/1 and 2.

[2] *Commentary on the Epistle to the Galatians 4: 26.*

[3] *Institutes of the Christian Religion,* B IV, ch. 1, entitled 'Of the True Church, the duty of cultivating unity with her, as the mother of all the Godly.' G. Henry Beveridge, James Clarke & Co. Limited, London, 1953 printing 2 vols., p. 253.

[4] *De sancta virginitate,* III P.L. 40, 397.

[5] J. G. Machen, *The Virgin Birth of Christ,* New York 1932, pp. 62–118; Biblica, 1956/4, pp. 455, 456.

[6] P. Gaechter, *Maria im Erdenleben,* Innsbruck-Wien 1954, discerns, by means of internal criticism, different stages in the account; the witness of

Mary; then transmission by a friend of Elizabeth, on the one hand, and by another woman on the other, and a converted Jewish priest; a collection of these narratives by another priest in Hebrew; and finally translation and incorporation into the Gospel.

NOTES ON CHAPTER 1: DAUGHTER OF ZION

[1] See Ps. 9: 15; Isa. 1: 8; 10: 32; 16: 1; 52: 2; Jer. 4: 31; 6: 2; 6: 23; Micah 1: 13; 4: 10; in the Gospels, Matt. 21: 5; John 12: 15.

[2] 1: 6; 2: 1; 2: 4, 8, 10, 13, 18; 4: 22.

[3] R. LAURENTIN, *Structure et théologie du Luc I–II,* Gabalda, Paris 1957, pp. 64ff.; 148ff.; J. GALOT, *Marie dans l'Evangile,* Desclée de Brouwer, Paris 1958, pp. 16ff.; S. LYONNET, 'Le récit de l'Annonciation et la maternité divine de la Sainte Vierge' in *L'Ami du clergé,* 66, 1956, pp. 33–46; H. SAHLIN, *Der Messias und das Gottesvolk* (*Acta Seminarii Neotestamentici Upsaliensis*) N XII, Upsala 1945; A. G. HEBERT, 'La Vierge Marie, Fille de Sion' in *La Vie spirituelle,* Août-Sept. 1951, Le Cerf, Paris, pp. 127ff.

[4] S. LYONNET, Biblica 20, 1939, pp. 131–41.

[5] R. LAURENTIN, op. cit., pp. 67ff.

[6] 'Dès que le Temple sera reconstruit,' *Bible du Centenaire,* Zech. 2: 10, note d.

NOTES ON CHAPTER 2: FULL OF GRACE

[1] J. GALOT, *Marie dans l'Evangile,* Desclée de Brouwer, Paris 1958.

[2] There are only two texts in the Old Testament Greek version which might be recalled here where the version suggests 'perfect, fulfilled, without reproach' (i.e. Septuagint version). Eccles. 18: 17, 'Lo, is not a word better than a gift? but both are with a *gracious* man.' Ps. 18: 26, 'With the merciful thou wilt show thyself merciful; with an *upright* man thou wilt show thyself upright'; J. GALOT, *op. cit.,* p. 26.

[3] A. MEDEBEILLE, 'Annunciation' in *Dictionnaire de la Bible,* Supplement I, p. 283.

[4] *Annotationes in Evangelium Lucae.* One finds in Luther also clear attestations of Mary's sanctity. See the very full anthology of texts from LUTHER, CALVIN, ZWINGLI and BULLINGER in W. TAPPOLET, *Das Marienlob der Reformatoren,* Katzmann, Tübingen 1962.

NOTES ON CHAPTER 3: POOR VIRGIN

[1] F. J. LEENHARDT, *La Parole et le buisson de feu,* Delachaux et Niestlé, Neuchâtel 1962.

[2] *Rouleau du combat,* 7, 3–4; G. VERMES, 'Quelques traditions de Qumrān in *Cahiers Sioniens 9,* 1955, p. 42.

[3] Midrash Petirat Mosheh; see R. BLOCH, 'Quelques aspects de la figure de Moïse dans la littérature rabbinique' in *Cahiers Sioniens 8,* 1954.

Explaining the complaints of Miriam and Aaron against Moses the *Sifri sur les nombres* underline that Miriam criticized Moses because he had ceased to practise the commandment concerning marriage. Rabbi Nathan then continues to show that Miriam had no intention except that of safe-guarding a divine law. However, she was punished and hence there is all the more reason to believe that those who speak not for the good, but for the evil, of others will suffer the same. J. BONSIRVEN, *Textes rabbiniques,* Rome 1955, 244, p. 54.

[4] See in the same mood the rabbinic history of the Priest Nir in *Ecrit du sacerdoce de Mathusalem, Nir et Melchisedech,* German translation by N. BONWETSCH, *Die Bücher der Geheimnisse Henochs,* Leipzig 1922.

[5] M. DIBELIUS, *Jungfrauensohn und Krippenkind*, Heidelberg 1932, pp. 22-8. The account of the birth of Isaac lent itself to such a miraculous interpretation: 'Yahvé visited Sarah as he had said and did for her what he had promised. Sarah conceived and bore to Abraham a son in her old age, at the time which God had indicated. To the son who was born to him by Sarah, Abraham gave the name Isaac.'

[6] We have developed this point in *Marriage and Celibacy*, Delachaux et Niestlé, Neuchâtel 1955, pp. 47ff.

[7] J. H. NICOLAS, O.P., *La virginité de Marie, étude théologique*, Editions universitaires, Fribourg, *Collectanea Friburgensia*. 'The grandeur and beauty of virginity in no way means that marriage is to be deprecated or human love despised. It asserts its own excellence without any detriment to other essential values, even when it may be preferred to them. However suspicious of himself man is, or uncertain of his choices, his natural inclination is to disqualify what he does not choose. It is for this reason, in fact, that it has at other times often happened that when virginity has been exalted it has been accompanied by a contentious discrediting of the marriage state, with a consequent forgetting of the greatness of Motherhood. Inversely, the return of more modern people to a just appreciation of a Christian and human value of love does not proceed without the perfectly unjustifiable question being raised of the pre-eminence accorded in the Church in all ages to virginity. The radiant image of this blessed Woman who, by the paths of perfect virginity, was led to the highest and most complete form of Motherhood has thus done much to reveal to men the true sense of virginity, which is not mutilation or limitation, but on the contrary shows a positive and expansive quality.

[8] Rabbi Nathan, *Sifre Nomb.* 12. 1, ed. Horowitz, Leipzig 1917, p. 98.

[9] *Marriage and Celibacy*, pp. 142-3.

[10] We are speaking here of the monk according to the ancient tradition but it is well recognized that that may well involve every man and every woman, every clergyman and every layman, who dedicate themselves to the Church whilst maintaining celibacy and seeking that individual poverty in obedience to the Church.

[11] *De bono conjugali*, XII.

[12] Chapter, 'Mary and the Church.'

[13] R. LAURENTIN, op. cit., pp. 176ff., and others with him.

[14] PLINY, *Hist. nat.* 5, 17; JOSEPHUS, *De bello judaico*, II, 8, 2; M. J. LAGRANGE, *Le Judaïsme palestinien*, Gabalda, Paris 1937, pp. 306-7.

[15] S. LYONNET, *L'Ami du clergé*, 66, 1956, p. 42b, note 10.

[16] This belief is a constant one with Luther throughout his whole life; cf. W. TAPPOLET, *Das Marienlob der Reformatoren Katzmann*, Tübingen 1962, pp. 49ff.

[17] ibid., pp. 240ff.

[18] P.L. 23, cols. 183-206.

[19] Comm. in Matt. 13: 55; cf. *Marriage and Celibacy*, p. 71.

[20] Comm. in Matt. 1: 25.

[21] *La Revue Réformée*, 1956/4, pp. 63-4.

[22] Invited by the Bishop of Belley, Mgr. Camus, to reply to certain questions concerning a former little work, Charles Drelincourt, a French Reformed Pastor (1595-1669), well represents the Reformed tradition of the seventeenth century and wrote a long treatise, *De l'honneur qui doit être rendu à la sainte et bienheureuse vierge Marie*. He stated concerning perpetual virginity, 'This happy Mother remained a virgin during the birth and after it.' He went further than Calvin's position in that the latter did not assert her virginity *in partu*. The important thing for him consisted in the Spiritual Virginity of Mary, in her virginity *ante et post partum*, and not in the physical fact of her virginity.

NOTES ON CHAPTER 4: DWELLING OF GOD

1 P. GAECHTER, op. cit., p. 20 quoting Strack-Billerbeck; see also PRAT, *Jesus Christ*, Paris 1938, I, p. 59.

2 M. J. LAGRANGE, *Evangile selon saint Luc*, Paris 1921, p. 13.

3 H. SAHLIN, *Der Messias und das Gottesvolk*, Upsala 1945, pp. 127–8; A. G. HEBERT, 'The Virgin Mary, Daughter of Zion' in *La vie spirituelle*, 1951, pp. 131–2; J. COPPINS, *La Vierge Marie dans l'Ancien Testament*, Eph. Theol. Lov., 1955, pp. 15–16.

4 R. LAURENTIN, op. cit., pp. 73ff.

5 See also the account of the baptism of Jesus with this same theme simplified (Luke 3: 22 and parallels).

6 E. BURROWS, *The Gospel of the Infancy and other Biblical Essays*, Burns Oates & Washbourne, London 1940, p. 47; R. LAURENTIN, op. cit., pp. 79ff.

7 The Septuagint uses the word six times in all; the version of Symnach has also 'Skirtan' in 2 Sam. 6: 16.

8 J. H. GREHAN, 'The Ark of the Covenant' in *Clergy Review 36*, 1951, pp. 301–11; R. LAURENTIN, *Marie, l'Eglise et le sacerdoce*, Lethielleux, Paris 1953; II, an index of the titles of the Virgin.

9 The Vulgate translates 'glorify and bear God (then) in your body.'

NOTES ON CHAPTER 6: MOTHER OF THE LORD

1 R. GUARDINI, *The Mother of the Lord*, Le Cerf, Paris 1961, p. 29. Romano Guardini here gives a sidelight which is a warning against a tendency of Protestantism rather than a faithful and always valid description of an attitude towards Mary: 'Perhaps it is on this fundamental issue that Catholics and Protestants are separated in the conception which they have of Mary. Protestants seem to consider Mary only as the Mother of Jesus the man, in a purely physical sense, excluding at the same time her status as the Mother of the Son of God Incarnate and the personal relationship which, as a mother, united her with the Redeemer. From such an approach there result consequences which, in the end, could affect the person of Christ Himself. The definitions of the Council of Ephesus relate to Mary just as much as they do to Christ.'

2 The Septuagint translates: 'the Kyrios said to my Kyrios: . . .'

3 *Genetrix Dei et Domini nostri Jesu Christi*, 'Communicantes' of the Roman Mass.

4 Translation of G. DUMEIGE, *The Catholic Faith*, L'Orante, Paris 1961, p. 191.

5 The contrast between Cyril and Nestorius to-day no longer appears quite so marked. It seems that Nestorius sometimes used the title of *theotokos* in an orthodox sense and that Cyril was himself not always clear in his teaching of the two natures. Non-theological factors played their part in the dispute of the schools. But a contrast of quite another kind has existed between tendencies which were insisting the one on the division of natures in Christ and the other on their fusion. The Councils of Ephesus and Chalcedon had to distinguish in favour of the union without confusion, and the distinction without division of the two natures of Christ, as true God and true man, born of the Virgin Mary, Mother of God, *theotokos*. On this matter see the very balanced historical judgment of G. JOUASSARD, 'Mary in Patristic writing, Divine motherhood, Virginity and holiness' in *Maria I*, Beauchesne, Paris 1949, pp. 122ff.

6 Martin Luther's works, *Weimar*, 50: 591, 22–592. 5.

7 'Von der ewig reinen Magd. Maria, der Mutter Gottes.' HULDRYCH ZWINGLI, *Collected Works*, Berlin, I, 391–428.

8 One should not normally embark on this subject until one has read the

magnificent book *Das Marienlob der Reformatoren* of W. TAPPOLET, Katz-mann, Tübingen, 1962. See the very good analysis of R. STADLER, 'The Holy Virgin in the Reformers' in *Choisir* 31, May 1962, pp. 17–20.

In regard to the Marian doctrine of the Reformers, we have already seen how unanimous they are in all that concerns Mary's holiness and perpetual virginity. Whatever the theological position which we may hold to-day, in regard to the Immaculate Conception and Assumption of Mary it is right to know, perhaps to our great surprise, that these two Catholic dogmas were accepted by certain Reformers, not of course in their present form but certainly in the form that was current in their day.

At the period of the Reformation the idea that Mary was exempt from original sin (the Immaculate Conception) was a matter of controversy and was even contested in Dominican circles. Most theologians held a middle position. They taught that the physical generation of Mary was within the scope of original sin, but that her soul had escaped this (following the Augustinian doctrine which teaches that the coming of the spirit into the physical embryo is subsequent to its conception). Luther shared this common idea; he declared in a long sermon for the 'Day of the Conception of Mary, Mother of God,' in 1527, 'above all it is necessary for us to see what original sin is in order to be able to understand how the holy Virgin Mary was released from it . . . as to the conception of the Virgin Mary whose body was procreated in the fashion of other children, until the soul was infused, it was not necessary that she should be conceived as was Christ; for she was able to be brought forth under the law of original sin, up to the time when her soul was bestowed. But, in that which concerns the other conception, that is to say the infusing of her soul, one believes with devotion and holiness that she was brought forth without original sin, in such a way that at the moment of her soul being infused she was also similarly purified from original sin, and at the first instant in which she began to live she was without sin, adorned with the gifts of God' (W. TAPPOLET, op. cit., pp. 29–30). Thus, for Luther, as we see from his very own words Mary's conception is to be placed between that of Christ and that of all other men.

In the years 1543–1644 Luther wrote again: 'Some relate this passage: "by thee all the nations of the earth shall be blest" (Gen. 12: 3) to the Blessed Virgin, Mother of the Child, and see there an allusion to the fact that the child would be born of a pure mother, a pure chaste and spotless virgin. It is indeed a devout and satisfying thought' (ibid., 32).

In connection with the purification according to the Law of Mary in the Temple, Bullinger, the successor of Zwingli, wrote: 'And if she who was wholly pure from her birth did not disdain to be purified, that is to say to receive the blessing of purification, is this not all the more reason why those who fall under the yoke of the law by reason of their real impurity should observe the same' (ibid., p. 282).

On the issue of the Assumption Luther does not speak precisely but is content to assert on August 15th, 1522: 'From this gospel one cannot draw any conclusion about the fashion in which Mary is in heaven; it is not necessary any more to know the fate of the saints in heaven. It is enough to know that they dwell in Christ as God says in Matt. 22: 32: "God is not a God of the dead but of the living' making reference to the text of Exodus 3: 6: "I am the God of Abraham, the God of Isaac, the God of Jacob"' (ibid., 55).

Bullinger wrote in 1565: 'The most learned theologians say that one cannot assert anything on the matter of the death or the assumption of the virgin. To wish to unearth or clarify certain facts on which scripture is silent is not without its dangers. Let us content ourselves with believing that the Virgin Mary is indeed active in heaven and has received every beatitude after her departing.' However, in 1568, he wrote on the same subject: 'Elijah was transported body and soul in a chariot of fire; he was not buried in any Church bearing his name, but mounted up to heaven, so that on the one hand we might know what immortality and recompense God prepares for his faithful prophets and for his most outstanding and incomparable creatures, and on the other hand in order to withdraw from men the possibility of venerating the human body of the saint. It is for this reason, we believe, that the pure and immaculate embodiment of the Mother of God, the Virgin Mary, the Temple of the Holy Spirit, that is to say her saintly body, was carried up into heaven by the angels' (ibid., p. 327).

Without enlarging on the position adopted by the Reformers, and without admitting that they are valid on every point, it is necessary to recognize that in their time the Marian issue was much more open and free than it is to-day.

[9] *Institution chrétienne*, 1560, IV, IX, 8; ed. Labor et Fides, IV, p. 163.

[10] Calvin, '*Lettres anglaises*' 1548–61, Berger-Levrault, Paris 1959, pp. 180–1.

[11] *Auf etliche scharfe* . . . Zurich 1557, 134.

[12] W. Tappolet, op. cit., p. 315.

[13] *De l'honneur* . . . op. cit., p. 4.

[14] Here Nestorianism and Docetism are united.

[15] Weimar, 36: 208, 19 to 26.

[16] Weimar, 45: 105, 7 to 106, 1.

[17] Such works as *The Hidden Years of Jesus* by Robert Aron, Grasset, Paris 1960, have their use in order to enable us to grasp this human background.

[18] Weimar, 37: 97, 3 to 13.

NOTES ON CHAPTER 7: MOTHER OF THE MESSIAH KING

[1] It would be finicky to refer to all the references in detail here: all that is required in order to note them is to refer to the Greek text in the edition by E. Nestle, *Novum Testamentum Graece*, or in the translation of *La Sainte Bible de Jerusalem*, full edition.

[2] R. Laurentin, op. cit., p. 85.

[3] *Mariae Lobgesang*, Wittemberg, March 10th, 1521.

[4] *Uber die selige Jungfrau*, May 18th, 1558; W. Tappolet, op. cit., pp. 284–5.

[5] Charles Drelincourt, op. cit., p. 16.

[6] 'Bible Studies in the First Chapter of St. Luke' in *Foi et vie*, 85–6, August–October 1936, pp. 509–10.

NOTES ON CHAPTER 8: MOTHER OF THE SUFFERING SERVANT

[1] Article 'Pur' in *Vocabulaire de theologie Biblique*, Le Cerf, Paris 1962, pp. 887–8.

[2] 'Not to be purified when one is impure (legally) is a sin (morally): not because of simple disobedience to the "order" of purification, but because of "opposition to God in his very Being" for God is the Holy One above all others' (Lev. 11: 44–5). Article 'Pur,' *Vocabulaire biblique*, Delachaux et Niestlé, Neuchâtel 1954, pp. 240–1.

[3] For this idea of memorial-presentation in regard to the Eucharist, see *L'eucharistie, mémorial du Seigneur, sacrifice d'action de grace et d'intercession*, Delachaux et Niestlé, Neuchâtel 1959.

[4] The Roman Mass and paraphrase from the *Eucharist at Taizé*.

[5] We have here reproduced some pages from *L'homme moderne et la vie spirituelle*, Editions de l'Epi, Paris 1962, 2nd edition, because it seems essential to us not to separate the Virgin Mary, the first Christian, the type of the Church, from all those who after her will have to know in faith this same sharing in the sufferings of the Crucified so far as their spiritual and corporeal resurrection is concerned.

⁶ The death of Joseph is not mentioned in the gospel but suggested by the fact that, after the entry of Jesus into His ministry, one only encounters Mary alone and by the fact that at His death on the Cross He will commit her to John.

⁷ op. cit., p. 10. This was written in the seventeenth century but in the midst of the nineteenth a collection of French Lutheran canticles will actually contain a 'Stabat Mater' describing the suffering of Mary:

'Jesus' tender mother
Stood in bitter sadness,
Close beside the Cross . . .'

The ten stanzas are poor poetry but have an authentic piety inspired by the Gospel of St. John; *Receuil de cantiques a l'usage des Eglises evangeliques de France*, Paris, Cantique 63.

NOTES ON CHAPTER 9: MARY AND THE CHURCH

¹ These two texts have been commented on by numerous exegetes or mariologists with great profusion and diversity. It would be vain to try and sum them all up. We are only quoting here what has struck us most forcibly by their authority or originality: M. E. BOISMARD, *Du baptême à Cana*, Le Cerf, Paris 1956; F. M. BRAUN, *La Mère des fidèles*, Casterman, Paris 1954; R. BULTMANN, *Das Evangelium des Johannes*, Vandenhoeck und Ruprecht, Göttingen 1953; O. CULLMANN, *Les sacrements dans l'Evangile Johannique*, P.U.F., Paris 1951; C. DILLENSCHNEIDER, *Le Mystère de Notre Dame*, Alsatia, Paris 1962; J. GALOT, *Marie dans l'Evangile*, Desclée de Brouwer, Paris 1958; M. de GOEDT, *Bases bibliques de la maternité spirituelle de Marie, I*, Lethielleux, Paris 1960. In this same *Bulletin de la Société Française d'études mariales* you can read the exegeses of the Fathers in the excellent article of TH. KOEHLER, 'The principal traditional interpretations of John 19: 25-7 in the first twelve centuries'; H. DU MANOIR, *Maria*, t. 6, Beauchesne, Paris 1961, art. by A. Feuillet.

² It is possible that the calling of Peter took place on the fourth day (that is, if we read 'at dawn' and not 'the first' in verse 41, as certain manuscripts have it); the removing of one day enables us to set the marriage at Cana just the same on the seventh day, because for St. John, Christ who died on Friday rose on the third day; i.e. the Sunday; it is less probable to place the calling of Nathanael on the sixth day, as does M.-E. BOISMARD, op. cit., pp. 95ff. Because of the schemata of the three 'next day after' phrases we prefer the chronology which is given here.

³ C. H. DODD, *The Interpretation of the Fourth Gospel*, Cambridge 1953, p. 299: 'It is certainly not without significance that this manifestation (of the glory at Cana) takes place on the third day. The difficulty of establishing a satisfactory chronology of the events from this date onwards is well known. But the 'third day' was in the Christian tradition, from the most ancient times, the day when Christ manifested his glory by his Resurrection from the dead.'

⁴ See in particular, on the calling of Nathanael and Jacob's ladder: M.-E. BOISMARD, op. cit., pp. 123ff.

⁵ K. L. SCHMIDT, *Der johanneische Charakter der Erzählung vom Hochzeitswunder in Kana*, Harnack-Ehrung, *Beitrage zur Kirchengeschichte*, 1921, pp. 22ff., which, however, sees in this a contrast of the Baptism by water and the Baptism of the Spirit (wine); O. CULLMANN, op. cit., pp. 39-40, who sees the connection between the Jewish purification and the Christian Eucharist.

⁶ See the references by M.-E. BOISMARD, op. cit., pp. 139-40, who prefers a non-sacramental interpretation.

⁷ Adv. Haer. III, 16. 7.

⁸ See O. CULLMANN, op. cit., pp. 9-28.

[9] O. Cullmann, op. cit., pp. 81–3.

[10] M. de Goedt, op. cit., p. 37.

[11] R. Bultmann, op. cit., p. 80: 'When the wine fails, the mother of Jesus draws his attention towards this, apparently to get him to do a miracle, which not only fits the reply of Jesus in verse 4, but which also bears a similarity to the style of all the accounts in which all is told and must be understood from the point made at the outset.'

[12] K. L. Schmidt, op. cit.; A. Wikenhauser, *Das Evangelium nach Johannes,* Regensburg 1948, p. 63.

[13] We are not discussing in detail this expression, which has been studied for a long time by numerous authors, and in particular those we have quoted. R. Bultmann, op. cit., p. 81: 'The *ti emoi kai soi* is a popular form frequently used in the Septuagint for rendering the Hebrew *mah-li va-lak,* often in the New Testament. The expression does not signify so much a refusal of communion, but refers to some particular concrete occasion.'

[14] M.-E. Boismard, op. cit., pp. 154ff., has suggested another interpretation of 'the Hour,' which would be that it is not the moment of the Crucifixion, but that of the glorious manifestation reached precisely on this day of the marriage at Cana. M.-E. Boismard's hypothesis would thus give the dialogue the following meaning:
Mary: 'They have no wine' = Disturbance, anxiety.
Jesus: 'Woman, what is there between thee and me?' = You are wrong to disturb me just because the wine has run out, for you reason in a human way, whereas you should remember that I am the Messiah.
Jesus continues: 'Has my hour then not come?' = Not a statement but a question (the hypothesis of H. Seemann, 1952); since the hour of the manifestation has come. In a human sense Mary has nothing to be disturbed about.
Mary, understanding the sense of the rebuke, says to the servants, 'Do whatever he tells you.' We would then have a transition from human anxiety to faith in the miracle.
It is difficult to fit this hypothesis to the sense given about the Hour in the passages of the Gospel which we have quoted.

[15] R. Bultmann, op. cit., pp. 81–2: 'The preparation is finished with verse 5: the mother has understood her Son; there is only one more thing to be done; to be ready for the orders of him who is going to accomplish the miracle. Thus she commands the servants to do whatever Jesus eventually commands.'

[16] It will repay study to consult the excellent article by Th. Koehler, 'The principal interpretation of John 19: 25–7, in the first twelve centuries,' *La Maternité spirituelle de Marie,* I. Etudes, *Bulletin de la Société Française d'Etudes Mariales,* 1959, Lethielleux, Paris 1960, pp. 119–55.

[17] Origen, Com. in Jo., I, 4–23, G.C.S. orig. 4, p. 8.

[18] *De praescriptione haereticorum,* 22, P.L. 2, 34B.

[19] In Joh. Hom. 85, P.G. 59, '62.

[20] Com. in. Ev. Joh. apost.

[21] See for these Fathers, and the others quoted later, Th. Koehler, op. cit.

[22] St. Epiphanius. *Panarion,* III, 78, P.G. 42, 713–14.

[23] In Joh. 19, P.L. 35. 1950.

[24] *Commentaire de l'évangile concordant,* Armenian version (fifth century). text and translation by L. Leboir, C.S.C.O. 1954. t. II, p. 117.

[25] Exp. Lc. II. 4. P.L. 15. 1554: *Sources chr.* 45, p. 73.

[26] Exp. Lc. VI. 38. P.L. 15, 1678; *Sources chr.* 45, p. 242.

[27] Epist. 63. P.L. 16. 1218B.

[28] Exp. Lc. X, 132. P.L. 15, 1836C–1838C; *Sources chr.* 52, p. 200.

[29] De inst. virg. 7, P.L. 16. 317C–318AB.

[30] Exp. Lc. X, 134, P.L. 15, 1838C; *Sources chr.* 52, p. 201.

[31] Exp. LC. VIII, 5, P.L. 15, 1700C; *Sources chr.* 52, p. 10.

[32] A. MUELLER, *Ecclesia Maria, Die Einheit Marias und der Kirche,* Fribourg 1955; on St. Ambrose, pp. 168–80.

[33] Hom. 8 in *Stabant autem* . . . P.G. 100, 1476D.

[34] ibid., 1477B.

[35] See the excellent article by H. BARRE, 'Mary and the Church, from the Venerable Bede to St. Albert the Great,' in *Marie et l'Eglise,* I, Bull. de la Soc. Fr. d'Et. Mar. 1951, Lethielleux, Paris, 1951, pp. 77ff.

[36] *Oratio I,* texte A. WILMART, R.A.M. 1938, p. 53.

[37] *Oratio 52,* P.L. 158, 957.

[38] *Tractatus* . . . P.L. 159, 315.

[39] In Joh. XIII, P.L. 169, 790C; A. THYES, 'John 19: 25–7' and 'The spiritual motherhood of Mary' in *Marianum,* 1956, p. 101, sees here 'a real turning in the direction of spirits.'

[40] See *Confirmation,* Delachaux et Niestlé, Neuchâtel, 1957, pp. 19–20 One can also link up here the quotation of scripture to the believer ('he who believes in me'), but the text is then less clear; it would be a question of the spirit, which flows from the believer, like living water; in spite of the precedent in John 4: 14, the image would not be coherent; it would be a matter of the reception of the Spirit, 'the Spirit which they would receive who believe in him.' We here prefer the more ancient tradition which applies the 'Scripture' to Jesus rather than to the believer.

[41] O. CULLMANN, op. cit., pp. 81ff; R. BULTMANN, op. cit., p. 525, also gives the sacramental interpretation, though considering that verses 24B–35 are an ecclesiastical addition of a later time in order to establish the sacrament on the mystery of the death of Christ; he thinks the same for John 3: 5 and 6: 52b–58. We cannot agree with R. Bultmann who considers the Evangelist as anti-sacramental and must therefore return to the idea of a later interpolation. Let us just note that he does not think that he can contest the sacramental interpretation of the text as we have it. Like R. Bultmann, we must think that the text of 1 John 5: 6, which also speaks of the water and the blood united by the Spirit, primarily concerns the reality of the Incarnation. (Jesus is manifested as the Son of God at His baptism and at His death.) Here the sacramental allusion is less certain.

[42] On the Comforter, see C. K. BARRET, *The Gospel according to St. John,* London 1955, pp. 385–6.

[43] G. KITTEL, *Theol. Wörterbuch zum N.T., IV,* article 'mētēr,' p. 646: '. . . she is indicated twice (John 19: 26)—almost with a proper name, only as "hē mētēr," the mother.'

[44] E. HOSKYNS, *The Fourth Gospel,* London 1947, pp. 529–30; LIGHTFOOT, *St. John's Gospel,* Oxford 1956, p. 317; A. FEUILLET, 'La vierge Marie dans le N.T.' in *Maria VI,* Beauchesne, Paris 1961, pp. 54–61.

[45] A. MUELLER, *Ecclesia Maria, Die Einheit Marias und der Kirche,* Fribourg 1955.

[46] 'In. Lc. X,' 134, P.L. 15, 1838C *Sources chr.* 52, p. 201; R. BULTMANN, op. cit., p. 521, who does not want to believe in the historicity of the scene, and gives it a purely symbolic meaning: he sees it as having to do with the unity of Jewish-Christianity (Mary) and pagan-Christianity (the beloved Disciple); he would have to honour in Jewish Christianity the 'mother' from whom he has come forth, and she would have to be considered 'at home,' that is to say, as an integral member in the great universal ecclesiastical community; there would then have to be on the part of Christ 'raised,' the commending of unity for two communities. the Jewish-Christian and the pagan-Christian, already met in the High Priestly prayer (17–20ff.). This ingenious exegesis is too beholden to the ecclesiastical, non-historical interpretation of R. Bultmann to be really valid. One notices all the time its similar parentage to that of St. Ambrose.

[47] Certain copies of the text have 'mother' in the singular. Is there here a trace of the ecclesiastical explanation of 'hundredfold'? The Church is to be this mother whom one discovers.

[48] *Kirchenpostille*, 1522; Weimar 10; 405, 12–406, 3.

[49] Sermon of July 2nd, 1523; Weimar 12; 615, 5–616, 1.

[50] Weimar 11; 144, 5–9, 12–14.

[51] W. TAPPOLET, op. cit., p. 91.

[52] There is here a play on the words, *schwanger gehen*, which in a physical sense means 'being pregnant,' and in a figurative sense, 'to meditate in her heart.'

[53] Sermon of February 2nd, 1534; Weimar 37; 287, 35–288, 2.

[54] *Kirchenpostille*, 1522; Weimar 10; 72, 19–73, 2.

[55] Weimar 11; 219, 24–7.

[56] Weimar 11; 224, 8.

[57] Weimar 28; 402, 29–403, 4.

[58] Weimar 29; 655, 26–656, 7.

[59] J. DE SAUSSURE, *Contemplation de la croix*, Delachaux et Niestlé, Neuchâtel 1961, pp. 55–70, has a very beautiful meditation on the 'mother of Jesus' which concludes as follows 'And since, on the cross, it is I who die in thee, she who was close to it is therefore also close to me, close to every one of us who die in thee; in her there was concentrated, and there assists us, the presence of thy Church, the Mother of the Faithful. She surrounds, with her tenderness, our agony as Christians and it is to every one of thy beloved disciples that thou hast given her for mother. God makes man, and you have loved in her thy Church made woman. O image of the invisible God, you have given to us in her the image of the invisible Church. Behold thy mother! Lord, thanks be to thee for granting us a mother so exquisite! Besides, since by thy mercy you have deigned to make us thy brethren, how can thy mother not be our mother? And even more intimately so; since she was thy mother, how may she not be ours for us, the members of thy Body, who share nought but the same spirit with thee?'

[60] The Eucharistic preface in the service of the dedication of churches expresses the motherly function of the Church in her prophetic and sacramental ministry: 'It is she (the Church), the unique and beloved Bride whom Christ has bought with the price of his blood and whom he causes to live by his Spirit. In his breast we are born anew by grace (Baptism), we are nourished with the milk of the Word (preaching), we are strengthened by the Bread of Life (Sacrament), we are warmed by the help of thy mercy (Absolution) . . . '

[61] For the presence and rôle of Mary in the Church, as a figure of spiritual motherhood, see *Dialogue sur la Vierge*, by several Catholic and Protestant authors, Vitte, Lyons 1951:

'Mary is therefore present in the Church, at the head of all the saints, mother of God and first Christian woman to be loved and to lead men to the love of Christ, to be imitated and leading to an imitation of Christ, called blessed and blessed amongst women and yet leading us to the praise of God: "My soul doth magnify the Lord."

'The spiritual consequences of the presence of Mary in the Church are important.

'It is first of all the humble and hidden life with Christ, the contemplative and mystical life which are set by her in honour in the Church, against spiritual and ecclesiastical pride and against useful activism.

'Hence it is a family spirituality which is revived in the heart of the Church, the family of God, with all the tenderness of Jesus Christ, and his gentleness and his friendliness, against this false virility and austerity which is too often the rule in ecclesiastical relationships, this hardness and dryness of a certain kind of puritanism.

'It is finally the rôle of women in the Church which is thus indicated by the attitude of Mary in the presence of her son. She is not a priest as he is, she holds herself behind him, she hides herself, she follows him. Her function is to take care of him, to love him and to prepare the way for him. She is capable of intuition and daring as at Cana; she is able to be the decisive catalyst of great events; she is compassionate and she suffers at the foot of the Cross; she understands everything, she bears everything, she hopes everything, she is indispensable to the work of salvation, but in her own place, like that other Mary, of Bethany, she sits at the feet of Jesus listening to his words' (pp. 119–20).

NOTES ON CHAPTER 10: A GREAT SIGN IN HEAVEN

1 On Revelation ch. 12 see: F.-M. BRAUN, *La mère des fidèles*, Casterman, Tournai 1954; J. COLSON, *Un roi fit des noces à son fils*, Desclée de Brouwer, Paris 1962; L. DEISS, *Marie, Fille de Sion*, Desclée de Brouwer, Paris 1959; H.-M. FERET, *L'Apocalypse de Saint Jean*, Corréa, Paris 1946; A. FEUILLET, 'Le Messie et sa Mère d'après le chapitre XII de l'Apocalypse' in *Revue Biblique* 1959/1 and 'La Vierge Marie dans le Nouveau Testament' in *Maria VI*, Beauchesne, Paris 1961; A. KASSING, *Die Kirche und Maria, Ihr Verhältnis im 12. Kapitel der Apokalypse*, Patmos, Cologne 1958; P. PRIGENT, *Apocalypse 12, histoire de l'exégèse*, Mohr, Tübingen 1959.

On the Book of the Revelation in general: J. BEHM, *Die Offenbarung des Johannes*, Vandenhoek and Ruprecht, Göttingen 1949; C. BRUETSCH, *Clarté de l'Apocalypse*, Labor et Fides, Geneva 1955; S. GIET, *L'Apocalypse et l'histoire*, P.U.F., Paris 1957; H. LILJE, *Das letzte Buch der Bibel*, Furche-Verlag, Hamburg 1958; E. REISNER, *Das Buch mit den sieben Siegeln*, Vandenhoek and Ruprecht, Göttingen 1949.

2 R. LAURENTIN, L'interprétation des Genèse 3: 15 dans la tradition jusqu'au début du XIIIe siècle' in *La Nouvelle Eve*, I, Lethielleux, Paris 1954; H. CAZELLES, 'Genèse III, 15, Exégèse contemporaine' in *La Nouvelle Eve*, III, Lethielleux 1956.

3 See chapter 1: 'Daughter of Zion.'

4 The writings of Qumrân reveal a similar awareness of this prophetic theme: 'In the waters of death (the Woman) there will be born a male child and in the sorrows of Sheol there will be thrust forth from the "spring" of its fatness a marvellous "Counsellor" endowed with power who will deliver the man from the waters.' The similarity between this text of the "Hodayoth' writing from Qumrân and that of the Book of Revelation is very striking. See A. FEUILLET, op. cit., *Revue Biblique*, 1959/1, pp. 64–7; J. COLSON, op. cit., pp. 139–40.

5 A. FEUILLET, 'Le Messie et sa mère d'après le chapitre XII de l'Apocalypse' in *Revue Biblique*, 1959/1, pp. 60ff.

6 It is worth noting here that even in the Roman Mass for the feasts of Mary the collects are never addressed *to* the Virgin but always to God in thanks for the graces received by Mary.

On the matter of praise to God for Mary: R. SCHIMMELPFENNIG, *Die Geschichte der Marienverehrung im deutschen Protestantismus*, Schöningh, Paderborn 1952; *Dialogue sur la Vierge* (by various Catholic and Protestant writers), Vitte, Lyons 1951; H. BARRE, *Les premières prières mariales de l'Occident*, Marianum, Rome 1959; E. FLICOTEAUX, *Mystères et fêtes de la Vierge Marie*, Le Cerf, Paris 1956; *Maria in Liturgie und Lehrwort*, Ars Liturgica, Maria Laach 1954; ABTEI MARIA LAACH, *Maria in der Kirche, Väterwort und Gottteslob*, Pustet, Regensburg 1955; 'La Vierge Marie dans la prière de l'Eglise' in *La Maison-Dieu*, no. 38, Le Cerf, Paris 1954; TH. MAERTENS, 'Le développement liturgique et biblique du culte de la Vierge' in *Paroisse et Liturgie*, 1954/4; P. REGAMEY, *Les plus beaux textes sur la Vierge Marie*, La Colombe, Paris 1942.

[7] See our article on the 'Commemoration of the Saints' in *Verbum Caro*, no. 49, 1959; P.-Y. EMERY, 'L'unité des croyants au ciel et sur la terre' in *Verbum Caro*, no. 63, 1962; *The Commemoration of Saints and Heroes of the Faith in the Anglican Communion*, S.P.C.K., London 1957; M. LACK-MANN, *L'Eglise luthérienne et la Commémoration des Saints*, Ed. Saint-Paul, Paris 1961.

[8] Acts of the Council in March 1526 and March 1530; EGLI, *Aktensammlung zur Geschichte der Zürcher Reformation*, 1519–33, Zurich 1879, nos. 946 and 1656.

[9] Commentary on Luke 1: 42, 45.

[10] These dates are still observed in the Roman Catholic liturgy and make doubles with March 25th and July 2nd; the 'Offices at Taizé' has adopted this observance of the Annunciation and the Visitation on the Wednesday and Friday of the third week of Advent: Presses de Taizé 1961, p. 411.

[11] op. cit., p. 414.

[12] op. cit., pp. 17, 20.

[13] op. cit., p. 389.

[14] The Lutheran and Reformed traditions which have retained the credal beliefs in Christ, true God and true Man, born 'of the Virgin Mary, blessed mother of God, humble handmaid of the Lord, our example of faith, obedience and saintliness' have not believed that the doctrines of the Immaculate Conception of Mary (though admitted in a certain sense by Luther) or the 'corporeal Assumption' of Mary (though admitted by the Reformer, Bullinger) must be held in the same fashion.

For the reasons outlined in the introduction to this volume it is not our purpose here to study these two latter dogmas of the Roman Catholic Church. We here simply point out, so as to be strictly objective, the two definitions of these dogmas.

The Roman Catholic Church professes the dogma of Mary's Immaculate Conception, promulgated by Pope Pius IX on December 8th, 1854, in his 'Apostolic Constitution, Ineffabilis Deus' as follows, 'We hold by this doctrine that the blessed Virgin Mary, at the very instant of her conception, was, by the grace and peculiar privilege granted her by God Almighty, and in view of the merits of Jesus Christ, the Saviour of the human race, preserved and exempt from every spot of original sin, and this we believe is revealed by God.'

The Roman Catholic Church professes the dogma of Mary's Corporeal Assumption, promulgated by Pope Pius XII on November 1st, 1950, in his 'Apostolic Constitution, Munificentissimus Deus' as follows, 'It is a dogma divinely revealed that Mary, the Immaculate Mother of God, even Virgin, at the end of her earthly life, was raised in body and soul to the glory of Heaven.'

The Orthodox Church similarly professes the doctrine of the corporeal assumption of Mary, though it has not defined it as a dogma.